The Body of the People

The Body of the People

East German Dance
since 1945

Jens Richard Giersdorf

The University of Wisconsin Press

The University of Wisconsin Press
1930 Monroe Street, 3rd Floor
Madison, Wisconsin 53711-2059
uwpress.wisc.edu

3 Henrietta Street
London WC2E 8LU, England
eurospanbookstore.com

Library of Congress Cataloging-in-Publication Data

Giersdorf, Jens Richard.
The body of the people: East German dance since 1945 /
Jens Richard Giersdorf.
p.   cm.—(Studies in dance history)
Includes bibliographical references and index.
ISBN 978-0-299-28964-5 (pbk.: alk. paper)
ISBN 978-0-299-28963-8 (e-book)
1. Dance—Germany (East)—History.
I. Title.   II. Series: Studies in dance history (Unnumbered)
GV1652.5.G54   2013
792.809431—dc23
2012013013

For my parents

Siegrid and Wolfgang Giersdorf

who never saw this, but always believed in it

Contents

Illustrations

Acknowledgments

The material in this book has been shaped by over fifteen years of research on dance in East Germany, though I have been engaging with the subject of this book for much longer than that. My early desire to dance in our local children's dance company in Quedlinburg was channeled into the much more respectable male exercise of judo. Nevertheless, in my twenties I became a member of one of the many East German amateur dance companies, the Karl-Marx-Universität's dance ensemble. This ensemble was a folk dance company that shared a theater with a children's choir, a pantomime ensemble, a theater company, and a world dance and music company. I had to learn how to stomp, turn, and lift women in an eclectic mix of Eastern European dances and pseudo–Latin American choreographies with revolutionary messages. My fellow dancers—Elke Hunstock, Paula Riediger, René Peter Schmidt, and Tom Güldemann—are still my dear friends and have been a part of my subsequent journeys through dance.

The leaders of this company, Silvia Zygouris and Evelyn Iwanow, eventually shifted the repertoire from folk to modern dance. We renamed the company the Tanzbühne Leipzig without even being fully aware of the complex history of that term; Rudolf Laban had named his company Tanzbühne Laban. Such ignorance was emblematic of East Germany's engagement with the German modern dance tradition. When I began to be more interested in dramaturgy than in dancing, Silvia and Evelyn made me the company's first dramaturge and pulled many strings to get me enrolled in the short-lived *Tanzwissenschaft* degree at the Theaterhochschule Hans Otto in Leipzig.

The head of the program, Werner Gommlich, helped us gain access to major dance companies and schools in East Germany. My modern teacher, Eva Winkler, forced me to improvise and exposed me to the *Ausdruckstanz* tradition. Petra Stuber, who taught aesthetics, not only became my model for how to teach but she also masterfully revealed the politics of art to me. My fellow student Susanne Ladopoulos introduced me to the modern dance tradition in Dresden, where her mother taught at the Palucca School, and nudged me to think against established discourses in dance history. I thank all of them for their decisive influences.

Soon after the gates of the Berlin Wall had been opened, several West German dance scholars came to talk to us. Among the first to visit was Claudia Jeschke, who provided an international context for our East German perspective on dance. The East German dance historian Marion Kant heard that I was interested in studying in the United States and put me in contact with the newly founded PhD program in dance history and theory at the University of California, Riverside. I am grateful to both of these scholars, who followed and encouraged this project for many years.

I remain indebted to the first cohort of professors in the dance history and theory program at the University of California, Riverside: Heidi Gilpin, Marta Savigliano, Sally Ness, Linda Tomko, Susan Rose—and of course Susan Foster—all of whom introduced me to the idea that agency, identity politics, and the questioning of historizations all unfold through embodied subjects. Susan Foster and Sue-Ellen Case pushed me into the critical engagement with dance in East Germany, and they have shaped my initial work on it like no other scholars. Susan remains a strong intellectual and personal presence in my life, and there is hardly anyone who makes me think more vigorously.

At Riverside, my fellow student Maura Keefe patiently taught me about U.S. American dance and culture. Jacqueline Shea Murphy and Jennifer Doyle were important to this project at different times. Silvia Ochs helped it along with her kindness. Becca Rugg opened my eyes to gender, sexual, and race politics, and to the importance of following a personal vision. She still does. Janet O'Shea was not only a fellow student but later a colleague at the University of Surrey, UK. Our ongoing personal and professional dialogues imbue this book. Balancing the demands of teaching and service to institutions and our field with writing a book is not always easy, and Yutian Wong provided the crucial—and unfailingly witty—perspective along the way. I am fortunate to have her as my colleague, collaborator, and friend.

This project took shape when Ann Cooper Albright started to guide it editorially. Her enthusiasm brought it to light, and I am grateful to her and the editorial board of the Society of Dance History Scholars for their support. Gay Morris took it to another level with her careful readings. Susan Manning—an inspiration as an academic and as a person—never stopped telling me how necessary this book is. Through her knowledge of the topic, she became its chief critical reader. The anonymous reviewers for the press provided valuable and constructive comments and suggestions. All my students over the years have given me a reason to write this book. Parijat Desnai and Ailina Rose

Mayer helped smooth the rough edges. I thank all of them, as well as the staff at the University of Wisconsin Press for their work during the last phase of the project. Thank you also to the Glass Shop for providing me with a frequent refuge for my writing.

This is a book about a country that no longer exists, meaning that my research in the many archives and my interviews with choreographers and dancers serves as more than just a scholarly method of information gathering. They helped me rethink and reconstruct East German embodiment. Above all, I thank the Tanzarchiv Leipzig and Gabriele Ruiz and Janine Schulze. Also thanks to Sabine Zolchow at the Archiv der Akademie der Künste, Axel Becker at the Palucca Schule Dresden, Cordula Reski-Henningfeldt at the Komische Oper Berlin, Katja Wildermuth from MDR, and the Stadtgeschichtliches Museum/Sportmuseum Leipzig for their help in my research. Arila Siegert, Fine Kwiatkowski, Jo Fabian, Patricio Bunster, Manuela Bunster, Raymond Hilbert, and Nejla Y. Yatkin gave me insight into their work, and their individual approaches to dance helped me understand what dance can do. Maryann Appel made it all look good. This book would not have been possible without them.

The University of California, Riverside, the University of Surrey, and Marymount Manhattan College supported this book with grants and fellowships. I also received a study abroad and senior academic research grant from the DAAD (German Academic Exchange Program), a small grant from the Arts and Humanities Research Board in the UK, and a scholar-in-residence award from Jacob's Pillow.

This book has been shaped by numerous conference presentations and publications. Material from chapters has been presented at conferences of the Society of Dance History Scholars, Congress on Research in Dance, International Federation for Theater Research, and the Embodiment of the Nation conference at the University of Hamburg. Early versions of chapters and excerpts are reprinted with permission as follows: "Border Crossings and Intra-National Trespasses: East German Bodies in Sasha Waltz's and Jo Fabian's Choreographics," *Theater Journal* 55, no. 3 (2003): 413 32, copyright © 2003 The Johns Hopkins University Press; "Dancing, Marching, Fighting: Folk, the Dance Ensemble of the East German Armed Forces, and Other Choreographies of Nationhood," *Discourses in Dance* 4, no. 2 (2008): 39–58; "Why Does Charlotte von Mahlsdorf Curtsy? Representations of National Queerness in a Transvestite Hero," *GLQ* 12, no. 2 (2006): 171–96; "Von der Utopie zum Archiv: Patricio Bunster und die politische Funktion der Choreographie," *Forum Modernes Theater* 23, no.1 (2008): 29–36; "Ideology and Dance: Competing Notions of Modern Dance and Ballet in East Germany 1945–61," *Dance Gazette*, May 2004, 27–29;

and "Technique as Ideology: Professional and Amateur Dance in East Germany 1961–1989," *Dance Gazette*, Aug. 2004: 23–25.

You can't live abroad and research your native culture without keeping a strong connection to it. This bond has been provided by my family and friends. The book is dedicated to my late parents, who supported my academic career in dance with a pride and interest in my vocation and research subject that pushed me and keeps pushing me, even though I am no longer able to talk to them. My siblings, Silke Berger and Sven Giersdorf, and their own families have heard way too much about this book over the years. They will be happy and proud to see it in print. So will my new family here in America. I thank Margot Steinberg and Michael and Virginia Gusick for their support. A special thanks to Anne Boswell Bertrand, our own fairy godmother.

Yet most of all I want to thank my own unconventional family. I know that none of my academic work would be possible or enjoyable without their love and the balance they provide. My partner Ned Gusick literally has not only been with me through every stage of this book; he helped so much that he is now an honorary dance scholar. And he secretly loves it. Our three-and-a-half-year-old daughter, Emma, has no idea what Papa is doing when he shuts the door in order to *arbeiten*. But one day she will read this book and will hopefully understand a bit more about how East Germany is not only a country that has vanished but how its culture and movement survived in some small way through her father and other East Germans abroad and in Germany, and how and why this is important. And if she can understand that, than hopefully the readers of this book can as well.

The Body of the People

Introduction

Spectacles
Between Utopia and Ostalgie

The Waning Archive

The archivist deposited a pile of binders, untouched in decades, on the wobbly table.[1] I sat surrounded by official memos and unofficial correspondences relating to the bygone era of the German Democratic Republic (GDR), in particular to the mass dance events that took place from 1954 until the fall of the Berlin Wall. There were very few colorful programs of official events. Instead, most of the materials were old-fashioned Thermofax and carbon copies— letters, reports, internal memos, proposals—held together by strings. When I opened the binders, the bureaucratic scent of East Germany wafted up at me.

The archive at the Sportmuseum Leipzig had been struggling to survive since the dissolution of East Germany in 1990; renovations of its temporary quarters were being undertaken to ensure at least the security of its collection.[2] As I sat in a cold and drafty hallway, a construction worker opened the door repeatedly, pushing a wheelbarrow in and out to dump old bricks. Each time the door opened, I flung my arms over the flimsy copies to prevent them from flying away, physically protecting the dingy remnants of my expired country of origin. I felt I was not only saving them from the January gusts. I was protecting these papers from time, from the waning institution of the archive that stored them, from public neglect, erasure, and nostalgia, and from my own conflicted academic and personal stance toward them.

The more I lay atop those papers, involuntarily pressing my body against their cushiony, fading surfaces, the more I felt doubt about having to engage with these banal relics of the country in which I grew up. The material only confirmed what I had already discovered about other state-sponsored dances

3

and about movement culture generally in East Germany. Yes, East German choreographers reinvented a tradition after World War II by tapping into selected areas of German dance, such as movement choirs, folk vocabulary, and Soviet and German mass movements.[3] These invented traditions were meant to validate East Germany as a progressive successor of German culture and to create a socialist national identification distinct from the West by updating movement traditions in relation to socialist corporeal ideals. That was especially true for the mass events that I was researching at the Sportmuseum's archive. Through choreography, the idealized East German body—a body that was clearly gendered and joyfully optimistic yet seriously dutiful, developing in its technical abilities over time—was invented, confirmed, and reinforced as rhythmically collective, healthy, and ready for the task of building a new country.

Leipzig became the center for these socialist mass choreographies by hosting all eight *Turn- und Sportfest* (German sports and gymnastics festivals), organized by the government. The opening ceremony, which included more than ten thousand participants and was staged in the newly erected central stadium, eventually became the signature event for all these festivals. The movements of participants' bodies on a stadium lawn typically expanded into the bleachers, thereby involving the audience. The general population also participated through choreographic routines that had been promoted throughout the country years before the mass events took place in Leipzig.[4] In bringing people together on such a large scale, these mass events corporeally generated a sense of national identity, which Benedict Anderson has labeled an "imagined community."[5] According to Anderson, through their collective imagination, the people of a group perceive themselves as a nation, even though they lack the close interaction normally necessary to constitute a group. Choreographed mass movements can also effectively substitute for such direct interactions, because they allow a kinesthetic empathy in the observing citizen.[6] This was especially true in East Germany, since the citizens were already familiar with the choreography through their participation in nationwide routines. As a result, mass choreographies became a powerful corporeal constituent of East German national identity as well as a means of affirming it.

Yet, more than twenty years after the fall of the Berlin Wall, all that is left of these once-powerful choreographies are flimsy and dusty carbon copies in a waning archival institution. The state of these archival holdings is indicative of the lack of historization of East German dance. I have been working on East German dance history for nearly twenty years. I have tracked down material in unlit and unheated warehouses and private collections, interviewed reluctant subjects, and followed archives that, threatened with closure, have been moved

Mass choreography on the stadium floor and in the bleachers creating propagandistic messages, Turn- und Sportfest Osttribüne, Leipzig, 1977. Bundesarchiv, Bild 183-S0727-121. Photo: Peter Koard.

several times since the reunification.[7] These archives mostly hold material on the official dance culture. Most of the rest of the material on East German dance, such as documentation concerning the extensive amateur dance world, the folk dance companies, and the dance ensemble of the armed forces, is scattered over personal collections, buried in former West German archival vaults, or simply gone.[8] Other materials that still exist will be lost over the next decade or so with the death of company directors, choreographers, and participants. As a result, nearly the entire dance production of a nation will have disappeared. Thus, when I refer to the waning archive of East German dance, I am not only speaking of the complex situation of the archival holdings on official East German dance; I am also evoking the vanishing of nonofficial dance, the repression or misreading of East German choreographic practices after the fall of the Berlin Wall, and the unacknowledged migration of socialist dance vocabulary into other national forms. Only the analysis of the relationship between all of these choreographic endeavors allows a comprehensive understanding of dance in East Germany.

Consequently, the main purpose of this book is to demonstrate how dance can serve an array of distinct functions in relation to a national structure, ranging from ideological affirmation to multileveled resistance against national standards. Just as East German officials utilized dance to create socialist citizens, so too citizens tapped into choreography's constructive potential to respond critically to state power. Therefore, I don't argue dance in East Germany had a coherent role and structure. Rather, I want to show how distinct circumstances in relation to the development and deterioration of national structures demand different choreographic decisions. As such, the chapters in this book are purposefully diverse in their approach, subject, and authorial voice. What unites them is their shared investigation of choreographic practices in East Germany and my act of interpreting them.

Throughout I make my own position as the analyzer visible in order to highlight the subjectivity of the analytic and theoretical choices I have made and my general position toward the described history. This performance of research and analysis is informed by what Yutian Wong labels "doubled ethnography."[9] The term refers to the dance scholar's self-reflexive engagement with self-representative choreographic practice. As an East German dancer and dance scholar, I was created as a subject by socialist dance and had to position myself in response to it. To make this subjective position visible is a political intervention, because it challenges analytic objectivity, theoretical objectification, and dance's often-assumed ephemerality.[10] In other words, in each chapter I allow my subjective, physical experience of studying, performing, watching, and reading about dance in East Germany to enter my writing as I move critically through East German dance history.[11] In addition, my physical engagement with the archival material on the mass choreographies demonstrates that my corporeal response to history is not merely reactive but is as constructive as the history itself.

East German Choreography and Embodiment as Dance History

My primary concern in writing this book is to perform a political act through the labor of historicizing. I want to introduce a non-German-speaking audience to a dance culture that is thus far not part of established dance history. In existence from the beginning of the last century until the early 1940s, German modern dance, referred to as *Ausdruckstanz* (expressionist dance), and its protagonists Mary Wigman, Rudolf Laban, Kurt Jooss, Dore Hoyer, and Harald Kreutzberg have been subjects of various historical treatments that are accessible to the international dance connoisseur and scholar.[12] Dance in West Germany after World War II, notably the influential *Tanztheater*, is also the subject of many academic and arts publications.[13] Even contemporary dance in postunification Germany has been analyzed in terms of its relationship to European and global dance.[14]

Yet a comprehensive discussion of dance in East Germany is absent from dance history in any language, even German.[15] This is surprising, because an investigation of East German dance and choreography has much to offer to the contemporary dialogue on embodiment, movement, dance, and choreography in the field of dance studies and related disciplines. It is one of the few cases in recent times of dance being purposefully utilized for the establishment of a distinct national identity at all levels of artistic practice and social discourse. East German dance and body culture became the battleground between German cultural tradition and socialist corporeal directives, first in the Soviet-occupied sector after World War II and then from 1949 on in the GDR until the fall of the Berlin Wall in 1989. In response to the control exerted by the Stasi (Ministerium für Staatssicherheit), one of the most developed secret service apparatuses in modern times, as well as to enforced socialist corporeal collective standards, dance and embodiment became important resistive and oppositional tools. Dance in particular became significant as a form of resistance due to its censorship-evading capacity and its ability to communicate multiple meanings that went beyond—and that contradicted—spoken language.

While there are indeed instances of the utilization of dance for indoctrination and resistance in other contexts, East German dance culture was unique in its confined temporal and spatial occurrence, as well as in its relationship to Western dance history. East German dance was developed both strategically and organically over the course of a little more than forty years, beginning in 1945 and officially ending with German reunification in 1990. For most of this time, from 1961 to 1989, East Germany separated itself from Western Europe by means of an impermeable border, symbolized by the Berlin Wall. It was further isolated from the West in its specific function as a battlefield in Cold War politics. Due to this isolation on one side and global importance on the other, East German choreographers and citizens embodied their national culture in a unique way. This conscious engagement and shaping of East German identity did not start with the founding of the GDR and end with the fall of the Berlin Wall. Rather, East German dance developed in response to post–World War II politics and continued to critically—or nostalgically—shape German culture after the reunification in 1990; hence my decision to expand the analyzed time frame to seven decades, beyond the forty years of the East German state's existence. I also explicitly extend the reach of East German culture by preserving distinct East German contributions to global social structures, thereby further resisting its disappearance.

Analysis of the rise and descent of East German dance and choreography and its subsequent role in a reunified, contemporary Germany and globalized world is facilitated by the relatively short time span of East Germany's existence and its spatial confinement. In sketching a hitherto unexplored history, I have chosen to provide examples of choreographies of indoctrination and resistance in loose chronological order. I am fully aware that chronological temporality has been critiqued as a tool used by dominant parts of society in historization. I avoid simplistic chronology by highlighting overlooked aspects of official choreographies, and by emphasizing neglected and nonofficial parts of the East German movement culture through a genealogical approach.[16] *The Body of the People* is thus not a traditional history of dance in East Germany, focusing on milestone stage productions, socialist dance education, important dance companies, and influential choreographers. Rather, it is a historical and theoretical analysis of dance, choreography, and embodiment in East Germany and an exploration of how all these organizing principles reflected social and political structures and how they created official and oppositional systems.

The Politics of Studying Dance

As much as this is a book about dance in East Germany, it is also a book about a critical commitment to dance, dancing, and a conscious theoretical engagement with both. I see my historicizing of East German dance not just as a disciplinary issue but a political one, and not only because I am inserting a largely unknown history into mainstream dance scholarship but also because I apply appropriate methodologies to each facet of this dance history, ranging from collective mass dances and stage choreographies to private events, as well as discuss disciplinary concerns connected with each of these facets. With this approach, I do not seek merely to insert East German dance into a dance history that otherwise would stand unaltered. I also want to provide models and viewpoints that question traditional discourses and hierarchies in our field and emphasize the significance of dance as a tool for an understanding of social structures.

At the same time, I want to denaturalize the analytic process and adopt a critical stance toward such applied methodologies so as to prevent them from dominating the complex processes I analyze. In telling the story of dance in East Germany, *The Body of the People* emphasizes a methodological investigation of traces of movement and physicality; for that reason, dance studies is an effective apparatus by which to problematize a history of the vanished East German choreographic landscape. Given the commonly held notion that dance is ephemeral, the discipline of dance studies has been forced to problematize disappearance and nontangibility repeatedly. Thus, looking at dance and embodiment and employing methodological frameworks from dance studies constitutes a logical means by which to understand the ephemeral state of East Germany.

I also want to be clear about my terminology and concepts such as dance and choreography. Definitions of dance in our field and beyond are numerous. Most focus on the aesthetic and artistic features of dance, its rhythmic nature, and its performative or social aspects. When I started my career in dance studies in the late 1980s in East Germany, a vast amount of educational and pedagogical dance material was available but only a very limited amount of literature on dance history. Thus I was thrilled to find a vintage copy of Max von Boehn's 1925 *Der Tanz* (*The Dance*). I soon realized Boehn, like many of his contemporaries, such as Fritz Böhme, Hans Brandenburg, Rudolf Lammel, and Frank Thiess, naturalize dance by emphasizing the biological origin of the form.[17] Boehn sees both animals and humans as capable of rhythmic movement based on heartbeat, breathing, and the symmetry of bodies. Yet he states that only humans are capable of turning this natural rhythmic movement into a conscious labor and ludic movement.[18] Boehn further naturalizes dance by denying that it is possible to notate even the technical aspects of dance.[19] An art historian and anthropologist, Boehn uses his general observations on the origin and specificity of dance to pursue an anthropological reflection on dance in the non-European world. This introduction sets the ground for a chronological narration of the progressive development of dance in the Western world that concludes with his pessimistic evaluation of Laban's philosophical utopia of a new dance culture and of the influences of Negro dances on Germany's social dance culture.[20] Dance is thus divided into the non-Western or primal urge to dance on one side and the evolution of a progressive Western art form on the other side.

My subsequent encounter with Curt Sachs's work in my first dance history course at the Theaterhochschule Hans Otto upheld this division. Sachs expands the notion of dance by including non-European dance in a tale of Western evolution. Sachs defines dance as "rhythmic motion not related to the work motif" but leaves the division between dance and other rhythmic movements purposefully open.[21] However, Sachs sees dance's purpose as part of a universal movement toward unity with a divine force; he thus understands it in terms of the ideas put forth by German Romantic writers, such as Heinrich von Kleist in his treatise on grace.[22] Sachs's project has been critiqued repeatedly for its Eurocentric, colonial, and naturalizing stance, yet it was important in conjunction with related studies (for instance, the work of Marcel Mauss and others at the Archives internationales de la danse in France) because it incorporated nonstage or social forms into the concept of dance and emphasized dance as knowledge and thus encouraged the development of dance studies into an academic discipline.[23]

Both aspects—the critique of the definition of dance as a naturalizing form and the recognition of its capacity to function as a knowledge system—are of

importance in my reading of dance in East Germany. I employ a definition of
dance that allows an opening of it beyond the rhythmical performance of steps
in front of spectators or with other dancers for aesthetic and social reasons. My
decision to begin this book with an anecdote of my corporeal engagement with
the materials documenting mass choreography at the Sportmuseum reflects this
expanded notion of dance. Understanding my spontaneous physical reaction
as a response to the multiple threats to the archival holdings on mass movement in East Germany requires as much a rethinking of traditional definitions
of dance as does the inclusion in its definition of mass sports exercises. For this,
I find Susan Foster's reconceptualization of dance, which I encountered in my
graduate work at the University of California, Riverside, in the early 1990s,
helpful. Foster defines training, technique, rehearsal, performance, and reception all as intrinsic parts of dance.[24] The advantage of this definition is the
visibility of less acknowledged parts of dance, such as the labor of dancing, and
its disciplinary and power structures. Her definition also positions agency in
every aspect of dancing. However, this definition, as I eventually realized, still
treats dance as geared toward a product, even when the process and constructive choices are highlighted.

To allow a more precise consideration of these constructive choices, I
started to distinguish between dance and choreography in my work. The concept
of choreography has undergone many changes over the centuries.[25] As established in Western dance historical discourse, the term originates in the combination of the Greek words for dance and writing. Raoul Auger Feuillet coined the
term for his scoring of dances around 1700. His dance notation depicted the
structure and layout of dance in relation to social standards and techniques of
upper-class conduct, but the term later came to connote the original creation of
dance pieces. Inspired by artistic musing and divine inspiration, the choreographer created choreographies as a means of reflecting his or her understanding
of society. The arrangements of steps and gestures in a staged space and to a
musical or seemingly natural rhythm served foremost as a mirroring device
for society. The material for these choreographies was newly created or at least
amounted to a surprisingly new arrangement of existing dance steps and gestures. To accomplish all of this for the audience, the executing dancer had to be
competently trained in the technique used by the choreographer and able to
follow choreographic instructions in the rehearsal process.[26]

Only with the rethinking of dance as mastery of technique at the end of the
nineteenth century did Western choreography start to engage with movement
in nature and labor, something various folk forms had already done much
earlier. Choreography also achieved the capacity to influence society beyond
providing a representation of it by incorporating female choreographers and

by engaging with the newly defined psychological sphere.[27] The conscious, if unacknowledged, incorporation of non-Western or indigenous dance techniques and structures were still considered products of the choreographer's genius rather than of skillful borrowing. It was not until the middle of the twentieth century that historians began to acknowledge the incorporation of non-Western and indigenous forms and structures into the movement pool and process of choreography. This acknowledgment of multiple influences, as well as a focus on improvisation, allowed for a departure from the idea that it was the individual choreographer's genius that propelled dance forward.[28] With this shift, choreography became a varied decision-making process about all aspects of structure and performance rather than solely a structuring of steps or gestures for a performance. The process could involve group or individual decisions, reconstruction, revisiting of traditional material, or rearrangement of existing structures.

On this account, choreography was situated outside any specific technique and thus not even necessarily tied to dance. I am interested in this kind of definition of choreography because it elevates decision making and thus assigns agency to the decision makers. It also allows the incorporation of movement material traditionally not defined as dance. As I eventually realized while teaching the genealogy of choreography to my own students at the University of Surrey, the problem with such a definition is the seeming neutrality of choreography, because it doesn't always acknowledge its ties to a specific cultural materiality. There is no such systematic neutrality, as Michel Foucault showed in his work, and it is important to recognize the possibility that the contemporary concept of choreography enables, or is at least complicit with, colonial, postcolonial, and economically globalizing projects.[29]

I also began to understand that the critique of choreography needed to be applied to the rethinking of the term and practice as a methodology in dance studies.[30] Foster proposes to employ choreography as theory that allows dance historians to construct both historical traces of dance and their stance toward these traces into a choreography. She writes that "to approach choreography as theory is to open up a space where dancing and all body-centered endeavors have an integrity equivalent to that of written documentation of them."[31] This political move attempts to emancipate both dance and choreography from a Cartesian grip and, without erasing the distinction between the written and the choreographed, elevates them near the permanent realm of writing and other textual and artistic products. Even though such an understanding of choreography does not eliminate the problem of practice as a universalizing instrument, it a least addresses the issues of ephemerality and disappearance, which have haunted dance since Romanticism.

Feminist dance scholars have frequently pointed to Western culture's view of the body as a problematic site.[32] Under the influence of Cartesian mind-body dualism, the body is equated with femininity, and dance as a female art form furthers this naturalizing emphasis. Dance and choreography are thus situated outside the bounds of reason and function on an intuitive and unconscious level. They are the transient expression of an essentialized body. This focus on dance's impermanence has been repeatedly addressed by scholars in different ways according to their disciplinary and national backgrounds. For instance Janet Lansdale at the University of Surrey and Kurt Petermann at the Tanz-archiv in Leipzig, two scholars who influenced the institutions I studied and worked at, have attempted to solidify dance and turn it into a tangible object for analysis and storage.[33]

Foster proposes to equalize dance and choreography as knowledge systems comparable to other forms of artistic and linguistic discourse.[34] She is fully conscious that they are not the same, but she suggests that they be treated equally at the same time that she problematizes their differences, which is the approach I take. Working though particular examples of indoctrination, resistance, and diaspora in this book, I situate agency firmly in specific bodies, dances, and choreographic acts and make my position and theoretical approach toward these past bodies and their traces visible.

Dance in East Germany: A Historical Context

Germany-based choreographers and modern dancers, from Mary Wigman and Hanya Holm to Harald Kreutzberg, Gret Palucca, Jean Weidt, Marianne Vogelsang, Dore Hoyer, and Kurt Joos, have been pivotal protagonists of twentieth-century Western dance history. They defined the German modern dance form that became known as *Ausdruckstanz* in Germany and abroad before and during World War II. After the war, modern dance in West Germany gained attention with the creation of *Tanztheater* (dance theater) by choreographers such as Pina Bausch, Johann Kresnik, Gerhard Bohner, Reinhild Hoffmann, and Susanne Linke. At the same time, John Cranko of the Stuttgarter Ballett, John Neumeier of the Hamburger Ballett, and William Forsythe of the Frankfurter Ballett propelled West German ballet to worldwide recognition. However, comparatively little is known of the developments in dance during the same time in East Germany.[35]

Cut off from the Western world, dance in socialist East Germany progressed more via its relationship to Soviet-dominated choreographic developments in the Eastern Bloc than through an exchange with West Germany or other capitalist countries. Few dance productions toured major theaters in the West, severely limiting the exposure those audiences had to East German dance. Even if Western dance connoisseurs managed to catch a performance by the ballet companies of the Staatsoper unter den Linden or Tanztheater der Komischen Oper in Berlin or the Semperoper in Dresden, they would only have seen a very small part of the East German dance landscape. The majority of dance was performed in small theaters or as part of mass sport and political events or in social settings by amateur companies, folk dance companies, youth and children's dance troupes.[36]

The East German state was, by self-definition, a dictatorship of the proletariat; this was evident not only in government politics but also in the socialist state's relationship to dance. Occupied after World War II by the Red Army and transformed (following the Potsdam Agreement of 1945) into the Soviet Occupation Zone, East Germany intensely de-Nazified the political, intellectual, and cultural elite at the time of its inception and declared itself antifascist. With the 1949 founding of the GDR on the territory of the Soviet Occupation Zone as a direct result of the early phase of the Cold War, East Germany replicated Soviet governmental and societal structures, including the authoritarian leadership of a communist party.

The establishment of socialism in the GDR unfolded in the 1950s, and the 1960s saw the stabilization of the Socialist Unity Party's (SED) political and economic leadership. The building of the Berlin Wall in 1961 effectively put an end to a damaging outflow of highly skilled citizens, including scientists, teachers, and academics (over two million, one-fifth of the labor force), while the introduction of the new central system of planning and management in 1963 led to temporary economic success.[37] Soon after, the GDR was ranked twelfth among the industrial powers of the world.[38] SED party conventions during the late 1940s and 1950s assessed socialist developments and communicated the party's plan for the coming years to citizens. These conventions also situated East Germany and its achievements in an international context.[39] In the wake of its economic achievements, the government turned its attention to realms of society that lay outside labor. The GDR government continued its efforts to create a distinct East German national culture, and this endeavor was especially important to the government because it sought to establish East Germany internationally as a state distinct from West Germany.

Dance inhabited a controversial position in the East German process of nation building. As an art form that was not based on spoken or written language, it was considered ambiguous and open to multiple meanings and thus arguably not always suitable for didactic propaganda. Still, dance became of particular concern to East German officials because it reached into numerous levels of social life. Not only was dance found in industrial and administrative centers such as Berlin, Leipzig, and Dresden; every midsized city in East Germany had its own theater or opera house, and these houses often had separate theater, opera, and ballet companies. The GDR provided sixty-five of these multidisciplinary theaters for its sixteen million citizens. Yet most importantly, dance was also performed in social settings and by community or amateur dance groups. The government sponsored numerous community theaters and dance companies that were affiliated with factories, organizations, and universities throughout the country to demonstrate the creative capacity of the working citizens.

As I show in chapter 1, these companies were guided by the example of several semiprofessional state-sponsored folk dance companies, among them the dance ensemble of the armed forces. In order to show how dance is both a symptom of socialist reality and an aesthetic practice, chapter 1 destabilizes fixed notions of socialist dance by revealing how the East German government's definitions of socialism changed and how artistic manifestations also shifted with those political structures. The choreographic content and movement vocabularies of dance companies were defined during national dance conferences. For instance, the Theoretische Tanzkonferenz of 1953 postulated that formalism (a socialist code word for modernism) was holding back socialist dance production and stated that socialist realism ought to shape the form and content of any dance production. The conference established firm guidelines on dance vocabulary, content of choreographies, dance education, dance research, and criticism. Other such conferences in later years focused on specific areas of dance production, such as children's dance, folk dance, adult education, social dance, and amateur dance.[40]

Yet what had the biggest impact on all art—not just dance—were the two state-sponsored cultural conferences at the chemical plant in Bitterfeld. The first conference in 1959 is the most notorious cultural conference in the history of the GDR; at it, the government declared that all arts had to focus on the life of the working class. Artists needed to experience labor conditions through active participation in factory and farmwork in order to write, choreograph, or paint about them and thereby fulfill this directive. Likewise, the East German government decreed that the working class had to contribute to and participate in artistic production. The enforcement of this mandate echoed earlier developments in the Soviet Union. The second conference in 1964—three years after the Berlin Wall had been built—demanded a renewed effort toward the creation of an East German national culture. Choreographers, dance pedagogues, directors of dance companies, and dancers had to adjust to each of these national mandates throughout the period that East Germany existed.

At the end of World War II, many dance teachers, choreographers, and dancers were initially able to continue where they had worked during the war;

Socialist realism and dance: cover of conference proceedings of the government-sponsored theoretical conference on dance art, Berlin, 1953. Berlin: Staatliche Kommission für Kunstangelegenheite, HA Künstlerischer Nachwuchs und Lehranstalten, 1953. Tanzarchiv Leipzig e.V.

dance was nearly overlooked during the de-Nazification process. Artists were needed for a quick start-up of production in all four occupied sectors.[41] For instance Mary Wigman had been teaching in Leipzig since 1942, when she had been forced to close her school in Dresden. She continued to teach in Leipzig after the war in the dance department at Leipzig's music conservatory and eventually even choreographed for the Oper Leipzig. Dresden and Leipzig, which had famous ballet companies and established dance schools, became part of the Soviet Occupation Zone and centers of postwar dance in East Germany, second only to East Berlin.

Wigman had been one of the key figures in dance during the early Nazi era and only later faced censure from the propaganda ministry because she was not willing to adjust her vocabulary to reflect wartime propaganda.[42] Despite her choreographic work for National Socialist events, such as the 1936 Olympics, and the close relationship of her choreographic philosophy to Nazi ideology, Wigman, along with many other major dance figures, received documentation from the occupying forces after the war that not only certified her noninvolvement but even established her as a victim of Hitler's regime. She was exonerated because her artistic status was too important to the Soviet

Strong group-leader relations in Mary Wigman's *Orpheus und Euridice*, Leipzig Opera, 1947. Tanzarchiv Leipzig e.V.

occupying force and to East German leaders returning from exile in the Soviet Union, who had a clearly defined strategy for the creation of a new socialist German culture. Wigman was thus able to present her famous choreography of Gluck's *Orpheus and Eurydice* at the Oper Leipzig in March 1947.

The choreography revisited Wigman's renowned interrogations into group-leader relationships and her employment of movement choirs. Wigman also relied on her trademark pathos to create strong, seemingly universal characters in this production. After the war, Wigman had pondered leaving Saxony because she wanted to establish herself in the more cosmopolitan city of Berlin. So despite the success of her *Orpheus and Eurydice*, she left East Germany soon afterward for the Allied-occupied part of Berlin, where she taught an influential generation of West German choreographers and dancers until close to her death in 1973.

The more classically trained choreographer Tatjana Gsovsky faced a different decision. In 1945, she became the head of the ballet company at the Staatsoper unter den Linden in Berlin. Very early on and with surprising speed, Gsovsky choreographed many classics of the ballet repertoire, such as *Romeo and Juliet, Cinderella, Sleeping Beauty, Firebird,* and *Don Quixote.* Despite the success of her choreographies and the establishment of the Staatsballett as a leading company in East Germany, Gsovsky faced increasing censorship by GDR officials. Her

Jean Weidt's *Das Opfer (The Sacrifice)*, Volksbühne Berlin, 1961. Tanzarchiv Leipzig e.V. Photo: Karl Deutscher.

movement vocabulary, which combined ballet technique with *Ausdruckstanz*, led to charges of formalism from cultural officials. Gsovsky's ballets were controversial because any investigation of formal matters or modernist attention to the material and structure of artistic production were considered reactionary and were eventually prohibited. Only the concentration on collective and essential experience in socialist society was deemed an appropriate socialist realist expression. As a result of this political pressure and censorship, Gsovsky left East Berlin in 1950 and reestablished herself with great success in West Berlin.

The choreographers and dancers who elected to stay in the newly founded state had to contend with continuous censorship, intrusion, and prohibition. The "Red Dancer" Jean Weidt was one of the few dance artists who emigrated from Germany during the Nazi period due to his sympathy with Communist views, first to France and then to the Soviet Union. On his return to Germany, he constantly had to defend himself against East German state officials, even though he was clearly a leftist choreographer. Weidt founded the Dramatische Ballett, a company that was supposed to allow members of the working class access to ballet and modern dance instruction. Yet without warning, the East German government removed him from his own company and transformed it into a folk dance ensemble. The radical elevation of folk dance vocabularies was one of the dominant political and choreographic devices by which modern dance was eradicated from East German stages. The government favored Soviet-influenced ballet and folk dance as tools of socialist realist representation and repressed *Ausdruckstanz* on the grounds that it was too individualistic and formalist.

Gret Palucca, another modern dancer, also had to fight government interference. Yet, Palucca was known for her ability to negotiate such intrusions. She was one of the pioneers of *Ausdruckstanz* and consequently was invited to dance a solo at the 1936 opening of the Olympics. Even though she had to close her school because of her part-Jewish heritage, she was the only modern dancer who performed her solo work for the duration of the war. Her career in East Germany demonstrates that she was also able to navigate the constraints of the socialist regime. With the help of the Soviet occupation forces, who saw in Palucca a valuable teacher and cultural functionary, she promptly reopened her school in bombed-out Dresden in July 1945. She continued to hold important positions in the administrative structure of East German cultural politics throughout her life. Renowned for her technical ability and her abstract choreographies that interrogated moods and expressions, Palucca never formulated a technique or pedagogy. Still, she influenced several generations of dancers and choreographers in East Germany owing to her determination to teach her own choreographic approach. Palucca's success and fame gave her and her school partial immunity from censorship. Yet even she had to justify her *Ausdruckstanz*-based vocabulary and teaching over the course her career in the GDR.[43]

Just as in the 1930s and 1940s in the Soviet Union, in the 1950s and 1960s in East Germany, there was a conscious turning away from modern dance in the direction of a ballet repertoire and the creation of a ballet-based dance education. But even ballets had to show that they were at least making an attempt to merge movement derived from folk dances. Restagings of Soviet imports such as *The Fountain of Bakchiserai, The Stone Flower, Gajaneh, The Flames of Paris,* and *Scheherazade* provided the necessary models for the productions of new socialist ballets.

Neue Odyssee (*New Odyssey*), which was choreographed by Lilo Gruber (Gsovsky's successor at the Staatsoper unter den Linden in Berlin in 1957), became a frequently restaged paradigm for an East German combination of ballet vocabulary and folk dance material in the service of a contemporary socialist narrative. The plot is loosely based on Homer's *Odyssey*. But the temptations the protagonist of this ballet endures on his journey home are capitalist-influenced elements that need to be overcome on the way to socialism. During the course of his journey back home where his wife awaits him, the husband fights off prostitutes and thieves makes his way through primitive dance bars

Gret Palucca teaching female students at the Palucca School, Dresden, 1982. Photo: Erich Höhne, Deutsche Fotothek.

with jazz music, and confronts black markets. The clear references to the German capitalist state in the West were not missed by the audience. State officials hailed the production as the first truly East German ballet. This political endorsement laid the groundwork for the ballet's triumphant journey through many East German theaters. It also established Gruber as one of the country's leading ballet choreographers.

Contrary to popular belief, the overnight erection of the Berlin Wall in 1961 actually saw a momentary break in the rigid government control of all aspects of life in the GDR and allowed artists a more critical engagement with socialist structures. The closing off of its borders to West Germany allowed East Germany to halt the damaging drain of qualified workers, among them many dancers. Yet the more liberal atmosphere was only temporary; two years later, the government renewed its strict guidelines for artistic production by closely censoring it and establishing direct governmental jurisdiction over the professional institutions and training facilities as well as the amateur movement in the now enclosed East German territory. Thus, the newly erected wall and secured borders changed and defined the artistic landscape in the GDR for the remaining twenty-eight years of its existence.

Part of the renewed governmental intervention was an effect of its desire to demonstrate to the international dance world that East German ballet companies were capable of mastering the ballet vocabulary at an advanced level. In order to stage classics such as *Swan Lake* or *Cinderella*, the companies desperately needed well-trained dancers. Thus, all three state-sponsored dance academies in Dresden, Leipzig, and East Berlin were called on to focus their education on ballet. Agrippina Vaganova's methodology became the influential model for dance education in East Germany, and Soviet teachers were imported to ensure the correct adoption of her approach. The Staatliche Ballettschule Berlin emerged as the dominant institution in this ballet-based dance education. Martin Puttke, the leader of the school until the fall of the Berlin Wall, researched the relationship between anatomical uniqueness of each individual and ballet technique, which enabled the development of a distinctive pedagogy for ballet training. He also became the coeditor (with Werner Gommlich) of translations of Nikolai Tarassov's *Classical Dance: The Dancer's School,* and Nikolai Serebrenikow's *Pas de deux in Classical Dance.* These publications, as well as Soviet training and Puttke's methods, enabled ballet technique in East Germany to achieve a high standard; East German dancers eventually received long-awaited recognition with medals and awards at ballet competitions in Osaka, Helsinki, Varna, Tokyo, Moscow, and Lausanne in the 1970s and 1980s.[44]

Dresden remained the only state school where *Ausdruckstanz,* subsequently renamed *neuer künstlerischer Tanz* (new art dance), was able to survive as a teaching method because no other school had the equivalent of a Palucca. The combination of rigorous ballet training with *Ausdruckstanz*-based choreographic and improvisational techniques yielded creative and skilled choreographers who defined the dance landscape in East Germany and subsequently in the united Germany.

Another dominant influence on dance in East Germany was Tom Schilling. Schilling, who achieved his greatest success in the 1970s, trained in ballet technique but also worked with Dore Hoyer and Mary Wigman in *Ausdruckstanz.* He became a protégé of Walter Felsenstein, the artistic director of the Komische Oper Berlin. Even though Schilling masterfully employed ballet vocabulary, he also turned toward other movement systems depending on each specific narrative and characterization in his different choreographies. This kind of investigation permitted more formal inquiries into movement vocabulary as well as choreography; the result of such inquiries were unique works that defined ballet and dance in East Germany for nearly two decades.

As chapter 2 establishes, Schilling emphasized the development of new choreographic forms as a means of rethinking the Soviet model of content-driven "revolutionary ballets" and as a way to include folk and other nonballet vocabulary into his socialist realist ballets. Chapter 2 seeks to disrupt art historical discourses that set socialist realism as a static and historically, politically concrete paradigm against modernism as a universal and apolitical aesthetic by tracing Schilling's shifting interpretations of socialist realism in concert dance. The technical demands of Schilling's works, in combination with the abstraction engendered by complex dramatic narratives, created powerful dancers, such as Jutta Deutschland, Hannelore Bey, Roland Gawlik, Thomas Vollmer, and Gregor Seyffert. The developments at Berlin's Komische Oper and the Staatsoper unter den Linden were complemented by strong productions at the Oper Leipzig and at the eventually rebuilt Semperoper in Dresden.

At the beginning of the 1980s, a shortage of oil imported from the Soviet Union forced the GDR to boost its brown-coal production to cover demands from its industry. The resulting strain on the environment led to a growing underground movement for environmental protection. This movement merged with an already existing peace movement, especially in the younger generation, which no longer identified with the socialist state. Particularly strong solo performances exploring new approaches to choreography reflected such resistance, and because the number of dancers performing in these events and the number of spectators attending them was smaller, they did not always show up on the radar of official censorship.

Fine Kwiatkowski's one-woman performance art shows provided a unique embodiment of a critique of state-sanctioned art and gender structures in the 1980s. With her shaved head and often painted body, Kwiatkowski engaged in improvised choreographies with contemporary sculpture and music, creating a postmodern approach to dance in a country that had not extensively explored what the West experienced as modern dance. Arila Siegert contributed to East German artistic resistance with the founding of the first independent professional solo dance company, a conscious revisiting of *Ausdruckstanz* vocabulary, and a rethinking of dance production. Chapter 3 situates these two theatrical choreographies of resistance in relation to choreographed pedestrian resistance in socialist East Germany. I analyze a seemingly isolated act of performance to expose frequently underestimated connections between aesthetic and political choices and to reveal the corporeal resistance that unfolded even in private moments.

Also beginning in the 1980s, the extensive amateur dance scene attempted
to question the government doctrine that required folk-based vocabulary and
revolutionary narratives depicting the working class's struggle against capitalism
in East Germany or abroad. Many choreographers who are still successful in
Germany today initially experimented with their new forms, movement vocabularies, and contents in those companies. For instance, Jo Fabian, recipient of
the prestigious German Producers' Prize for Choreography in 1999, started his
unique interrogation into movement and language systems at a university-
sponsored community theater in Leipzig in the 1980s. As I explain in chapter 4,
his formalistic investigations into spatial compositions and abstracted pedestrian movements stood in direct opposition to the doctrine of socialist realism,
in which dance, movement, and choreography was never emancipated from
narrative and message. Contrary to this doctrine, Fabian assigned agency to
the moving body, liberating it from story and theatrical characterization. But
his dancers' bodies still engaged with history and society by ironically reconstructing significant events, such as German reunification in 1990. Chapter 4
sets up a dialectic relationship between Fabian's aesthetic strategy and West
German choreographer Sasha Waltz's depiction of East German working-class
life. The chapter relates these two theatrical approaches to the political reality
and conscious pedestrian choreography of the East German citizens who
breached the Berlin Wall on the morning of November 10, 1989. I also connect
Fabian's and Waltz's work and the fall of the Berlin Wall to a restaging of that
event by Turkish choreographer Nejla Yatkin in 2009 in New York City.

Other community dance groups likewise attempted to move away from
the doctrine of folk movement vocabulary by revisiting German modern
dance vocabulary. For instance, the Tanztheater der Deutschen Post, a dance
company that was sponsored by the East German postal service, and the
Tanzbühne Leipzig, the student dance ensemble of the University of Leipzig—
typical examples of East German state sponsorship of community dance
companies—incorporated a movement system developed by Patricio Bunster.
Bunster taught modern dance for over ten years in the GDR. He was trained in
Chile by immigrant German members of Kurt Jooss's company, and in 1954
he became a soloist at Chile's national ballet company as well as its chief
choreographer, until he immigrated to East Germany in 1973 in the wake of
Augusto Pinochet's coup. Bunster created a unique movement vocabulary that
merged Kurt Jooss and Sigurd Leeder's method with Chilean folk dance. During
his residence in East Germany from 1973 to 1985, Bunster taught at several
dance schools and his pupils became influential dancers, pedagogues, and
choreographers in East Germany and, after 1990, in the united Germany.
Upon his return to Chile in 1985, Bunster continued his work with *Ausdruckstanz*

Geschlossene Gesellschaft with Elke Hunstock, Katrin Filipiç, Wolfgang Maas, and Jens Richard Giersdorf, Tanzbühne Leipzig, 1988. Tanzbühne Leipzig.

vocabulary at the Espiral dance center, which he cofounded with Joan Turner at the Universidad Academia de Humanismo Cristiano. Chapter 5 explores the complex network of diaspora and the migration of East German cultural production as a site for visionary utopian imaginations and regional and global critique. My final analysis of East German contributions to global cultural production leaves the reader with a glance at the potential impact of the East German national body on today's global cultural exchange.

Amateur dance companies under the direction of Bunster's pupils in East Germany revived some of the early German modern dance traditions, now enriched by Bunster's use of South American folk vocabulary. This combination of German and foreign folk movement with modern dance and the eventual integration of ballet into it as a training method allowed community dance companies to approach topics outside of traditional folk narratives. Increasingly, community dance companies even staged carefully choreographed critiques of the political and social situation in East Germany. For instance, the choreography of *Geschlossene Gesellschaft* (*Closed Society*) from the Tanzbühne Leipzig explored issues of space, enclosure, and conformity. The dance featured four dancers in a confined space in which they performed solitary everyday tasks, such as reading, combing hair, and washing the floor. Forced by their proximity they eventually broke out of their isolation and engaged with each other in seemingly harmonious group and pair configurations, only to fall back into a violently repetitive re-enactment of the opening movement sequence. The absence of a clear narrative and the emphasis on distinct movement vocabularies for the depiction of the different stages in the dancers' circular development permitted a variety of interpretations. As much as the choreography could be read as a familiar representation of social and personal relationships, the members of an East German audience would also have been aware of the dance's correspondence to the political situation in their own country, specifically the inability of individual citizens to break out of repetitive socialist rituals in the enclosed society.

Community companies critiqued political and social situations not only through narrative but also through a thoughtful exploration of choreographic approaches, different dance styles, and vocabularies. These positive developments in community dance were accompanied by an increased interest in Western techniques, such as those of Martha Graham and José Limón, on the part of professional dance companies and ballet schools during the late 1980s. Dance in the GDR was no longer able to ignore international developments, which reached even the walled-in dance community through workshops and performances. Dance had already surpassed clearly ideological endeavors both in topic and technique, and as a result, many East German dancers and choreographers were ready to play an important role in the united German dance landscape after the fall of the Berlin Wall.

With the fall of the Berlin Wall, many socialist countries, including East Germany, that had heretofore been prominent players on the world stage began to quickly, and in many cases, literally, vanish from the world map. In the years following the fall of the wall, some former socialist countries such as Poland were able to recast their experience under Communist rule as part of a national narrative of ongoing resistance, while others, such as the former Yugoslavia, experienced a violent breaking apart into smaller national, ethnic, or religious units. Yet others, such as the former Soviet Union, configured their national identities by way of reference to czarist colonialism and Bolshevik rule.

However, East German national identification went on a completely different trajectory from that of the other socialist states. Not even a year after the fall of the wall, the country was subsumed into the West German national structure. Retrospectively, the fall of the wall can be seen as simply a step toward reunification. As a result, the distinct political systems, institutions, and cultures that characterized East Germany have nearly completely vanished. In some instances, this history was actively—and physically—eradicated by the unified Germany: witness the destruction of the Palace of the Republic, the seat of the

East German Parliament, the *Volkskammer*, in other cases, the history of the GDR has disappeared from neglect and disinterest.

The fact that the GDR no longer exists becomes important for a discussion of East German dance and choreography; its cultural artifacts are only available in the form of archival documents and as oral culture. Hardly any of the country's dances are still in the repertoire of any dance company. The embodiment of its citizens still endures, yet it has been overlaid by the unified Germany's corporeal codes. The East German utopia of a progressive socialist German state has been replaced by its former citizens' *Ostalgie*, the consumerist nostalgia for East German products. Such unproductive nostalgia lacks a comprehension of East German culture's constructive power. My analysis of East German dance, choreography, and conscious physicality attempts to restore what I deem a significant aspect of that era: the body of its people.

1

Dancing National Identity
in Daily Life

A New German Folk (1945–61)

My aim in this chapter is to expose English-speaking readers to a swath of German dance history that has heretofore been neglected. I illustrate how the East German government utilized folk, a term whose definition I complicate, to create a distinct nationality in an international arena. The era of the East German state offers a fruitful case study for a reevaluation of the idea of the folk because it was one of the last times in recent history that a government directly and overtly employed folk dance to influence its citizens in regard to state-sponsored goals. In a time of economic global erasure of national dividers and simultaneous violent reassertion of localized identification and cultural difference, a study of the creation and subsequent decline of national identity—especially a national identity that was formed outside of global capitalist societies—enables a critique of current political and cultural globalizing developments.[1]

I provide an initial overview of the history of folk in Germany in order to contextualize the philosophical and political dilemma posed by the government's belief in the transformative potential of it. My subsequent discussion of the extensive and unique amateur dance scene and the government's attempt to indoctrinate social dance serves as an illustration of the state's reach into all areas of dance production.

The chapter culminates with a study of the Erich-Weinert-Ensemble, a dance ensemble of the East German armed forces that became one of the major tools for the socialist state's creation of a national identity and its correlated effort to shape its citizens into *sozialistische Persönlichkeiten* (socialist personalities). To illustrate how the Erich-Weinert-Ensemble became one of the main institutions involved in this redefinition of East German nationhood and citizenship, I discuss the company's genealogy and chart the evolution of its repertoire. My analysis of *Canto General*, which was the Erich-Weinert-Ensemble's largest and ultimate dance production prior to the opening of the Berlin Wall in 1989, demonstrates that such state-sponsored projects reinforced East Germany's national identity and situated it as part of the socialist system. More importantly, this large-scale choreographed hymn connected East Germany to the global proletarian struggle through its emphasis on transnational folk.

I am especially interested in the formulation of utopian societal visions through dance and in embodiment as archival practice in East Germany. In this chapter, I attempt to rereference folk not only as defined by its preservationist or traditional value but also through its potential as a vehicle for manufacturing community identification, whether localized or nationally demarcated. These two focal points—tradition and community—are complemented by an investigation of folk's emphasis on corporeality as a knowledge resource. Such an understanding of folk extends notions of archival practice into corporeality and movement. Tradition, community, and corporeality, which define my exploration of folk, are not clearly distinct from each other, and indeed, the cases in which they overlap are the most interesting.

Thus, my goal in this chapter is twofold: I want to reclaim unknown parts of East German dance history and insert them into a larger historical discourse. At the same time, I want to provide an understanding of folk that goes beyond the often narrow definition of it as a traditional and community-based dance practice. In other words, I wish to expose the English-speaking world to the dance history that ensued in the aftermath of *Ausdruckstanz*'s interrupted supremacy in Germany, but I am also interested in a critical analysis of the potential employment of culture—and specifically folk dance—for the visionary rethinking and restructuring of societies more generally.[2]

Folk as a Nationalizing Movement in Germany

Germany has fostered an intense and complex relationship to its folk dance vocabulary, so much so that lederhosen-wearing men slapping their calves in high jumps and lifting feisty women in dirndls has become a symbol of German identity worldwide. Yet Germany's attention to its folk dances and other peasant traditions is a fairly recent phenomenon. The focus on and creation of a regional, and subsequently, national tradition was part of the construction of national identity that occurred in nearly all European countries in the wake of the French Revolution of 1789.[3] In Germany, writers and poets spearheaded projects intended to evoke national spirit and patriotism. Writers in the Sturm und Drang period (approximately 1765–85) questioned the Enlightenment's insistence on the supremacy of reason. Artistic exploration returned to emotion, feelings, and the natural as knowledge sources. Most famously, the poet Johann Gottfried Herder turned to peasant language and folk songs, seeing them as an expression of the seemingly unconscious creative and artistic sources of a nation.

The idea of individual genius, so important to Romanticism in Germany, found its collective counterpart in the concept of the original and the instinctive creative capacity of the *Volk*.[4] Folk songs, fairy tales, and legends were established as artistic products in their own right and were specifically freed from the scrutiny of reason. Due to its worldwide popularity, the famous collection of fairy tales by the Brothers Grimm became one of the most visible projects in the reevaluation of folk production. Even though this attention elevated folk into the realm of artistry, it also situated folk outside the realm of critical evaluation. This classification of folk as original, natural, and instinctively creative still defines our modern reception of it.

Throughout the nineteenth century, the predominantly arts-driven creation of a national cultural identification eventually expanded into a political force in Germany. Even though German national identity initially was defined mainly in the fields of literature and music, specific attention has been paid to the corporeal component of the nation since the middle of the eighteenth century. For instance, Johann Christoph Friedrich GutsMuths and Friedrich Ludwig Jahn established the national sport movement that instituted the (predominantly male) healthy national body, created through exercise. This attention to sport and exercise, in combination with the hygiene movement arriving from England and Sweden (which included the female body), spawned a whole network of sporting and hiking associations at the end of the nineteenth century and beginning of the twentieth century.[5] In her interdisciplinary survey of dance and physical culture in Germany during this period, Inge Baxmann confirms this turn away from individual physicality toward an emphasis on group movement.[6] These collective movements were synchronized through rhythm, and rhythm also became the main focus in dance.

In 1925, Max von Boehn closed his history of dance by arguing that rhythm had the potential to elevate dance into a major art form. While he dismissed Émile Jaques-Dalcroze's rhythmical focus at his dance school in Hellerau as too narrow and naively artistic, Boehn still commended Jaques-Dalcroze's pupil Rudolf Bode for building on his mentor's interest in intensifying "the expressivity of the entire body."[7] In 1934, Bode explicitly called for the establishment of a "connection between physical training and the cultural expression of a nation" and employed dance and folk dance in carrying out this plan on the grounds that they were "the noblest expressions of German cultural convictions."[8] Bode went on to become the head of the Fachgruppe Körper-bildung und Tanz inside the Kampfbund für Deutsche Kultur under the National Socialists. So while the Nazis did not invent the connection between dance and national expression, they were able to utilize and manipulate existing ideas and an extensive network of physical culture.

The Nazis streamlined dance and physical culture by melding disparate ideas into a single-minded force, most notably through the extensive employment of folk dance and songs for education of the Hitler Youth. Starting in 1936, all girls had to join the female branch of the Hitler Youth, the Bund Deutscher Mädel (BDM). This organization and its subdivisions focused on the physical and mental indoctrination of all girls. One important aspect of this education became the study of German folk dances, mostly in connection with folk songs. Twice a week, nearly every German girl would learn to sing German folk songs and to dance German folk dances. They would perform in age-based groups at nationwide festivities or during holidays celebrated in their hometowns or regions. Groups drawn from Glaube und Schönheit—a subdivision of the BDM—would even perform these folk dances in front of their führer, Adolf Hitler, at national gatherings and other large-scale events.[9]

Choreographing an East German Nation

Given this appropriation and abuse of German folk tradition under the Nazi regime, any employment of folk after World War II in the Soviet Occupation Zone and subsequently in East Germany seems surprising.[10] But artistic developments in East Germany were determined by the Soviet Union, and it had already promoted folk as the most important cultural expression of the Soviet people.[11] East German officials focused on folk material not only for its preservationist or traditional value but also for its potential to manufacture localized and national community identifications. East Germany, constructing itself out of the war-torn German nation, depended on the creative powers of folk culture.

Baxmann rightly points out that times of social and political uncertainty generate a need for cultural reassurances, which can typically be secured by directing oneself toward the past.[12] East Germany was in a doubly uncertain situation: not only was the state coping with the aftermath of World War II but it was also grappling with the task of constructing a national identity distinct from that of West Germany, which laid claim to all of German history and culture.[13] Thus, an integral aspect of this renegotiation of Germanness became the East German claim to Germany's cultural inheritance in literature, theater, and dance. Yet, in line with the Soviet emphasis on socialist realism, the East German government incorporated only select parts of Germany's culture into its new national culture. The focus was classical literature, such as the work of Johann Wolfgang Goethe and Friedrich Schiller, as well as folk traditions in literature, music, and dance.

Folk allowed a unique connection to the seemingly unspoiled distant German past. And with its symbolic associations with agrarian labor, it aligned with the new socialist ideology. In Marxist-Leninist theory the relationship to labor was the determining factor for any individual in a social system. Under the capitalist system, the proletariat was exploited by the process of production, while under a socialist one, it was no longer disconnected from the instruments of production but rather owned them. Thus, the ruling class under socialism was the industrial working class in collaboration with farm workers. Folk culture, originating in labor movements and community festivities, permitted a seemingly timeless artistic depiction and celebration of labor.[14] Such folk-based artistic depictions also contributed to the socialist state's growing emphasis on socialist realism, which was thought to reveal underlying principles of socialism. Folk dance with its still traceable and recognizable features linking it back to the labor movement was seen by East German officials as working with socialist realism to uncover the essence of socialist labor culture.[15]

Consequently, the East German government made considerable efforts to create a working archive of folk dance by commissioning collections and publications of folk material and by supporting an extensive amateur dance scene whose participants performed folk dances or drew on folk material to choreograph new dances. Publications ranged from ideologically focused manifestos, such as Aenne Goldschmidt, Rosemarie Lettow, and Albin Fritsch's 1952 *Der Tanz in der Laienkunst* (*Dance in Amateur Art*), to manuals explicitly for training and choreography, such as the 1953 *Material für die Bildungs- und Erziehungsarbeit der Volkskunstgruppen: Tanz* (*Material for the Educational Work in Folk Dance Companies*). *Der Tanz in der Laienkunst* reads like an archetypal Cold War document in its denunciation of capitalist degeneration in the United States and Western Europe and in its stressing the necessity of focusing on untainted national folk material for its values defined by labor and naturalness. The collective of authors producing these writings also situated folk in relation to other dance vocabularies and struck out against *Ausdruckstanz* as formalist, decadent, and cut off from socialist experience. Moving from critique to implementation, the authors also provided strict rules relating to the appearance, training, and repertoire of any East German amateur dance group.

Material für die Bildungs- und Erziehungsarbeit der Volkskunstgruppen supplemented this doctrinaire guidance with two syllabi for the education of beginners and advanced dancers. Each of these syllabi was divided into sessions on cultural politics and aesthetics, general body training and movement exercises, folk dance techniques and rhythm, specific folk dance styles, and finally, the history of dance. The history of dance was also broken down into readings and exercises. Readings included general writings on folk dance, its importance for the creation of a socialist society, dance historical essays, and also speeches and publications by Stalin such as, for instance, his "Marxism and the Question of Linguistics" and "Dialectical and Historical Materialism." The anonymous authors emphasized the political capacity of folk dance by stating that the aim of the movement exercises was to provide training in "discipline, collective spirit, self control, and endurance."[16]

Of particular interest in this publication are the sessions on folk dance techniques, because they offer an overview of what officials and dance historians in East Germany considered essential elements of German folk dance vocabulary. The material was divided into steps, holds, and formations. The steps were further divided into walking, striding, bouncing, jumping, and combinations of these moves. Examples were simple walks, triple steps, and changeover steps in different time, such as two-four, three-four, and four-four time. The authors also described triple and changeover strides, simple jumps on one or two legs in two-four and three-four time, jumps on one leg while the second leg shuffled from the back to the front, jumps in which the stretched out second leg tapped the ground in the front, and so on. Holds between two dancers were categorized as one- or two-hand holds while holding the arms at various heights and at different angles, holds crossing arms in numerous ways, holds on hips or shoulders, open and closed holds, and backward holds. Finally, the authors described numerous formations, such as a circle with dancers in line, side by side, or in pairs; various rows; and mills, which were created by joining hands in various constellations in the middle of a circle.

All of these generic steps, holds, and formations were expected to be taught as part of specific regional folk dances that had unique styles and required specific execution. The curriculum started with simple dances and moved into more complex material toward the end. As an example, the first dance explained was a dance in pairs called *Spinnradl* ("spin wheel" in a German dialect) that required the dancers to turn and change partners.[17] Both the name and movement of the *Spinnradl* referenced the spinning of yarn. Women and men organized themselves into couples in a circle, greeted one another with a nod of the head, and performed earthbound steps and simple knee bends. The man turned the woman under his lifted arm—a figure reminiscent of a spindle spinning in a woman's hand, giving the dance its name. Then the couples all turned repeatedly in a *Kiekbusch* hold, in which the man, standing behind the woman, held her hands out to the sides at shoulder level and the woman looked back over one of her shoulders to see her partner.

As complex as this might sound, *Spinnradl* was actually a simple dance consisting of walking and turning, emphasizing two kinds of earthbound walks, various holds, and two kinds of turns, all of these emblematic of German folk dance. The authors included specific goals for the execution of these movements. The circle forms were intended to educate dancers in collective spirit; the earthbound steps celebrated naturalness; the holds promoted a "healthy" relationship between dancers of both genders; and the turns created liveliness. The steps, turns, and holds in *Spinnradl* and all the other dances in the manual were never seen by the East German government as solely folk dance movements; they were also movements capable of carrying an ideological message and transforming practitioners into better East German citizens.

No wonder then, that the government provided manuals describing these dances and detailed instructions for how to perform them to the amateur dance ensembles and that officials ensured that these steps and dances became a living archive of socialist values through performance. This archive extended far beyond the research and notation of dances into the continuous reenactment and reconfiguration of them. Thus the East German government utilized the constructive power of the folk material instead of just preserving it as a cultural artifact. As a result, East Germany had one of the most extensive amateur dance scenes in the Eastern Bloc. Nearly every town, village, large factory, mine, transportation company, university, store chain, and agricultural collective had a dance company. This network of folk dance companies was closely monitored and ruled by a central organ that was founded in 1952, the Zentralhaus für Kulturarbeit, which oversaw the work in all fifteen district cultural affairs offices and subdivisions of these offices in all boroughs. The Zentralhaus für Kulturarbeit offered workshops for folk dance teachers, organized conferences, seminars and festivals, and published journals and the two education manuals already mentioned.[18] *Volkstanz*, one of these journals, rhetorically asked in a headline, "Can you agitate with folk dance?"[19]

To guarantee a positive response to this question, the government, besides creating the amateur folk dance scene, established a large showcase for these dance companies. Beginning in 1955, the annual Fest des deutschen Volkstanzes in Rudolstadt staged successful incarnations of government cultural policy.[20] Dance companies from every part of the republic gathered to present their programs to each other and to a jury, to learn new dances, to discuss developments in folk dance research, and to receive new instructions from officials for the coming year. The first gatherings even included mass folk dances that featured up to three thousand dancers.[21] These practices were not just repetitions of an idyllic past, aimed at preserving it for posterity. They aimed to shape the present. In training people using strict guidelines and by enforcing the

Folk dances for the masses at the annual Tanzfest in Rudolstadt, 1969. Tanzarchiv Leipzig e.V.
Photo: Gerhard Jllig.

repeated performance of tightly choreographed movement, the state sought to create a certain kind of citizenship. Simply put, in doing something over and over, East German bodies were supposed to be conditioned to move in a specific way.

All the layers of control, exchange, and instruction on shared guidelines and correct execution merged East Germans to an extent into the state's project and also led to the creation of a living archive of East German movement. This archive represented not only the preservation of material valued by the government for its localized and ideological functions but more importantly the transformation of its citizens' existing embodiment through repeated execution. Dancing material from the past became a means by which to restructure the present East German social system. In addition, the East German state attempted to set the stage for a future in which everyone would have a socialist way of moving. Through this danced labor, the state ensured a path toward communism, the Marxist-Leninist utopian future.

State-controlled, professional folk dance companies provided models for public engagement with folk throughout East Germany. The Erich-Weinert-Ensemble, the first professional folk dance company, was founded in 1950. It was joined in 1952 by the Staatliches Volkskunstensemble as well as the Staatliches Ensemble für sorbische Volkskunst, and two years later by the Staatliches Dorfensemble.[22] The Erich-Weinert-Ensemble, in conjunction with these other companies, provided funding for professional ethnographic research of folk dances in East German towns and villages. Eventually such research found its way back onto the stage and into community performances through these professional ensembles.[23] These performances in turn became examples to be followed by the amateur ensembles. Even though these facets of engagement with folk dance material cast a wide net, the government realized that it was not reaching all East German citizens. In particular, young people were not always engaged by folk dances. To expand the influence of folk dance into the realms of youth culture, GDR officials embarked on a campaign that would come to be characterized as one of the most bizarre incidents in German dance history.

Folk Dance as Social Dance

In 1952, the dance publication *Der Tanz in der Laienkunst* called for the creation of new socialist dances in East Germany. The authors, who were choreographers and directors of professional dance companies, declared that new choreographies had to focus on the transformation of folk into material that could have an immediate political impact. In this way, dance could become a weapon of class struggle.[24] To access a broader public, they suggested that everyone in dance turn their attention to social dances, since those dances reached the majority of citizens and most importantly the youth. Even though social dances, such as the waltz or French tango, were identified with the middle class and not the working class, the authors felt its collective form was enough to transform it into a progressive tool for the creation of conscious East German citizens.[25] Another publication went so far as to call social dances corrupted folk dances that had lost their connection to their original creative sources. To reverse this destructive regression, social dances needed to be revitalized through movement material and choreographic principles from folk dances.[26] The government campaign for new social dances continued for years and became increasingly dogmatic. Finally at the beginning of 1959, the campaign bore fruit; at the annual folk dance festival in Rudolstadt the government was able to present a new social dance.

Two ballroom dance teachers, Helmut and Christa Seifert, had choreographed a dance called *Lipsi*, named after Lipsia, the Latin name for Leipzig, its city of origin.[27] The choreographers freely mixed existing social dance steps with German folk vocabulary. The dance figures were kept simple so as to be accessible to beginners. The *Lipsi* began in a regular social dance embrace and combined synchronized chassé steps with half-turns in waltz steps. These traditional social dance steps were regularly interspersed with pivoting steps on both feet and kicking steps forward and backward in promenade position.[28] These steps and turns under raised arms were quoted from dances such as the *Spinnradl* and *Laendler*. This quoting of the folk became more evident when the woman was positioned in front of the man with her back facing him, looking over her shoulder. Despite the missing handholds in the *Lipsi*, the position was clearly a variation of the *Kiekbusch* hold that is part of the *Spinnradl*.

Except for one movement sequence in which the woman turned the man under her raised arm, the entire movement vocabulary clearly gendered the participants. The woman was assigned the more stylized movements and the man control over the turns and tilts. This prescribed assignment of gender roles satisfied the socialist state's desire to guide young people into heterosexual couples.[29] Despite the fact that women in East Germany were supposed to participate equally in the production process and that this participation was supported by an extended network of child care and public services, the government never attempted to challenge gender binaries or heteronormative constellations.

The resurrection of folk dance vocabulary in relation to social dances paralleled this endorsement of fixed gender connotations. Folk was seen as pure and less influenced by effects of socialization and conditioning because folk

Heinz Weihmann und Frau — Sonderklasse

Hasso Busch und Frau — Sonderklasse

72

Ein neuer Gesellschaftstanz:
LIPSI

Nach Abschluß der Redaktionsarbeiten für diese Broschüre erreichte uns die Nachricht, daß von Mitgliedern der Arbeitsgemeinschaft der hauptberuflich tätigen Lehrer für Gesellschaftstanz der Deutschen Demokratischen Republik in Zusammenarbeit mit Komponisten ein neuer Gesellschaftstanz zu einer rhythmisch entwickelten Musik im 6/4 Takt unter dem Namen „Lipsi" geschaffen worden ist. Die Leser der Zeitschriftschrift „Der Tanz" werden sich erinnern, daß wir in unserer Ausgabe 12·1958 über die DDR-Konferenz der Lehrer für Gesellschaftstanz in Erfurt berichteten. Dort wurde ausführlich über die Anordnung des Ministers für Kultur in der DDR über die Bildung einer Arbeitsgemeinschaft der hauptberuflich tätigen Lehrer für Gesellschaftstanz und deren Aufgaben geschrieben, die unter anderem darin bestehen „Formen des Gesellschaftstanzes zu entwickeln, die auf unseren nationalen Traditionen beruhen und einer sozialistischen Lebensauffassung entsprechen." Der „Lipsi" ist das erste praktische Ergebnis zur Erfüllung dieser Aufgabe.

Wir geben **Helmut** und **Christa Seifert,** den Schöpfern der Choregraphie des neuen Tanzes das Wort zu einigen Ausführungen über die Entstehung des Lipsi:

Wir haben uns bei der Entwicklung der Tanzschritte zuerst von der Musik leiten lassen, die einen modernen Charakter hat und in einem mittleren, heute am häufigsten üblichen Tempo gespielt wird. Ferner haben wir den knappen Raum in Betracht gezogen, den ein Tanzpaar hat, wenn es zu einer öffentlichen Tanzveranstaltung oder zum Dielentanz geht. Die Schritte sind also klein und benötigen wenig Platz. Sie bewegen sich immer in Tanzrichtung fort, so daß Zusammenstöße weitgehend vermieden werden. Da der Tanz für die Allgemeinheit bestimmt ist, mußten die Figuren entsprechend einfach und leicht lernbar sein. Es ist kein Problem, einen Anfänger in kurzer Zeit mit dem Tanz vertraut zu machen. Wir sind auch von der Partnerbeziehung ausgegangen. Die Pare tanzen in Tanzhaltung, aber mit Abstand, können in verschiedenen Positionen die Tanzhaltung lösen. Sie tanzen Grundschritte, Drehungen sowie Platzwechsel und Schritte in Stellung hintereinander. Somit wird den Paaren eine größere Ausdrucksmöglichkeit als bei der ständig geschlossenen Tanzhaltung gegeben. Der Tanz ist in seinem Aufbau modern. Wir wollen mit ihm einen Tanz entwickeln, der den Erwartungen unserer Jugend und überhaupt des heutigen Menschen entspricht.

Announcement of the *Lipsi* in a government publication from 1959. Leipzig: Zentralhaus-Publikation, 1959, 72. Tanzarchiv Leipzig e.V.

traditions were defined by a way of life predating industrialization. Bodies involved in preindustrial agrarian labor were perceived as closer to nature and the natural—an ideological construction in itself. The East German government ascribed to folk material the capacity to penetrate layers of socialization to the presumed natural essence of bodies. By positioning bodies in a paradigm of the natural, bodies were defined as biological entities not yet socially constructed. So instead of reflecting a more contemporary understanding of gender as socially constructed, the reconstructed folk movement reduced gender to biological differences. Because of the folk dances' biologically based gender connotation, the East German government in effect endorsed a heterosexist paradigm for relationships among its citizenry.

Western dance movements, such as dances based on "rock 'n' roll," were thought to be a product of a degraded capitalist society. Prior to the erection of the Berlin Wall in 1961, the government could not prohibit rock 'n' roll and other Western dance movements. Consequently, the state tried to provide a socialist alternative to the capitalist and decadent way of moving. The *Lipsi*, with its incorporated folk material, was fostered to enable young GDR citizens to spend their spare time dancing in company without imitating Western dances. This alternative consisted of exclusively East German movement vocabulary, free from any external material. In this manner, folk was utilized as an internal force, as an attempt to establish a unique East German culture and with it to create an East German national identity.

Not surprisingly, the *Lipsi* was rejected by young East German citizens.[30] On November 2, 1959, forty young people marched through the city of Leipzig and shouted, "We don't want *Lipsi*! We don't want Alo Koll! We want Elvis Presley and his rock 'n' roll!"[31] Yet the official reaction to the demonstration in Leipzig proved how important the East German government deemed the *Lipsi* to be in its fight for an East German culture. Fifteen of the demonstrators were sentenced to jail with sentences ranging from six months to four and a half years.[32]

The failure of the *Lipsi* did not put an end to the East German government's attempts to influence the national corporeal identity through the employment of folk vocabulary in dance. Officials had already turned their attention to the potential for reaching citizens of a younger age—children. One endeavor was a collection of children's dances published by the central committee of the government youth organization Freie Deutsche Jugend (FDJ) in the 1950s titled *Volkstanz-Sammlung (Folk Dance Collection)*. This collection featured a dance that involved an interaction between children and a set of state policies known as "the Plan." The Plan was the economic plan issued every five or seven years by the East German government that centrally regulated the GDR's industrial development and outlined the political strategy for that period.

This dance was a message piece organized around the young dancers' questions about the Plan's impact on their lives and their possible contribution to the Plan's endeavors.[33] Their questions were expressed in song, and the music and lyrics of this song were accompanied by a brief movement sequence. The choreography employed simple forms and movements, such as running in circles while holding hands, elevation to half toes, rhythmic clapping, and lifting of arms to front and side. These were no longer direct quotations from specific folk dances. Rather the circle patterns, handholds, and claps now only evoked the geometry and movements of a more abstract folk or even general dance vocabulary. The only directly quoted folk form in this dance was a mill, in which two children jumped around each other while holding hands with crossed arms. This cross-hold appeared in various folk dances, such as the *Wechselhupf* dance.[34]

This kind of abstract employment of folk forms accompanied by dia-logue increasingly defined many choreographic endeavors of government-commissioned works. Part 2 of the 1976 *Kolloquium des Staatlichen Folklore-Ensembles der DDR* (*Colloquium of the State Folklore Ensemble of the GDR*) distinguished three different choreographic approaches to the use of folk. The first still demanded the direct and truthful reconstruction and performance of folk dances. The second outlined how to use folk vocabulary in stage productions of newly choreographed folk dances. The third approach insisted that choreographers expand their engagement with folk material by utilizing it as a template for developing more abstract socialist and realist dances for the stage.[35] These guidelines called for a kind of engagement with folk that would move beyond a simple replication of steps and spatial arrangements. Folk now became an essence to be evoked in contemporary choreographic work. Significantly, this progressive engagement with folk material eventually liberated choreographers from the restrictions of more traditional East German folk material and opened them to a global perspective.

Dancing, Marching, Fighting:
The Dance Ensemble of the East German Armed Forces

Even a company such as the Erich-Weinert-Ensemble—created as a model for the reconstruction and reinvention of folk material—eventually had to abandon its exclusive reliance on folk.[36] It was founded in 1950 as an imitation of the famous Alexandrov Ensemble, which was established as a division of the Red Army prior to World War II.[37] The Soviet dance company drew on folk dances as symbolic of the mother country, national unity, and, most importantly, labor. The East German Erich-Weinert-Ensemble mirrored this strategic use of folk culture as part of its own mission to promote the proletariat as the new ruling class.

The Erich-Weinert-Ensemble was a conglomerate of various artistic ensembles. It consisted of a male choir, orchestra, cabaret, and dance company. During the first years of its existence, the independent divisions collaborated on most of the performances. The dance company was originally comprised of nine men and three women. These early dancers were amateurs who received all their dance training from the company. Later, the group recruited professional dancers to serve as dancing soldiers. In her 1972 thesis "Das Profil einer sozialistischen Tänzerpersönlichkeit im Erich-Weinert-Ensemble der NVA" ("The Profile of a Socialist Dance Personality in the Erich-Weinert-Ensemble"), Rita Langfeld, who trained the dancers of the company over many years, described the folk vocabularies she taught and her training objectives. Training included learning repertoires from East European countries, alongside German folk vocabularies. Ballet technique was transformed and channeled into a specific approach to folk dance training and repertoire. For example, Langfeld described how she taught a classical port de bras as a folkloric port de bras and how she trained dancers to execute lifts and jumps in different national styles.[38]

On average, the company gave fifty performances a year for fellow soldiers and the general public. Their repertoire included folk dances from other socialist countries, but the majority of the repertoire eventually consisted mainly of German folk dances, predominantly from regions located within the borders of East Germany. Steps from these dances also provided the raw material for any new choreography with contemporary themes about the everyday life of the soldiers. The creation of an embodied archive such as this became East Germany's key strategy for inventing a unique East German tradition.

During its first years of existence, the Erich-Weinert-Ensemble operated inside the definition of the archive as East German and was exclusively concerned with folk. Folk was recuperated from abuse during the Nazi era, reclaimed as specifically East German and socialist, and then utilized to play out societal visions. By presenting a combination of artistic, intellectual, and ideological material, including strong reference to collective labor through the folk, the ensemble aimed to evoke a quasi-cathartic transformation in the audience and thereby foster a socialist reality. In particular, viewers were intended to develop into *sozialistische Persönlichkeiten* (socialist personalities).[39] The definition of "personality" in the *Philosophisches Wörterbuch*, an East German philosophical dictionary, was distinct from that of the individual. It highlighted the function of human beings in society as well as their political, cultural, and moral qualities.[40] A socialist personality was thus cultivated through societal work. Under the guidance of the Marxist and Leninist party and in collaboration with other human beings, socialist personalities were also expected to take increasing charge of their lives. This process was thought to lead to a development of the personalities' distinct capabilities and to allow the personalities to have more impact on the production process.

According to the definition, socialist personalities valued general and ideological education and were always interested in expanding their professional knowledge. They also drew on this knowledge in producing art and defending of the socialist state against its enemies. The dictionary listed high socialist moral standards, community spirit, and the courage to take risks as important characteristics of the socialist personality, who developed all these qualities by being actively involved in a collective production process. The dictionary stressed, however, that the individual did not disappear into the masses. On the contrary, the higher material and cultural living standards resulted in a blossoming of human individuality in all citizens and not just in the ruling elite, as had been the case in previous societies. These developments could only be achieved after the capitalist means of production was overthrown and private ownership of production instruments was eliminated. Building on these new material prerequisites for the development of socialist personalities, the Marxist-Leninist Party, in conjunction with the socialist state, educated citizens in the art of cultivating their personalities.

This definition of socialist personality stressed the impact of labor and the collectivity on the development of East German citizens. Through collective labor, the socialist personality was expected to become a sophisticated, well-educated individual who strove to advance socialist society. Any artistic collective—which included any dance ensemble—was required to stress and support the development of the socialist personality. And the Erich-Weinert-Ensemble was tasked with leading the way.

Dancing into a Globalizing World

In 1972, the GDR was officially recognized as a state and was thus able to establish diplomatic relations with other countries.[41] Both German states became members of the United Nations in 1973. This recognition gave East Germany greater visibility in the international arena and thus forced the political leadership to adopt a more democratic stance toward its citizens. The state also strove to instill in its citizens national pride in past economic and cultural accomplishments as well as in the now internationally recognized state, which in turn led to a temporary artistic autonomy.[42]

Already by 1964, fourteen years after its founding, the Erich-Weinert-Ensemble had begun to rely more heavily on professional dancers. As an arm of the army, the dance company was able to use the general draft for male citizens to attract the best male dancers from major dance ensembles and the three state-sponsored ballet schools. In order to secure female dancers, who had to be employed, the Erich-Weinert-Ensemble offered good working positions in a major company. The infusion of professionally trained dancers in conjunction with the slight democratization of East German society changed the nature of the ensemble. Ballet vocabulary and even modern dance became important components of training and choreography. In 1972, Peter Buettner, a Palucca pupil, took over the company's leadership and adopted Palucca's approach to *Ausdruckstanz* by moving away from larger productions. The merging of different vocabularies combined with smaller-scale productions allowed the ensemble to engage with contemporary issues in much more abstract works. These dances and their high-caliber male performers started to earn awards at national and international ballet and choreography competitions. From the 1960s to the 1980s, the company received twenty-six awards at East Germany's national ballet competition.[43] And at the 1981 ballet competition in Moscow, Thomas Vollmer, one of the ensemble's soloists, received the bronze medal.[44]

Also in line with the changing political situation, some of the new choreographies displayed more critical views of East German society and soldiers' lives. It became possible to raise issues such as the protection of the environment from industrial pollution and the discrepancy between socialist doctrine and socialist reality. Socialist realism as the exclusive artistic mode was no longer insisted on, and other forms of artistic expression were tolerated. Artists in East Germany began to return to the project of modernism, which had been cut short for them by National Socialism and World War II.[45] An investigation of artistic form as content became an important part of this process. In dance, this led to a utilization of new vocabularies and an exploration of the relationship between spoken language and movement. This shift also led to an internationalization of choreographic endeavors; artists began to move beyond the constrictions of the national to venture into global approaches and vocabularies.

Enno Markwart, who had been one of the main choreographers of the Erich-Weinert-Ensemble for many years, choreographed *Korrelationen* (*Correlations*) in 1985, which earned him and his two performers first prizes at the annual East German ballet competition. This duet was for two soldiers, connected at the waist by their uniform belts, and it effectively illustrated the incessant proximity, codependence, and homosociality of the military environment without sugarcoating it with the usual socialist glorifications. Struggling against each other and the tie, the two dancers attempt unsuccessfully to free themselves from the

Enno Markwart choreo-
graphs soldiers' relationships in the Erich-Weinert-
Ensemble's *Korrelationen*,
1985. Photo: Siegfried
Prölss.

connecting device. Once they both realize the inevitability of their condition, they each try to dominate the shared space and movement. Eventually, the soldiers realize that they can achieve far greater range of movement and spatial freedom by working together.

As much as the dance still seems to relate a classic socialist narrative about the progression from individual to collective motion, the choreography departs from common socialist realist representations of reality by rendering the story abstract. More importantly, the choreography depicts a generalized situation through the exploration of movement and compositional principles, such as movement initiation and the structuring of space. This investigation of formal movement structures became much more emblematic of progressive artistic productions during the early 1980s in East Germany. These productions also bore more similarity to choreographic productions in Western Europe and North America.[46]

The professionalization of the Erich-Weinert-Ensemble and its successes at ballet and choreography competitions led to an astonishing touring schedule.

Of course the company toured all the socialist countries, but it also performed in Egypt, Algeria, Syria, Yemen, and Iraq.[47] Tours to these countries might sound surprising today, but those nations were included within the Marxist-Leninist mapping of the world for the construction of an international proletariat. Countries such as Yemen and Iraq were seen as part of the sweep of national liberation in postcolonial countries, and the Marxist-Leninist vision was that those postcolonial movements would combine forces with the proletariat in capitalist countries and with the already-established socialist systems. In this conception of world history, the 1917 October Revolution supposedly inaugurated the era of a transition from capitalist world order to socialist domination and subsequently communism. During the transitional period, these three main revolutionary forces—postcolonials, proletariats, and socialists—would cooperate to ensure the victory of the communist idea.

These three revolutionary forces became the focus of the Erich-Weinert-Ensemble's last large-scale choreography, *Canto General*, a coproduction with the Tanztheater der Komischen Oper Berlin. The choreography was performed in 1989 at the Palast der Republik as part of the cultural program for the national mass gathering of the FDJ.[48] *Canto General* is based on poems by Chilean communist poet and Nobel Laureate Pablo Neruda with music by the leftist Greek composer Mikis Theodorakis. Neruda's poetry and Theodorakis's music connect the struggle of postcolonial countries in Latin America to that of the working class in capitalist countries such as Greece. In addition, the proletariat in all three countries—Chile, Greece, and East Germany—fought against their indigenous fascist dictatorships during earlier decades, epitomizing the abstract Marxist-Leninist notion of three revolutionary forces. On a movement and choreographic level, these forces are symbolized in *Canto General* through a blend of *Ausdruckstanz* movements and ballet, as well as through the use of choreographic principles from Latin American and European folk traditions.

Utilizing these eclectic movement vocabularies to illustrate eleven poems from Neruda's famous cycle, the Erich-Weinert-Ensemble performed a utopian vision of global peace and social justice. This piece represented a tremendous shift in how folk was being used in choreography. At the time the dance company was formed, East Germany had been attempting to establish its national identity through a direct employment of East German folk vocabulary; by the late 1970s, the company's invocation of folk was no longer concerned with national specificity but with global interconnections. Although the company shifted from using folk as a nationalizing tool to using it as a globalizing mechanism, it was still concerned with the creation of a community, just a community that extended beyond the national borders of East Germany into the global proletarian community. More important, the nationalizing vision of the early years gave way to a globalizing utopia, which envisioned a worldwide uprising against capitalist oppression.

Still *Canto General* is not a simple depiction of global proletarian struggle. It choreographs East Germany into the center of this struggle. Both the program notes and reviews emphasize that East Germany had a vested interest in global social formations. Even though press releases and interviews with choreographer Harald Wandtke stress the abstract nature of the libretto, the choreography stays close to both Neruda's poetry and Theodorakis's music. In his poems, Neruda evokes revolutionary struggle and colonization in the Americas and anchors these cultural movements in a vivid description of natural beauty and ancestral mythology. Theodorakis underscores the revolutionary and celebratory aspects of the poetry by relying on hymns as the main musical mode. The choreography mimics Theodorakis's grand music through the extensive employment of mass movement choirs and strong geometrical patterning. Duets and solos break off from these larger groupings and return to the collective. At first sight, such an illustration of class consciousness seems to fit comfortably with the doctrine of socialist realism and seems to function as a simple propaganda tool. But a closer analysis reveals a more complex undertaking. *Canto General* amalgamates Neruda's eleven poems into an abstract narrative of a revolutionary uprising. Even though the libretto and costuming situate the story in a preindustrial, imaginary Latin American country, the story transcends national specificity.

The libretto, written by Bernd Köllinger, one of East Germany's major dance dramaturges, starts by depicting masses of people being born from the rumbling earth. These masses in turn give birth to the Poet, an indigenous young man. Evoking and interacting with natural powers and mythical figures in carnivalesque settings, the Poet encounters the Woman. Their fleeting relationship produces the Tree of Freedom, out of which the Liberator steps, a creation of man and nature. The Liberator wakes the people and organizes them into a revolutionary force. Meanwhile, the Poet joins a group of traveling performers, who stage a satiric critique of their capitalist rulers. The dictator sends in soldiers and the Poet is shot dead. His father's death rouses the Liberator, inspiring him to lead the masses into revolutionary uprising. The insurgence memorializes and invokes the Poet and he is resurrected; he joins the people, who become one with nature by returning to the earth. The revolutionary cycle is renewed when the earth trembles and gives birth to the masses again, from which another young man emerges.[49]

The libretto repeatedly evokes rural settings through references to the earth, trees, and maize fields as well as traveling performers. However, nature in *Canto General* not only connotes the countryside but also becomes a mythical

The Poet (Thomas Vollmer) and the people are created by mythical nature in the beginning of Harald Wandtke's *Canto General*, 1989. Archiv Darstellende Kunst, Akademie der Künste, Berlin. Photo: Reinhard Kaufhold.

Collective uprising moves the Liberator (Raymond Hilbert) toward the Girl (Angela Reinhardt) in *Canto General*, 1989. Archiv Darstellende Kunst, Akademie der Künste, Berlin. Photo: Reinhard Kaufhold.

force. This double sense of nature is emphasized by the choreography of the segment that follows shortly after the birth of the Liberator. Having emerged from the Tree of Freedom, the Liberator organizes the chaotic masses into a circle. The Liberator performs a solo with both balletic and abstracted everyday movements in the center of the circle. Eventually the circle of observing men and women rise and perform a folkloric circle dance with joined, raised hands and simple sideward walking steps, recalling East European and Latin American circle forms. Organizing themselves into pairs, dancers join their hands at shoulder level and perform mills counterclockwise and clockwise, and then they sit down in the circle for another solo by the Liberator. The Liberator, a synthesis of nature and human beings, initiates this short folk sequence. The choreography celebrates his arrival as well as nature through the abstracted folk patterns and vocabularies. Here nature, personified by the Liberator, becomes a revolutionary force that eventually leads the masses into the battle for justice. The abstract movement vocabulary no longer specifically references East German folk material but rather evokes the universal folk as a revolutionary principle.

As I have shown throughout this chapter, the East German state's journey from using folk dance as a nation-building instrument to using it as a globalizing one was systematically executed. Whereas the beginning of the socialist state saw a direct employment of East German folk vocabulary and dances, during subsequent years folk became a source for the development of new dances through the borrowing of already-abstracted folk vocabularies and principles from transnational folk. This amalgamation of choreographed ideology and technical mastery resulted in *Canto General*, a spectacular mass event that displayed the capacities of East German dance and choreography in service of state-sponsored goals. Yet form, content, and scale of *Canto General* felt already dated to an East German audience in 1989. As it turned out, *Canto General* was the swan song of a disappearing official national dance culture, whose unique vocabularies and structures were inextricably linked to the political history of East Germany from the time of the building of the Berlin Wall in 1961 to its unexpected collapse in 1989.

By 1989, it was surprising to see a dance production such as *Canto General*; it already seemed to belong to a different era. This production was the last to make visible the discrepancy between East Germany's official doctrine of dance in service of socialist ideology and alternative productions by community dance companies at smaller venues. These productions bore more similarities to international developments in dance content and technique. The amateur dance companies that produced them were able to develop choreographies that depicted relevant social issues or investigated formal concerns in dance. Jo Fabian is an example of such progressive developments; he staged his first main productions with the amateur dance and theater ensemble at the University of Leipzig and became a leader in East German dance around the time of the fall of the Berlin Wall.

Fredric Jameson's assurance that "all class consciousness of whatever type is Utopian insofar as it expresses the unity of a collective" reflects the East German government's official shift of emphasis from a national to a global utopia. "Such collectivities are themselves," Jameson adds, "figures for the ultimate concrete collective life of an achieved Utopian or classless society."[50] This shift was intended to move East Germany closer to its communist goal; however, as it turned out, it foreshadowed the end of the socialist state and the loss of that utopia. From the exclusive utilization of folk during the early years of its existence to the abstract use of folk in *Canto General*, the Erich-Weinert-Ensemble endeavored to restructure society through choreography. Yet the intrinsic nature of folk was at its bottom incongruent with East Germany's Marxism-Leninist ideology, because folk emphasized the regional or national and differentiated people into clearly gendered individuals. Marxism-Leninism, on the other hand, imagined universal social structures and equal subjects in a classless society. Throughout its existence, East Germany struggled with this contradiction, and in the end, this contradiction became one more factor in the fall of the socialist state. The following chapter addresses one strategy for overcoming a related incongruity between the state's stagnant ideology and its more progressive dance productions embodied in the tension between socialist realism and modernism by exploring the Tanztheater der Komischen Oper Berlin's uniquely East German take on *Tanztheater* (dance theater).

2

East German *Tanztheater*

Reconsidering Socialist Realism and Modernism (1960s and 1970s)

Scholars often reduce the East German state to its dictatorship and compare it solely to developed capitalist states, especially West Germany, rather than assessing it in relation to other socialist countries. These unfavorable evaluations tend to compare East Germany with capitalist states on economic and political grounds and use Western concepts of labor, market structures, and political systems as gauges.[1] When compared with other socialist countries, East Germany fares well. But drawing on universalized Western concepts of modernity and progress, as well as the so-called triumph of capitalism as a global political and economic structure, of course it becomes easy to label socialist ideological formations and their accompanying cultural productions as antiprogressive.

However, the advanced industrialization, efficient mass production, strong bureaucratic administration, extensive surveillance capacities, secularization, and break with traditional gendering of labor structures that characterized the GDR made it a modern state from its inception.[2] While the establishment of socialism in the Soviet sector marked the 1950s, the 1960s saw the stabilization of the SED's political and economic leadership. In 1960, after the death of the GDR's first president, Wilhelm Pieck, the Staatsrat was created, which strengthened the ruling position of the SED as well as its Stalinist head Walter Ulbricht. As described in chapter 1, the building of the Berlin Wall in 1961 then brought a brief period of economic improvement. At that time, the government realized that, in addition to labor, other realms of life needed to be taken into account in order to construct a modern East German identity. The state's commitment to improvement in living conditions, leisure, and entertainment would convince East German citizens of the advantages of socialism over capitalism.

49

Concepts like socialism, capitalism, and modernity are not static entities. As discursive models they rely on other historically determined discourses that accompany them. Modernity and its related concept of modernism require a counterpart against which to be defined.[3] For decades, socialism and socialist realist artistic productions that emphasized political engagement with the social served as antagonists to capitalist modernity and modernism's autonomous formalism. Recalling the now-famous debate between Sally Banes and Susan Manning in which Manning challenged Banes's America-centric and chrono-logical periodization of modern dance, Mark Franko emphasizes how the characterization of early modernism in American modern dance depends on an accompanying formalist discourse.[4] Franko also highlights the way what counts as modernism in dance is constantly adjusted in relation to social develop-ments and dance's own history and demands a reevaluation of modern dance "in light of its own artistic, cultural, and political context."[5] At the same time, Franko considers modern dance to be impure or even in parts antimodernist because of its "political intentions" and its unambiguous engagement with class and gender politics.[6] Correspondingly, Fredric Jameson argues that the concepts of modernism and realism "are drawn from two unrelated systems, and like those two well-known lines which, prolonged into infinity, never meet, they are incommensurable with each other." He elaborates on this point by noting that "modernism is an aesthetic category and realism is an epistemological one; the truth claim of the latter is irreconcilable with the formal dynamic of the former."[7]

Tom Schilling's East German *Tanztheater*, I maintain, refutes the idea that modernism and socialist realism are incommensurable.[8] Artistic production can be understood as both aesthetic investigation and political engagement with social structures. Despite modernism's claim to formalism and autonomy from the social sphere, it still explores social systems, and despite socialist realism's focus on representation of an essence of reality, it investigates aesthetic forms. As an East German choreographer, Schilling was forced to comply with socialist realist doctrine. At the same time, however, in his shifting choreo-graphic approaches throughout the 1960s and 1970s, he engaged with key aspects of modernism: artistic autonomy, formalist self-reflexivity, the achieve-ment of the essence of human experience by eliminating subjectivism and purging emotionality.

It is usually assumed that socialist realist art contested modern art—or, in socialist realist terminology, "formalist art"—and thus sought to bypass moder-nity as a societal period.[9] In dance historical discourse, productions of socialist choreographers and dancers are reduced to their political dimension and not investigated for their contribution to modern art.[10] The West German dance historian Jochen Schmidt's view on *Tanztheater* is an example of such reductive thinking. In his book titled *Tanztheater*, Schmidt categorically dismisses Tom Schilling's dance theater as old fashioned and politically corrupt.[11] In Schmidt's view, Schilling's work does not deserve to be called "Tanztheater," which by the 1980s had become a term of approbation used to refer to West German contemporary dance productions internationally associated with the work of Pina Bausch.[12] Schmidt argues that Schilling's work displayed neither a "serious engagement with the *Ausdruckstanz* tradition nor with modern dance over decades due to the political pressure."[13] This stance casts the West German dance scene as modern, progressive, and constantly changing and the East German dance scene as political, reactionary, and stagnant. In short: Western dance was modern and East German dance was not.

Parallels to this East-West dichotomy abound in the German art world, and similar analyses have been made of German visual art and art historical discourse. In her discussion of art historical discourse about East Germany, Ulrike Goeschen lays out the challenges for artists: "East German artists and art historians . . . wanted their art to be seen as independent of the social system and the individuality of each artist's work to be recognized. In their opinion one should not talk about the art *of* the GDR but rather of art *in* the GDR."[14] In contrast, the outside position—often voiced by West Germans—lumps all East German art together and "rejects it all as pre- or anti-modern, totalitarian state art."[15] Susan Manning speaks to the same issue in dance when recounting reactions in East and West Germany to the first united exhibition on dance in both parts of the divided nation at the Akademie der Künste in 2003. East Germans did not see their dance history represented in its full gamut, while West Germans did not understand why East German dance merited inclusion in such an exhibit in the first place.[16] Goeschen suggests that we question the status of Western art as normative and start seeing art in East Germany as increasingly emancipating itself from cultural doctrines. East German artists' stance toward modernism and the growing incorporation of selected parts of it into East German art serves for Goeschen as an indicator of developing artistic independence from state-sponsored artistic visions.[17] I expand on Goeschen's view by showing in this chapter that East German socialist realism was neither unadulterated by modernism nor an unchanging doctrine. Rather, even inside state-sponsored structures, socialist realism was constantly adapted to fit the needs of the changing political landscape in East Germany.

While scholars have analyzed the development of East German visual art in relationship to socialist realism, as well as to fascism, similar analyses of the connections between dance production and the East German political land-scape have yet to be conducted.[18] Filling this research vacuum is critical to our understanding not only of dance and dance history but also of socialist realism itself. As is the case in relation to visual art, socialist realism in dance also opened itself to varying degrees to modernist principles and incorporated them at specific points in the artistic production process. For instance, Schilling's *Tanztheater* challenged Western capitalist supremacy over modernism by relating socialist realism to modern artistic production. To illuminate these subtle shifts in socialist realist dance production, I discuss three works by Schilling in relation to the dance historical and ideological discourses surrounding them. Through a comparison of the dances and discourses we can see the development of socialist realism in East German society and the adjustment of socialist realist rhetoric in response the changing artistic productions.

Modernism: The Capitalist Project

Even though I am rethinking socialist realism in relation to modernism in a specific national and historical context, I am challenged by the fact that both concepts take on different meanings in the context of artistic practice versus art critical discourse. These terms have also been redefined or reexpressed based on the changing political situation. In order to rethink modernism and socialist realism historically and politically, I first work through some of these semantic challenges, thereby providing a clearer terminological framework for my analysis of Schilling's choreographies.

The contested term "modernism" is often theorized in relation to the term "modernity," yet they are not interchangeable, serving as they do different sets of agendas. Modernity commonly connotes a period of social development of Western society and of its fundamental philosophical, technological, and economic systems.[19] In the humanities, modernity refers to the formation of nation-states and the increasing domination of Europe by bourgeois and capitalist values. The beginning of modernism is often dated to the Enlightenment, whose values of reason, rationality, and causality modernism is said to share. Modern progress is attained through the development of social institutions and a radical rethinking of the position of human beings in relation to nature, each other, and society. History is no longer seen as a narrative of society's development but rather as a form of shaping and influencing it.[20] This vision is imported into other parts of the world through domination and colonization. As much as this account has become commonplace in academic discourses, the story of dance in the East German state offers us an important opportunity to complicate it.

As Jürgen Habermas points out in his seminal article "Die Moderne—ein unvollendetes Projekt" ("Modernity: An Unfinished Project"), the word "modern" was first used in the late fifth century to distinguish the official Christian present from the pagan Roman past.[21] For many epochs thereafter, the term became a code word for differentiating the new from the old, even as critics sought to maintain a dialogue with the classical period. Habermas detects a break from this engagement with classicism only with the onset of Romanticism; from then on modernity connotes a counterpoint to tradition and history.[22] Other theorists such as Henri Lefebvre and Jameson agree with the definition of modernity as always new, a term capable of being imbued with different meanings and structures. Jameson also points to national differences in the understanding of the time frame and application of the term: the German definition begins with the Enlightenment and emphasizes humanism, whereas the French definition commences with Baudelaire and Nietzsche and includes wariness toward progress.[23]

From language to language, we also see semantic and usage differences. In the English language, there is a distinction between modernity and modernism: Jameson suggests the first is a historical period and the second is an aesthetic, philosophical, and ideological reaction to that context that can be either negative or positive.[24] In German, the term "die Moderne" is used for both meanings; a distinction is made by adding "ästhetische" ("aesthetic") to reference modernism. To avoid confusion when discussing U.S. and German positions, I employ the English term "modernism" to talk about the array of artistic productions in the period from the second half of the nineteenth century through the second half of the twentieth century. Given the scope of this chapter, I am mostly interested in developments during the Cold War era, though I reference earlier developments when necessary.

In the same way that "modernity" has different meanings in different contexts, so too "modernism" is defined very differently depending on the artistic field or disciplinary discourse, period, or national context. The only general agreement is about the rupture caused by and reflected in modernist art. Susan Stanford Friedman offers the following diverse definitions in various disciplinary aesthetic discourses:

> Critics of modernist poetry often identify a poetics of fragmentation, parataxis, image, and idiosyncratic rhythms and sound patterns. Art historians often focus on the rupture from realism and increasing attention to form, especially pure geometric shapes and planes. Architectural historians often look to the stark, functionalist minimalism of Bauhaus design or cityscape towers as the expression of modernity and its aesthetic in the age of the machine. For music historians, the embrace of primitivism and atonality in a composer like Stravinsky might constitute modernism. Media critics look to the radical impact of the new mechanical means of

reproduction—photography, radio, cinema, television—for the sights and sounds of modernity.[25]

Dance and dance history—which are missing from Friedman's list—are often informed by the artistic practice and discourse of other art forms, as in, for instance, the engagement with art nouveau in the choreography of Loïe Fuller or the exchange between Gret Palucca and the Bauhaus movement as well as expressionist artists such as Ernst Ludwig Kirchner and Wassily Kandinsky.[26]

In her analysis of Kandinsky's drawings of Palucca, Susan Laikin Funkenstein acknowledges the discrepancy between the Bauhaus's narrow definition of modern art as independent from culture, social structures, and politics and the reality that it engaged with contemporary German and European societies in the 1920s. Funkenstein's focus on modernism's engagement with seemingly antithetical movements such as physical culture and the women's movement allows her to challenge the established binaries in modernism of masculine/feminine, mind/body, and high art/mass culture, which would be thoroughly solidified after World War II by Clement Greenberg.[27] Complicating the seeming regendering of Palucca's female body in Kandinsky's drawings in line with his constructivist depiction of her moving body and thus the images' male connotation, Funkenstein concludes that the abstract modernism of Bauhaus is not gender neutral. Rather, she argues that the neutralization of Palucca's femaleness reflects the New Woman's androgyny; it was thus an expression and celebration of newness, cosmopolitanism, and urban technological innovation and a challenge to traditional female gendering in society at that time.[28] Even though Kandinksy's constructivism was associated with maleness, his engagement with dance and the presence of Palucca's personality in his work demonstrates an incorporation of femaleness, an undermining of established binaries, and most importantly, an interaction with contemporary social structures and politics.

Funkenstein's argument is important for my own rethinking of the binary between socialist realism and modernism in dance because it problematizes key features that appear to split them into opposites. On one hand, socialist realism art is required to realistically represent political structures in order to communicate universal and essential truth. To achieve this goal, socialist realist art has to emphasize content over formal investigations as well as eliminate subjectivity and a distinction between high art and mass culture. On the other hand, modernism strives for artistic autonomy from social structures through abstraction and formalist self-reflexivity, the upholding of the distinction between high art and the popular, and an erasure of emotionality. Interestingly, modernism also works toward an essential truth, albeit through the artwork itself and not through any social or political relevance.[29]

These characteristics appear in different national discourses on modernism and socialist realism. For instance, Gay Morris recounts Gertrude Lippincott's assurance in 1948 that "true art could not be political because 'it transcends national and political boundaries and appeals to all mankind,'" which she issued in reaction to the Soviet censorship of modernist composers, among them Dmitri Shostakovich, Aram Khachaturian, and Sergei Prokofiev, on the grounds that they were formalists.[30] Morris points out that Lippincott's remarks affirmed modern dance's endangered post–World War II position as authentic art that universalized essential components of human experience independent from politics. Such a forceful affirmation of modernism's political autonomy in dance in the face of the Soviet prohibition against formalism contributed significantly to the development of U.S. modernism and its globalizing discourse. This perspective also contributed to the designation of socialist realism as anti-modernist. The development of U.S. modernism in general and modernist dance in particular has to be read at least in proximity to Greenberg's celebration of abstract expressionism in his 1955 "American-Type Painting," which became an important part of the U.S. struggle to establish global leadership in the field of modern art.[31] In "American-Type Painting" Greenberg generalized a highly subjective history of modern art in which non-Western influences and all European art culminated in American abstract painting.[32]

Among many critics of such hegemonic historization, Amelia Jones highlights the masculinist purification of artistic practice, reception, and content in Greenberg's essay and his other writings on abstract expressionism and specifically on Jackson Pollock.[33] Jones asserts that normative masculinity in modernist artistic production and reception also includes other identitarian positions of power, such as heterosexuality, whiteness, middle classness, and—I would add—nationality.[34] Yet the crisis of male embodiment in the United States after World War II caused by the anxiety regarding the uniformity and conformity of mass culture, its consumption by predominantly female citizens, and the emergence of a new female post–World War II subjectivity challenged seemingly independent modernist art.

Consequently, key features of modernist artistic practice and reception are executed and contested at the same time. U.S. modern art is defined as abstract or at least formalist, universal, elitist, and independent from political/social structures and thus as gender neutral. Yet as Kandinsky's drawings of Palucca suggest, modernism also incorporates all of the negated categories. Its abstract, formalist, universal, elitist, independent, and gender-neutral stance is built by evoking and simultaneously disguising a privileged masculinity. Thus modernism does engage with social structures. This is also evident in its anxiety around mass culture, the nationally specific construction of this masculinity, and so on.

Of course, all of these processes are infinitely more complex when thought through for dance, where embodiment cannot be as easily disguised or even removed, as in the visual arts. And in dance, female embodiment dominates. Thus, as Franko establishes, modern dance has to engage with "a variety of polemics over gender identity."[35] Even male, abstract choreographers of modern dance have to grapple with this issue. Philip Auslander describes the choreographer Alwin Nikolais's strategies in relation to Greenberg's definitions.[36] Nikolais disguised dancers' bodies through the use of full body costumes that did not adhere to the human form and through lighting and set design that fragmented, covered, and disguised the body. But most importantly he focused on motion rather than on the dancers' bodies. As Auslander points out, this approach complicates issues of representation and dancers' agency, yet he celebrates Nikolais's and other modernist artists' freedom to experiment with "form as an end in itself. Both Abstract Expressionism and Nikolais' dance thus enacted the tension between the twin modernist desires to shake off the universal human subject as the referent of art and to celebrate a universalizing idea of form."[37] This might be true, yet Auslander's analysis rests more on Nikolais's rhetoric and goals than on an analysis of his actual work. Seemingly abstract, many of Nikolais's choreographies in fact rely on narrative, slapstick, and absurdities in interbody relationships and thus emphasize human bodies and shatter the pure relationship to formalism.

Morris distinguishes between expressionist and objectivist modern dance and counts Nikolais among the objectivists but also recognizes Nikolais's work as permitting an exploration of "more fundamental energies than the human psyche."[38] Yet unlike Auslander, Morris is conscious of the political implications of rethinking modern dance in relation to art historical demands on modernist art. Morris analyzes the move away from strong individualism toward an exploration of form in the 1950s. Modern dance maintained its vanguard modernist position by eliminating "communication of essentialized emotion" and narrative and by emphasizing such elements as improvisation, chance procedure, the independence of music from dance and by deemphasizing such features as romantic relationships.[39] Morris points out that modern dance's attempt to focus on form and autonomy is in agreement with definitions of modernist artistic practice, yet its divorce from social structures also conformed to a Cold War emphasis on secrecy and censorship.[40] Her solution for modern dance does not stress motion, as does Nikolais's, according to Auslander. Rather, Morris sees modern dancers and choreographers highlighting an unconscious, "kinesthetic sympathy" between audience and dance that is specific to dance because it is embodied. According to Morris, dance's unique ability to communicate body to body allows it to convey an essential truth, so important to modernism.[41]

Interestingly, East German *Tanztheater* also appealed to the rhetoric of the body's ability to convey essential truths. Schilling often emphasized dance's unique ability to communicate ideas and truths to an audience strictly through movement, and he also claimed that this capacity distinguished dance from all other art forms. Yet, when he stressed such kinesthetic empathy, Schilling firmly situated his rhetoric in socialist realism. For Schilling, who matured as a choreographer inside East German ideological structures, socialist realism enabled dance to communicate the essence of socialist life to the entire audience, without any initiation or education. Thus, in his opinion, dance was actually one of the most valuable socialist art forms.

East German Socialist Realism

Born in 1928, Tom Schilling received his classical training as a child dancer at the theater in Dessau and later from modern dance pioneers Mary Wigman, Dore Hoyer, and Gret Palucca. He performed in Wigman's famous *Orpheus* production in Leipzig in 1947 and then as a soloist at the opera houses in Leipzig and Dresden until 1962. The Dresden opera then offered him the position of main choreographer, which he held until 1965.[42] Even though Leipzig and Dresden were important cultural centers of East Germany, Schilling longed to work in East Berlin, where theaters were more prestigious, government funding was more abundant, and there was less censorship.[43] The opportunity for a move to Berlin came in 1964 when Walter Felsenstein, the director of the Komische Oper Berlin, was searching for a choreographer to establish a dance company at his institution.[44] As a well-known East German dance legend recounts, after seeing an early version of Schilling's *La Mer*, Felsenstein exclaimed, "You are all hired."[45] As a member of the unique and privileged institution of the Komische Oper Berlin, Schilling was able to rethink and shape East German stage dance for several decades like no other choreographer.

The Komische Oper Berlin was established through decree in 1947 by Alexander Dymschitz, then the cultural commander of the Soviet occupational forces. It was housed in a famous 1892 theater building near Unter den Linden, one of Berlin's major streets. The building had a long tradition of mostly German-language light musical entertainment in the form of revues and operettas. Even the Nazi German government integrated the theater into its *Kraft durch Freude* (strength through joy) program. Revue and operetta held an important place in German culture, yet they were often perceived as entertainment without higher cultural significance. Felsenstein set out to rethink artistic and directorial approaches in this area of musical theater by breaking down the divide between opera and theater.[46] In the program notes for the performance of Johann Strauss's *Die Fledermaus* that opened the Komische Oper Berlin in December

1947, Felsenstein expounds his directorial philosophy: "Elements of this always sparkling, boisterous and life affirming work—the sometimes veiled humor and the partly revolutionary irony that expands into social critique—confirm that only significant fun—taken seriously—leads to true and everlasting delight. Far away from inconsequential amusement and unpopular experiment, the Komische Oper shall give joy."[47] This statement touches on all the benchmarks of Felsenstein's innovations by evoking a search for the true and original intent of a work and, with this, the value of tradition and a rejection of artistic experimentation. Yet at the same time, he comments that musical productions should display a critical capacity in relation to social structure and provide stimulating joy—without slipping downward into mindless entertainment. Felsenstein confirms this approach in his defense of his 1949 production of *Carmen*, for which he was attacked by critics because he reconstructed the opera's original structure with lyrical texts. He explains that his directorial work was not an experiment with an established opera but a reinstallment of original intent against a widespread practice of falsification.[48]

Such insistence on a work's original intention seems to situate Felsenstein in a conservative camp of opera directors who attempt to reproduce and reconstruct operas in a museological fashion as historical documents worthy of preservation. Nonetheless, Felsenstein's so-called *realistisches Musiktheater* (realistic music theater) broke with established conventions of opera by valuing all elements of an opera production equally. In his understanding, lyric, music, design, and performer had to function under the unifying umbrella of dramaturgical necessity and not the display of a star's virtuosity or an opera's aesthetic dazzle.[49] Felsenstein's dramaturgy of opera productions aimed to make libretti and protagonists' actions not only understandable but to demonstrate that the story constituted the only possible narrative for the depiction of a specific historical situation. By the same token, the accompanying music needed to be the only possible expression for that situation. Or, as Felsenstein puts it, "The heart of music theater is to turn music-making and singing on the stage into a communication that is convincing, truthful, and utterly essential. All problems of the drama and of staging are secondary to this. Music theater exists when a musical action with singing human beings becomes a theatrical reality that is unreservedly believable."[50] These "unreservedly believable" productions allowed audiences to see the realistic depiction of a specific dramatic situation, follow the opera, understand its true intent, recognize the critical capacity of that view, identify with the performance onstage, and finally leave the theater altered. Such an understanding of realism was partly influenced by naturalism, yet Felsenstein was fully aware of opera's artificiality and purposely utilized it. In other words, Felsenstein believed in the revolutionary capacity of artistic production, specifically that of opera, and he manipulated this theatrical artificiality in an effort to change social structures.

When Schilling joined the Komische Oper Berlin in 1965, it already had a nearly twenty-year tradition. Schilling situated his work fully in relation to Felsenstein's approach, stating, "I believe . . . that realistic dance theater does not only gain its realism through the content—by being a slice of reality and real life converted into theater—but by achieving such translation and the scenic creation strictly through dance and unmistakable as dance. As such, dance—of course in correlation with music—has to be a truly believable narration of history, a story, or a musical template in a way that the danced representation justifies itself and legitimates itself as the only possible expression."[51]

Protected by his privileged position at one of the nation's prime cultural institutions, Schilling employed any dance vocabulary that he deemed suitable for his communication with the audience, even questioning the dichotomy between ballet and modern vocabulary enforced by cultural functionaries in East Germany.[52] Schilling first staged his unique blend of dance vocabularies in his rechoreography of established repertoire such as Werner Egk's 1948 *Abraxas*—a ballet based on Heinrich Heine's *Doctor Faustus*—in 1966, *Der Nachmittag eines Fauns (Afternoon of a Faun)* in 1967, *Cinderella* in 1968, and *Othello, der Mohr von Venedig* in 1969. Yet he also produced new symphonic and classical ballets to Berlioz's *Symphonie fantastique* (1967), his final version of *La Mer* to Debussy's composition of the same name (1969), and Darian Bozic's *Concerto grosso* (1969), as well as Tchaikovsky's *Grand pas classique* (1971). Eventually, he created new contemporary works, such as the 1969 didactic socialist ballet *Der Doppelgänger (The Double)*, in which an East German working-class man cheats on his wife with a foreign dancer and is taught a lesson by the two women that brings him back to his wife.

On the occasion of the premiere of *Der Doppelgänger* in 1969, Schilling positioned himself in relation to the ongoing debate about realism in East Germany. He stated that the term "realism" needed to be modified for dance, citing Bertolt Brecht's famous statement that "realism is not how real things are, but how things really are" to voice his belief in the necessity of artistic solutions and specific forms that went beyond unambiguous gestures or miming of reality.[53] By referencing Brecht, Schilling indicated his awareness of the director's role in the shaping of East Germans' interpretation of socialist realism. Brecht had been one of the editors of *Das Wort*, the journal that printed the famous Expressionism debate in 1937–38, in which exiled German artists and art historians established their position regarding tradition and modernism in art.[54] This debate, which was influenced by and was a reaction to the original definition of socialist realism in the Stalin era Soviet Union, disputed the function of art in the twentieth century and the relationship between artistic expression and societal conditions. The expressionism debate, along with the influence of the Soviet definition of socialist realism, paved the way for a specific East German transformation of realism into socialist realism after World War II.

The concept of socialist realism was based on the definition of the term by Andrej A. Zhdanov at the first Congress of the Soviet Writers' Union in 1934. The definition demanded "a true-to-life" and historically concrete "representation of reality in its revolutionary developments."[55] The portrayal of the totality of all manifestations in society and the penetration beneath the surface enabled one to grasp the underlying laws of historical change.[56] Truth and historical concreteness were required of the artistic work because it had to further the socialist goal of ideologically transforming and educating the working people.[57] Socialist realism's double task of representing and educating thus combined realism as an artistic principle for a representation of reality with the politics of socialist ideology.[58] This approach departed from the employment of realism in other societies; socialist realism not only depicted and critiqued social structures but also supplied the way out of the contemporary societal system and into a brighter future via socialism, which subsequently would give way to communism.

Reacting to Stalinism, the fear of rising fascism, and the threat of war, exiled German communists relied on this definition in an attempt to deploy art as a weapon in a united political battle against imperialism in the 1930s expressionism debate. Yet their understanding of what constituted such art divided these artists and art historians into two camps; Georg Lukács, Béla Balázs, and Alfred Kurella on one side emphasized continuity with a classical tradition and Klaus Mann and Ernst Bloch on the other side demanded new content, forms, and even a redefinition of the structure and function of art in response to the new realities of their time.[59] Mann and Bloch postulated the independence of art and challenged the idea of a one-dimensional connection between politics and art as well as the notion of a simple correlation between reality and artistic depiction. They defended expressionist techniques such as fragmentation, collage, and montage. Balázs, Kurella, and Lukács criticized such uses of form and material in art on the grounds that they lacked content, were signs of bourgeois decay, and were deficient in relation to the people. This new art did not reflect reality in its essence because it remained on the surface of visible manifestations. For instance, by depicting reality as fragmented, these new art forms did not realize the correlation between manifestation and essence (which cannot be fragmented). Even though capitalism might appear as fragmented and torn, Marxism demonstrated the underlying unity of the condition of production. The avant-garde, lacking an understanding of that unity, did not represent its essence in its art and instead translated the seemingly fragmented environment into its fragmented or montage form.[60] In opposition, Balázs, Kurella, and Lukács called for an art that modeled classical humanism.[61]

Brecht eventually entered the debate by opposing Lukács's position, and the two writers came to represent antithetical viewpoints in the debate. Lukács admired German literature's classical period, holding in high regard both its principal representative, Wolfgang Goethe, and the critical realism of Thomas Mann. Brecht regarded both of these authors and the literary schools they represented as requiring critical revision. Brecht employed new critical methods, such as reportage, montage, and distancing to depict contradictions in modern society. He utilized a broad range of theatrical techniques from various historical and cultural realms to prevent the identification of both the actor with his or her part and the audience with the theatrical event. Brecht emphasized his actors' corporeality and strove to emphasize the depicted reality over the way it was represented onstage. Lukács, on the contrary, regarded all these techniques as bourgeois and decadent and demanded that art represent the essence of reality in a unifying form. He called for a congruence between the representation of reality and reality itself.

The East German theater historian Petra Stuber defines the latter employment of realism as apparently noncongruent with Marxist materialism. Socialist realism, according to her, favored illusionary and ideal depictions of reality. She argues that Lukács's definition of art was influenced by Hegel's and Aquinas's philosophy in which the essence of reality hides behind its manifestations and concepts but is nevertheless capable of revealing itself. Realism on Lukács's account thus reexposes the essence of a society as completely as possible. Such an understanding of art treats concepts and manifestations in society as social constructions. Yet the laws that construct these manifestations as well as an underlying essence remain outside of and uninfluenced by these concepts and manifestations. The notion that it is possible to work through all the concepts, names, and manifestations to advance toward the unchanging essence is an idealist position. Thus, the realists were actually idealists and subsequently socialist realism was an idealist art form.[62] Only through a complex historical redefinition of realism were the communist leaders of the GDR able to employ it as the main tool for the development of an East German national identity after World War II. Socialist realism depended on the socialist definition of reality; thus East German officials were able to constantly redefine socialist realism to make it match their ideological needs.[63]

Following World War II, East Germany's employment of socialist realism initially adhered to the Soviet example. The Soviet government used its presence on East German soil to ensure the ratification of its own view of realism. This manipulation was often disguised and mediated, yet it induced political debates, which influenced East German reality and artistic production over several decades.[64] The formalism debate at the beginning of the 1950s was one of those influential controversies, and it resulted in the state's official definition of art. As prescribed by the fifth plenum of the Central Committee of the SED (March 1951), the content of art determined its revolutionary effect on socialist citizens.[65] Art needed to help citizens understand reality and provide a means of moving reality toward the ultimate goal: communism. The form and structure of art needed to follow and support this goal-oriented content. In 1951, Hans Lauter, the secretary of the Central Committee, issued the following guidelines for how East German artists should depict a socialist citizen:

> We don't demand photographic faithfulness or naturalism from the artist; we demand something else. If, for instance, an artist depicts a progressive person, an activist, a young freedom fighter—although we don't want to say that there should only be representations of activists—then we demand that the representation of such persons expresses their readiness to work, their high quality, and their pride in their accomplishment. We want— when our best people are represented—the typical traits, which are the characteristics of a progressive person, to find their embodiment in the work of art. And we have the right to demand that, not only because such persons exist in reality and it corresponds with their dignity but most of all, *because these people embody the new that will lead us into the bright future.*[66]

Reflecting Lukács's ideology, the fifth plenum established German *Klassizismus* (neoclassicism of the mid-eighteenth to the end of the nineteenth century) as the foundation for socialist national art. German *Klassizismus* expressed the two related functions of art for East Germany. By recalling the classical past, officials emphasized the development of a German national identity in East Germany. Thus, the GDR established itself as the real successor to German prewar society, establishing a continuity in German history. In addition to legitimating the claim of the GDR to being the main inheritor of German history, the emphasis on *Klassizismus* revitalized that moment in German history in 1871 when the idea of a unified German national state was at its peak.

To create this unique East German history, the GDR not only excluded undesirable parts of German history but also fought against the influence of international concepts of art.[67] State leaders attempted to nurture an isolated national identity in the face of the growing globalization of art, economics, and politics. Only influences from the Soviet Union were welcomed by the GDR because of their ideological brotherhood. Thus, the GDR incorporated the Stalinist definition of a nation that regarded a "common culture" as a characteristic feature of nations.[68] There was no question about the kind of art that ought to serve as a foundation for this national culture. The SED newspaper *Neues Deutschland* published a list of endorsed arts and artists in 1951.[69] The list included folk tales, Johann Sebastian Bach's oratories, Ludwig van Beethoven's Ninth Symphony, Johann Wolfgang Goethe's lyrics, and Albrecht Dürer's paintings. These artists and their work became the foundation of the educational process in East Germany. The new socialist art idealized reality in the same way classical literature did.

However, realism was an idealist representation ultimately at odds with the Marxist materialism that served as the ideological foundation of East German national structures. To undo this contradiction, East German officials not only redefined socialist realism but also attempted to restructure reality by changing work environments and incorporating German folk traditions into socialist realism. In the opinion of SED officials, this method rooted the new socialist art in labor. To be able to create such art, the division between artist and the rest of society needed to be erased. The erasure of that distinction would change artistic reality by qualifying the socialist citizen to understand the conventions of socialist realism, thereby ensuring an unambiguous reading of the representation of socialist society's essence. Artists were told that to achieve that goal they needed to go out and teach the producing population about art history and artistic methods. In return, the workers were supposed to show artists how they worked and lived so as to enable these artists to depict them in their art. Art would finally move away from being an elitist occupation. Every socialist working collective encouraged their members to produce art and would go to great lengths to attend performances. This approach transformed art to an ideological and pedagogical tool and sought to break down the separation between social structures and artistic production.

For dance—despite its ambiguous form—to serve the state's goals, it needed to be specific in content as well as form. In 1953, dance practitioners and theorists gathered in Berlin for a conference to draw up clear guidelines on the deployment of socialist realism in East German dance. As a subsequently published treatise titled *Realism in Dance* observed, ballet masters, pedagogues, dancers, and theorists met under the official slogan "Fight for a realistic dance art, fight for the appropriation of the methods of socialist realism, fight a steady and consistent fight against all formalist appearances."[70] Officials at the conference provided unambiguous examples of socialist realist dance for the participants by showing Soviet documentaries about a production of the *Nutcracker* as well as Korean, Uzbek, and Polish folk dance ensembles. The chosen dances made clear that ballet and folk were to be stressed and that modern dance was to be excluded. Performances by the two state dance schools, two dance companies from Berlin, and the state folk art ensemble reinforced this emphasis.

An article by Martin Sporck published at the end of 1952 in the influential *Weltbühne* had already launched dance in this direction by calling on dance practitioners to engage in a public discourse on their art form.[71] Sporck, who felt dance was lagging behind the other arts, called for an investigation of the specificity of dance's form and structure. However, he only demanded that form be investigated for the purposes of arriving at a better understanding of how form could support the unambiguous communication of socialist content in dance. Quoting the director of the USSR's folk dance ensemble, Igor Moiseyev, Sporck defined dance as an artistic expression of emotions, ideas, and characters through rhythmic and spatial movements. Here again, dance was reduced to a tool for communication that had to be specific in its language and convey a political message. Each dance form fares differently in Sporck's subsequent brief analysis. In line with socialist doctrine, he saw ballet as carrying with it aesthetic and historical baggage but nevertheless as having potential for development if the vocabulary was reevaluated and utilized to relate socialist narratives as in Soviet ballet. Not surprisingly, Sporck wanted to revitalize ballet through an incorporation of German folk material and vocabularies. Startling is the fact that Sporck did not flat out dismiss *Ausdruckstanz* but nevertheless rejected it for its generalization of emotional states, such as lament or despair, and its subjectivism.[72]

Sporck's article sparked widespread comment among East German dance practitioners from diverse fields, all of them defending a move toward socialist realist dance. As it turns out, the *Weltbühne* solicited the respondents. The fact that the dialogue was staged accounts for the unified opinion among the featured ballet masters, choreographers, and cultural functionaries. All of them affirmed the need for such an exchange and the necessity of developing a socialist realist dance culture. In slight variations of the same argument, the respondents demanded better-trained dancers (in 1953 the dance schools in Berlin and Dresden only provided training for dancers fourteen years and older) and "realistic" librettos or at least a collaboration between choreographers and writers that would yield new socialist realist ballets. They also asked for the incorporation of Stanislavski's methods into dance (a Stanislavski conference had been held only a few months earlier in East Germany) as well as a study of and training in German folk dance and its absorption into ballet vocabulary and choreography. Interestingly, the respondents varied in their degree of criticism of *Ausdruckstanz*.[73] Some dismissed it wholesale, others wanted to preserve so-called progressive elements, and yet still others wanted to incorporate even such contested elements of *Ausdruckstanz* as improvisation.

Less surprising was the complete silence of any *Ausdruckstanz* protagonists. Neither Marianne Vogelsang, who still taught modern dance at her former school in Berlin, nor Palucca participated in the discussion. The *Weltbühne* editors repeatedly solicited Palucca's opinion, because she was the most visible modern dancer in East Germany and even collaborated with official cultural organizations such as the Akademie der Künste, yet as she did so many times before and after, she remained consciously silent. To compensate for this notice-able gap in the discussion, the editors opted to print a short piece by the music editor Ernst Krause, who had visited the Palucca School in Dresden. As Krause reported, Palucca worked simultaneously on two fronts, studying and analyzing baroque dances such as the pavane, allemande, and gigue so as to be able to utilize their structure for contemporary choreographies and also attempting to develop a teachable methodology for dance pantomime. "Dance pantomime" was basically code for a more accessible dance in which content and not form was the focus and whose message was clearly readable.

Palucca's seeming collaboration with socialist realist demands for readable dances through her work on dance pantomime and her quotation of established historical forms kept the opponents of modern dance temporarily at bay. She appeared to be moving toward communicating unambiguous meaning, just using modern dance vocabulary to do so, and seemed to be avoiding abstraction by engaging with set choreographic practices in baroque dances. However, her strategy did not work in the long run because the dance conference clearly demanded that modern dance engage with folk dance and eradicate tendencies toward cosmopolitanism and mysticism, yet she did not adopt folk dance and instead continued her investigation into choreography and improvisation.[74] This became another step in the long crusade against modern dance in East Germany.

The discussion in the *Weltbühne* was timed to initiate and influence the incorporation of socialist realism in East German dance, which became the focal point of the 1953 conference. Participants proudly highlighted the unique method of the conference whereby discussions centered on actual dance pro-ductions. In their understanding, this method instantiated Marxism's definition of the relationship of theory and practice, in which practice defines and creates theory, and not the other way around. As the *Weltbühne* reported, the partici-pants made it clear that socialist realism was not a style but "a method of observing the world and representing it in artistic productions from the working class's point of view and guided by Marxism-Leninism."[75] This definition of socialist realism allowed the participants to avoid having to prescribe one technique or choreographic form over others. Yet, in line with Soviet practice, they favored ballet technique and folk vocabulary and maintained that modern dance should be permitted only so long as it was in service of a concrete message and was informed by German folk dance.[76] The conference organizers felt compelled to clarify that this did not mean that only contemporary and realistic plots could be the focus of new dance productions. Fairy tales such as "Sleeping Beauty" could very well be socialist realist owing to their depiction of the battle of "light and good over evil and destruction and the victory of brightness over darkness." In the same way, a love scene could be legitimately socialist realist.

These clarifications and revisions created a conundrum that would haunt East German dance to the end; there was at one and the same time a seeming tolerance toward diverse techniques and narratives in dance practice and choreography and yet a constant condemnation in discourse of modernism, modern dance, and nonrealistic plots. The conundrum led to censorship and denunciation but at the same time to a perpetual redefinition of socialist realism in relation to dance. Depending on the latest interpretation of socialist realism, at any given moment a dance production could be attacked for its formalism, decadence, abstraction, and cosmopolitanism or on the contrary hailed as an example of a creative and up-to-date execution of socialist realism. Thus the context and rhetoric around dance productions became defining factors in the success of choreography with East German officials. The relationship between Tom Schilling's choreographic work and the rhetoric around it confirms this constantly shifting interpretation of socialist realism in dance.

Choreographing Socialist Realist Modernity

To analyze what modernist principles Schilling explored in his choreography it is necessary to comprehend which definition of modernism socialist realist rhetoric challenged.[77] The 1979 edition of the *Jugendlexikon Philosophie* (*Philosophical Youth Dictionary*) provides the staple East German view of modernism. The dictionary defined "Modernismus" as an "artistic development of the final stage of capitalism that reduces artistic progress to a constant change of formal approaches. That led to formalism, a rejection of tradition, and a separation of art from the people."[78] The dictionary listed a barrage of modernist styles, such as cubism, expressionism, futurism, and even neorealism, in order to illustrate the definition. Also important was the fact that modernism was apolitical, since it only rejected earlier bourgeois art and did not turn against the capitalist system. The people couldn't engage with such art, because they were not able to understand an "antirealist" modernism that focused on formalist exploration over a depiction of reality. Consequently, modernism was the decadent manifestation of a decaying capitalist society in deep crisis.[79]

This definition evoked all the hallmarks of the Greenbergian model of modernism but offered a negative rather than positive evaluation. What Clement Greenberg celebrated as the focus on the essential qualities of the artistic medium became in East German discourse a formalist exploration or simply formalism. Greenberg's emphasis on political autonomy and his rejection of mass art as kitsch was seen as apolitical and decadent leading to a separation of art from the masses, an inability to communicate with the people.[80] From the beginning, socialist realist rhetoric appealed to the notion that formalism was decadent to denounce modernism, and eventually this idea came to serve as a shortcut by which socialist realism could reject any art.[81] Formalism was defined as a specific artistic approach that focused on formal matters while neglecting content and emotionality. It was the highly subjective product of a genius cut off from regular society. Examples of formalism in East German dictionaries ranged from Gertrude Stein's poetry and Piet Mondrian's and Wassily Kandinsky's paintings to abstract art solely "composed of blotches and paint drippings."[82] This reference to Jackson Pollock and thus Greenberg's celebration of abstract expressionism was indirect but obvious. Though "decadence" could be an umbrella term for any sort of social decay, in East German rhetoric it was mostly utilized to label formalist art that upheld a division between art and the people, serving the financial and representational needs of a small elite and leaving only mass art in the form of "pornography and horror movies" for the people. It was thought that such art manipulated the people for profit, especially poorly educated, unemployed youth.[83]

Schilling, therefore, had to situate his choreographic endeavors in relation to such socialist realist rhetoric. To achieve his choreographic visions, Schilling took advantage of the changing rhetoric of socialist realism and the resulting unpredictable freedom to employ modernist principles in dance. In light of the uncertainty of that freedom, he engaged with different principles in developing each of his choreographies. *La Mer*, Schilling's signature piece, provides a compelling example of his strategic employment of modernism in socialist realist choreography.

Originally choreographed in 1964 to the first and second movement of Claude Debussy's orchestral work by the same name, the dance was expanded by Schilling in 1968 to encompass all three movements. Schilling was primarily inspired by the music, but he also engaged with a famous East German painting by Walter Womacka titled *Am Strand (At the Beach)*.[84] Painted in 1962, *Am Strand* became the most reproduced and iconic painting in East Germany, distributed on postcards, in calendars, and even as a stamp. It was exhibited at the state art show in Dresden in 1962 and was featured on the cover of one of the most widely circulated magazines, *NBI (Neue Berliner Illustrierte)*. In 1963, the original was given to head of state Walter Ulbricht for his seventieth birthday. The firm guidelines for socialist realist visual art at the time resulted in a predominance of depictions of work environments. Departing from this trend, Womacka painted a young couple. The woman sits in the foreground in a relaxed position, one leg drawn in, the other under her, looking past the viewer. The man lies on his stomach, propped up on his forearms, and looks up to the woman. The

Walter Womacka, *Am Strand*. Oil on canvas, 30 × 40 cm, 1962. Staatliche Kunstsammlung Dresden. © 2012 Artists Rights Society (ARS), New York / VG Bild-Kunst, Bonn.

bright colors and body postures are reminiscent of paintings by Gauguin, yet the waves in the background seem to threaten the couple from a distance, indicating a setting not typical of Gauguin's paradises.

Am Strand depicts a very private moment in a clearly public setting. Despite the painting's representation of a couple in a moment of leisure and not at work, it was celebrated by East German officials as nonmodern and socialist realist. An association for the fine arts stated at its nineteenth meeting that "without fear of being called by some an embellisher, Walter Womacka consciously elevated with his picture the beauty and inner richness of our maturing youth to beauty in art and with it he arrives at the aesthetic generalization of the truth (essence) of our life."[85] Such language evaluates the painting in line with the requirements of socialist realism, which called for art to depict the essence of socialism through a representation of socialist everyday life. Looking at the painting today, however, I find it hard to read as a prime example of socialist realism. Rather, it looks like many other not particularly realistic

Final scene of Tom Schilling's *La Mer*, Tanztheater Komische Oper Berlin, in a restaging from 1979. Archiv Darstellende Kunst, Akademie der Künste, Berlin. Photo: Arwid Lagenpusch.

portraits and scenes of Germany or United States in the 1960s that can be found in thrift stores.

Similarly, Schilling's *La Mer* relates more to abstract symphonic dance works popular in Europe during that period in both the East and West, such as those by John Neumeier in Hamburg, John Cranko in Stuttgart, Kenneth MacMillan in London, and George Balanchine in New York City, than to socialist realist principles. In strong relation to Debussy's music, Schilling depicts an interaction between a man and a woman at a beach. Neither setting nor costuming provide specificity; the stage is empty, the background an abstraction of waves and reflections on the horizon; the dancers' costumes are different versions of a leotard.[86] Sitting alone in the middle of the stage, the male dancer reacts to, or at times embodies, the imaginary waves, winds, and birds with a combination of ballet, modern, and pedestrian vocabularies. The choreography depicts him as being familiar with, and in control of, the natural environment. In contrast, the female dancer, who enters the stage later, is amazed by the beach and is careful in her exploration of the unfamiliar forces. While this difference between them produces a dynamic relationship, it also genders the characters according to heteronomative socialist standards.

Such traditional gendering is reinforced in the subsequent encounter between the woman and man: he leads, holds, and lifts her, jumping and turning powerfully. She is on point, reaching for him coquettishly, spiraling, leaning on him, and joyfully giving into the climactic embrace. Afterward, the man lies down exhausted and rests on his stomach while the woman sits, one leg drawn in and the other under her, caressing the man's head and back in a tableau reminiscent of Womacka's couple. Reflecting Debussy's final movement, Schilling's choreography uses images of natural forces to evoke danger to the couple's happiness. The woman detects the danger immediately but is not able to warn the man, who upon awaking just wants to continue the duet. He only realizes the imminent threat after the woman—who simultaneously reacts to and embodies the fight with the waves and birds—goes down to the ground vanquished. The man sweeps her up in several high lifts bringing her to safety; then both sink to the ground into an exhausted embrace, him reaching out to the conquered nature while holding her.

The dancers, Hannelore Bey and Roland Gawlik, received first prize at the 1968 International Ballet Competition in Varna for their interpretation of the roles. The piece remained in the repertoire of the Tanztheater der Komischen Oper Berlin for many years. The Swedish choreographer Birgit Cullberg restaged the ballet for her company. As late as 1983, the East German drama-turge and dance scholar Bernd Köllinger was claiming that the "concrete and meaningful interpretation by the two dancers, who brought their whole contemporary being and feeling into their roles, corresponded to the ability and the willingness of the audience members to identify fully with the events onstage." Köllinger reasons that "there is thus for an audience in Berlin, Dresden or Karl-Marx-Stadt no question that they can discover and detect people like themselves."[87] Köllinger's evaluation situates *La Mer* as an exemplary socialist realist work. Even though the situation seems specific, the experiences of every-day people are reflected in the source of the choreography and the interpreta-tion of the dance. Most importantly, from the standpoint of socialist discourse, the audience is able to relate to the events onstage because they represent the essence of socialism. Köllinger writes: "From the protagonists' relationship in their 'small world' one can deduce information about their lives, their way of living in the 'large world.' . . . It is not too far fetched to see in the mastery of the flood a symbol for the mastery over human destiny by the people. In this message, Schilling's optimistic conception of humankind can be summarized. The history of the work's impact proves that audiences experience and understand such values as socialist."[88]

In Köllinger's discourse, none of the elements of modern art, such as autonomy from political and social structures and formalist self-referentiality, can be detected in *La Mer*. However, if one looks at the movement vocabulary used in the choreography, it can be seen that *La Mer* clearly engages with modern principles. Schilling attempts to essentialize an encounter between a man and a woman. The setting eliminates concrete references to the time or space of the encounter. The movement vocabulary draws on classical, modern, and pedestrian vocabulary without national or political specificity. Even the prominent East German dance historian Eberhard Rebling admitted in 1974 that "in contradistinction to plot-driven ballets, Tom Schilling's ballets consciously omit any depiction of a specific milieu or time frame in order to provide every single audience member with ample space for fantasies and thoughts."[89] Nature as the driving narrative force is not represented in any naturalistic fashion. Only the protagonists' reaction to nature is shown, and at times, their movement vocabulary embodies nature, as in the case of the man's birdlike posture in which he lifts both arms out and stands in an arabesque or the woman's wavelike back-and-forth motion.

These moments are also when Schilling's choreography is the most self-referential. He investigates the combination of vocabularies for their technical and communicative potential. With this, he experiments inside the form rather than using dance to communicate a story. Even though the dance seems to narrate an emotional encounter between a man and a woman and to show how they overcome an external threat, the nonspecificity of the encounter suggests that the narrative serves only as a template and that the "expression" of the choreography rather than the emotionality of the encounter is what is important to Schilling. Mark Franko suggests that expression serves as a "depersonalized universal embodiment of subjectivity" that allows the choreography to become self-referential and universal. Franko posits a conversion of emotionality into expression as one of the early markers of modernist dance's utilization of the primitive. Drawing on Jacques Rivière's analysis of Vaslav Nijinsky's *Rite of Spring*, Franko explains that the primitive is used to defamiliarize the movement, thereby to erase emotion from the performance, and to create instead universal expression.[90] Schilling employs a similar strategy by combining varied vocabularies and by focusing on their expressive potential. Schilling not only highlights a unique corporeal way of communicating an encounter between man and woman but, more significantly, he focuses on dance's ability to communicate the essential quality of such an encounter. In other words, he experiments with a unique combination of ballet, modern, and pedestrian vocabulary to investigate dance as the only possible language for representing essential humanness.

Schilling's search for the essential expression of dance technique in *La Mer* separates the choreography—at least aesthetically—from a specific political and social system. In its representation of an essence, disengagement from the political, and its self-referential investigation of dance as a unique aesthetic system, *La Mer* fulfills the major criteria of modernist art. At the same time, its historical reception classifies it as part of socialist realist dance productions in East Germany and clearly binds it to the politics and economy of socialism. The East German critic Friedrich Dieckmann agreed with Schilling's vision for a specific understanding of realism in dance, remarking in 1970 that "the art of dance operates in its representation inside a much more specifically defined area than other representational art forms. Every attempt to leave this area, for instance, to embellish on details, leads dance away from an essential effect. Instead of creating a true, qualitative realism that is dance-specific in its form, the result would be a quantitative, insignificant, and formalistic realism."[91] In other words, if dance attempts to become realistic through formal elements, such as costuming, stage design, or plot, it gives up its most important means of specificity, as it is no longer communicating through its vocabulary. Endorsed by a statement that allowed that dance might take a more formalist approach to socialist realism, Schilling was able to broaden the sanctioned dance vocabulary of ballet by including modern and pedestrian movement as well.

Yet such experiments were not always welcomed, and there were limits as to what vocabularies would be accepted into socialist realist doctrine. Just a few years later, Schilling caused a controversy when he attempted to experiment with jazz and improvisation in his 1971 *Rhythmus* (*Rhythm*). The main critique was that the work lacked content and formal rigor. *Rhythmus* was used to punctuate an evening of a compilation of several other shorter works, among them *Match*, a very popular, humorous take on gender relations in the form of a tennis match, a restaging of Jerome Robbins's *Fancy Free*, and Tchaikovsky's *Grand pas classique*.[92] *Rhythmus* has no plot; rather it depicts a moment in the everyday life of a dance company. After several dancers pick up scattered items on an empty stage, turn the lights off, and leave, a male dancer returns to retrieve a forgotten robe. Stumbling over a drum, he starts improvising on it. A percussionist arrives, clearly horrified by the dancer's lack of percussion techniques, and after a short verbal and physical quarrel takes over. The dancer—ready to leave—is taken in by the drum's rhythm and begins improvising to the music. He moves in and out of various movement styles—African-influenced undulations of the torso,

Tom Schilling's *Rhythmus*, Tanztheater der Komischen Oper Berlin, 1971. Archiv Darstellende Kunst, Akademie der Künste, Berlin. Photo: Arwid Lagenpusch.

standard jazz sequences with turns and Fosse-style hands, and even flamenco. More and more dancers (or dancers dressed as hair, makeup, and lighting technicians) arrive and join in. Before the entire group breaks into individual and frantic improvisation at the end of the piece, they participate in a longer unison jazz sequence. *Rhythmus* ends with the dancers becoming self-conscious of how much fun they are having and leaving one after another while still laughing.[93]

A week before *Rhythmus* premiered on May 9, 1971, the seventy-eight-year-old Stalinist head of state Walter Ulbricht was forced to resign as a result of an intervention by the general secretary of the Communist Party of the Soviet Union and head of state Leonid Brezhnev. Ulbricht was an adamant believer in socialist realism and only six years earlier, at the ninth meeting of the Central Committee of the Socialist Unity Party, had cautioned against a reconciliation of socialist realism and modernism.[94] Erich Honecker succeeded Ulbricht, and the change initiated a brief period of tolerance of political expression that also applied to art. There was a slight improvement in living conditions, too, and citizens started to focus on individual needs, desires, and pleasures. The choice of improvisation and the rejection of plot in *Rhythmus* must be read in this political context, because the dance allowed a focus on individual choreographic choices and enjoyment of dancing over an execution of a choreography in service of an ideology.

David Gere asserts that improvisation "should be recognized for the great demand it places upon a performer, including the demand for nearly instantaneous responsiveness to a broad palette of sensation and perception."[95] Such a definition highlights the individual choice and responsibility of the improvising dancer. Agreeing, Susan Foster expands on this definition by emphasizing the two-sided nature of improvisation: the immediate decision making and the engagement with known material. Known material can range from the performance context, structural guidelines or predetermined rules, training, dance traditions, relationships between the dancers and the musicians to even any material previously improvised.[96] *Rhythmus* emphasizes this negotiation between the known structure and a spontaneous restructuring of elements through the way dancers move back and forth between set choreographed sequences and improvised parts. The audience is left guessing how much of the performance is being created in front of their eyes, adding an air of realism and authenticity to the dance. And the two-sidedness of *Rhythmus* situates it—uncomfortably—in both a socialist realist and modernist paradigm of the authentic on one side and the formal self-referential on the other. At the same time that the choreography can be seen adhering to definitions of either paradigm, it also challenges them.

At first glance, the choreography complies with socialist realist requirements. It depicts a mundane, behind-the-scenes-look at life at a theater. In addition to dancers, *Rhythmus* incorporates characters who have working-class vocations. The choreography also focuses on the labor of dancing, as the dancers clean up the stage area, and on dance creation, demonstrating the development of movement material by individuals and as a collective process. Finally, it reinforces socialist ideals through its positive and joyous stance toward group dynamics. Thus, it seemingly couples a representation of the essence of a socialist theater environment with an affirmation of socialist life. Above all, in line with the changing political landscape, the choreography provides room for individual self-expression through improvisation and thus allows an—even slightly critical—negotiation of individual and collective identities. For instance, at one point in the choreography, a guard in uniform appears to crack down on the unruly behavior onstage, a clear reference to the East German police state. Yet the dancers force him to join in by simply ignoring his authority and pulling him into dancing. Such seemingly minor choreographic resistances connected the dance in a critical way to political structures, and those references never went unnoticed in the highly censored East German artistic landscape.

As already mentioned, *Rhythmus* utilizes a variety of dance forms. Dancers improvise using polka, flamenco, or Eastern European folk dance vocabulary. Classical ballet vocabulary, such as turns and jumps, are mostly employed in solos to demonstrate technical mastery that is then acknowledged by other dancers. However, the vocabulary that was most consistently used when it was performed in the early 1970s in both the set choreography and improvisation was a form of jazz dance, or *Showtanz* (show dance), as it was called in East Germany. *Showtanz* was an unloved child of East German dance, because of its emphasis on both form and entertainment over content and message. In one of the few East German publications dealing exclusively with *Showtanz*, Werner Gommlich labored intensely to establish the socialist value of the form.[97] Drawing on Marx's theories of production and consumption, he argued that *Showtanz* was not to be dismissed as low art. Gommlich defined enjoyable consumption as a *Produktivkraft* (productive force), a central term in Marx's political economy that refers to the forces that are applied in the production process, such as the means of labor, including human labor power.[98] Simply put, this definition elevated entertainment and its consumption not only to the level of human labor but also to that of factories and machines, key elements of socialist structure and ideology. Gommlich thus maintained that entertainment was a very important part of socialist life.

The problem of entertainment in relation to *Rhythmus* was demonstrated by the fact that as late as 1983, one finds Köllinger devoting two pages of his book *Tanztheater* to defending the choreography against reviews that criticized it as mindless entertainment lacking content and message.[99] Köllinger sought to demonstrate that *Rhythmus* was a bridge between high and low art and between stage and audience by observing that "what happened fictitiously onstage— and what could not have become alive and have an effect without the dancers' relish, active engagement, and them being seized by the dance—should have activated, inspired, and energized the audience. And it did exactly that."[100] Drawing on socialist realist rhetoric, Köllinger defined the realism of the choreography as being authentic owing to both the dancers' active engagement with the material and their ability to communicate their authentic fun to the audience, who could be positively influenced by the joyful events onstage. This rhetorical elevation of the choreography's form and effect was of course problematic inside the paradigm of socialist realism. The relationship between content and form had been the central question in socialist realism, especially in dance and even more specifically for *Showtanz*, a form that valued form over content, entertainment over message. In order to resolve this problem, Gommlich argued that the content of *Showtanz* could not be reduced to a dramatic structure; rather it constituted a "thematic orientation, a mental claim, or a *Leitgedanke* [basic idea]." And the form was not a technique, but an "aesthetic quality."[101] If not reinstalling the primacy of content over form, these definitions at least bound form and content so closely together that they could no longer be evaluated independent of each other. Of course, Gommlich had to justify his discussion of the problematic of content and form by citing a Soviet publication on Marxist-Leninist aesthetic that assured a unity of content and form and the necessity of their being treated as dependent on each other.[102] Thus *Showtanz*—along with choreographies such as *Rhythmus*—was subsumed rhetorically under the umbrella of socialist realism.

Yet, Gommlich departed in his definition of socialist realism from early definitions of it that valued content over form and thus treated the two aspects of artistic production as separate. The changing political situation in East Germany at the end of the 1970s made formal investigation even more possible, and aesthetic theorists struggled to redefine socialist realism to fit the new approach to formalism. Not only did theorists begin redefining the relationship between content and form but they also started to address such problematic issues as individuality, abstraction, and improvisation. Gay Morris and Mark Franko note that these issues were likewise significant in debates concerning early modern dance.[103] For instance, Franko discusses the tension between early modern dancers' charismatic individualism and the required impersonality in modernism as well as the social activism called for in left-wing dance theory.[104] Morris highlights modern dance's anxiety regarding its mainstream appeal and its fear of losing its vanguard status.

Given that these issues were so central to both socialist realism and modernism—albeit not always from the same ideological position—it is not surprising that Schilling continued to struggle with them through a variety of approaches in his choreographies. Most of his efforts over subsequent years involved choreographing new versions of established ballets; in 1972, he choreographed *Romeo und Julia* (*Romeo and Juliet*) and in 1975 *Cinderella*. This allowed Schilling to stay inside the form of ballet and experiment with narrative. For instance, in his *Romeo and Juliet* the reason the young lovers' marriage is impossible is not because their families are feuding but because of their differing class backgrounds. This kind of change moved his ballets firmly into socialist realist territory, yet they were not always critically successful.

Partly in response to these unpopular ballets, Schilling attempted to find a new solution for the incorporation of modernist principles into socialist realist choreography in 1975 by choreographing *Schwarze Vögel* (*Black Birds*). The narrative ballet is based on a libretto by Bernd Köllinger and reached back to Schilling's early dance training in *Ausdruckstanz* but also expanded the company's existing vocabulary through an excursion into folk dance and Asian martial art forms. Depicting peasants' uprisings in medieval Germany, the project was part of a large-scale reevaluation and rewriting of German history by the East German government.

The year 1975 marked the 450th anniversary of the German Peasants' War of 1525, the deciding battle of which occurred in Bad Frankenhausen, a small town in the territory of East Germany. The battle was one of many uprisings of peasants and poor townspeople throughout the sixteenth century in Swabia, Thuringia, and Franconia. The uprisings were ignited by the effects of centuries-long exploitation of peasants by the nobility, as well as by the decline of smaller-level nobilities, the simultaneous rise of guilds, which demanded that patricians were allowed access to city councils, and last but not least, the challenge to Catholicism by the Protestant Reformation. Thus the participants of the uprising were not only peasants but also the urban poor, members of the lower nobility, and radical priests. The important differences in the 1525 uprising compared to earlier ones was the sheer number of participants, exceeding ten thousand in certain skirmishes, and the fact that the conflict spread across local areas, both of which owed to the leadership of members of the lower nobility, including Florian Geyer, and of priests, such as Thomas Müntzer, who had loftier goals for the uprising than the localized improvement of the peasants' lives. Thomas Müntzer was also the leader of a collection of a number of peasants' groups that eventually joined other factions in facing the united nobilities' armies in a doomed final battle in Bad Frankenhausen. Around eight thousand insurgents without much real weaponry were brutally defeated on May 15, 1525, by a six-thousand-strong army of well-organized and armed soldiers, which broke an armistice.[105] Nearly all the peasants were either slaughtered in battle or executed afterward. Thomas Müntzer was imprisoned, tortured, and publicly executed outside Mühlhausen, the city of his last residency.

This uprising became an important part of East German revisionist history because it fit perfectly into East German Marxist/Leninist historization with respect to its aim, outcome, parties, and locality. The fact that the epicenter of earliest revolutionary uprising was located in the territory that would become the German Democratic Republic allowed officials to cast East Germany as a rightful successor to German revolutionary forces. This interpretation was further supported by the interest that both Karl Marx and Friedrich Engels paid to the uprising. Engels even published a treatise on the revolutionary events in 1850 in which he compared the uprising to the revolution of 1848–49.[106] Such evaluation of the events in light of later revolutions established a clear genealogy of class battle, necessary for demonstrating Marxist/Leninist progression toward communism. The unified action of various social strata such as peasants, craftsmen, and priests added to this revolutionary narrative by foreshadowing the required collaboration of proletariat and farmers in a socialist revolution. Finally, the complex participation of clergy also fit the atheist stance of East Germany. Thomas Müntzer was originally a follower of Martin Luther but eventually turned against his teacher. Luther first supported the uprising that was influenced by his famous 1517 Ninety-Five Theses, though he eventually strongly condemned the peasant insurgents.

Because the uprising had such significant symbolic value, in 1975, East Germany initiated a full-scale celebration of its 450th anniversary. Artistic projects were commissioned in many forms all over the country, the most famous one being a panoramic painting by Werner Tübke, who created one of the world's largest paintings for the Panorama building constructed at the site of the final battle in Bad Frankenhausen.[107] The government issued a set of commemorative stamps, conferences were held, academic publications were printed, and for the day of the final battle, a parade wound its way through Bad Frankenhausen. And of course, there was Schilling's *Schwarze Vögel*.

Bernd Köllinger, Schilling's dramaturge, reported that the premiere of *Schwarze Vögel* received fifteen minutes of standing ovations and concluded that the "audience was fascinated by the coherence, emotional impact and assured style, that made this largest and most daring experiment in GDR ballet history; a master work."[108] He asserted that "not realist movement but moving realism determined the scene."[109] In addition to updating his socialist realist rhetoric, Köllinger also allowed formal investigation to become part of his discourse by highlighting movement as an important communicative tool for realism. Köllinger repeatedly emphasized movement vocabulary and spatiality as "translating real occurrences" into a scenic and poetic representation. He even called the choreography "an antinaturalistic movement concept" and clearly stated that "not so much the set or props but bodies and space should communicate."[110] The dramaturge justified his assessment by pointing out that none of the fight scenes utilized props, such as swords and halberds, but used corporeal means, such as karate, and that thoughtful repetitions of movement motifs were employed throughout the choreography. Pantomime, a much utilized socialist realist vocabulary, hardly appeared at all.

In his choice of libretto and characters, Schilling complied with all the requirements of an East German state-commissioned piece for the momentous anniversary of the Peasants' War. Florian Geyer, the nobleman who denounced his wealth to lead the peasants into the uprising and who was referenced in Engels's book on the Peasants' War, becomes the central figure of the choreography. Making him the protagonist allowed Schilling to demonstrate revolutionary spirit as independent from class affiliation. The libretto loosely narrates the story of Florian's growing awareness of the plight of the peasants and a love affair with a woman who is abused and eventually killed by another nobleman. Together with a priest, Florian leads the peasants into battle against the brutal and decadent nobility. Yet the uprising is bloodily defeated, and Florian is killed with the help of the deceiving cleric. Florian is one of the few characters that develops over the course of the dance. Most of the secondary characters, such as other noblemen, peasant women and men, a female and male joker, and a cleric, remain in their initially established characterization. For instance, the cleric is erratic and dangerous throughout and eventually betrays and kills Florian to save himself. Such a portrait was in line with East Germany's atheist stance.

Even though a narrative development provides an underpinning for *Schwarze Vögel*, the choreography does not strictly follow a linear story. The score by the East German composer Georg Katzer demanded a much more modern treatment of narrative and character. Katzer, a student of the famous modern leftist composer Hans Eisler, was one of the few composers working in the field of so-called *Neue Musik*, a term that defined a musical style similar to what in English is called "contemporary classical music." Originally influenced by Schönberg's Vienna school, Katzer became known for his incorporation of electronic music into the classical form. His score for *Schwarze Vögel* relies on traditional instrumentation, but the work's atonality, strong percussiveness, and complex rhythmic structures are more reminiscent of Stravinsky's work. The music contributes dramatic arches, yet with its complex layering it also provides the opportunity to represent several dramatic actions simultaneously. Schilling emphasizes these layers by allowing the setting to become an abstract backdrop for the changing choreographic investigations of individual and group actions rather than treating the stage space as clearly defined and separated sceneries for specific events. As a result, the choreography, structured into twelve scenes framed by a prologue and an epilogue, supplies vignettes and tableaux that establish situations and relationships more often than coherent developments.

The content of *Schwarze Vögel* made it appeal to East German officials; however, it is the spatiality and Schilling's vocabulary that lends it a modernist aesthetic. Schilling uniquely blends *Ausdruckstanz* and folk vocabulary while retaining the overall aesthetic of a narrative ballet. Ballet vocabulary is used sparsely in jumps, turns, and pointed feet. Women are rarely on point, and when they are, it is mostly to connote a decadent noble environment or when one of the female protagonists imagines a flight to freedom like a bird. Yet Schilling moves from groups to duets in a manner that a ballet audience accustomed to corps de ballet and pas de deux would be able to relate to.[111] At the same time his specific investigations of the relationship between group and individual are not at all dominated by ballet's representational spatiality but also include folk forms and most importantly *Ausdruckstanz*.

The prologue in particular attests to this strong revisiting of Schilling's earlier training. A group of masked men with arms raised high and crossed at the wrists face outward inside a circle of women, who stand upright and apart from each other, facing the men. The dancers wear earth-toned, worn-out clothes. The women wear dresses and the men, whose torsos are nearly bare, wear shorts. The women start stomping toward the men while lifting their bent arms slowly backward. Suddenly, the women move both of their arms straight forward and outward into a V-shape at chest level and bend forward, still facing the men, yet with their legs turned along the circle clockwise. Simultaneously, the men fall flat to the ground with their arms and legs spread out into a star-like formation, revealing a man who arches his torso up and back. The women continue along the circle's periphery, jumping with their upper body crouched over one leg with the other leg bent forward. Strong, polyrhythmic percussions emphasize the downward quality of the stomping and jumping. Dancers move with the drums without being dominated by them. Engaging their bodies' cores in contractions, bends, and turns as well as in going to the floor, the group jumps, turns, and falls through various constellations of the strong circle formation. Eventually, they form two close circles around the central male figure, holding hands, the outer circle traveling counterclockwise and the inner circle clockwise, leading to a frenzied sequence from which the central figure breaks free. The group hovers together and moves as a group timidly around the stage while the male leader jumps and turns around them, seemingly controlling them. He eventually jumps up to be held by the group high above their heads. The entire group, still in concentric circles, crouches down to the floor bent over and then lifts up the central figure in worship again, screaming out loud in ecstasy. A starting strongly atonal symphonic music begins, forcing the group, sensing doom on the horizon, to look around and up.

The prologue evokes the choreography of *Le sacre du printemps* in its reference to ritual, its relationship between group and individual, and the rhythmic complexity of its sound and movement.[112] Interestingly, Pina Bausch premiered her version of *Le sacre du printemps* in West Germany only three months after *Schwarze Vögel* had its premiere.[113] Bausch also utilizes *Ausdruckstanz* vocabulary, yet she incorporates many more pedestrian gestures into her much more emotional and emphatic choreography than Schilling does. Schilling remains inside an abstract modern dance vocabulary, making occasional references to worship and medieval circle dances. His dancers bend over and contract; however, these movements never achieve the existential quality of Bausch's choreography, in which dancers release their upper bodies and perform falls and contractions to near physical exhaustion. Bausch's vocabulary and execution elicits audience members' empathy, whereas Schilling depicts the essence

Prologue of Tom Schilling's *Schwarze Vögel*, Tanztheater der Komischen Oper Berlin, 1975. Archiv Darstellende Kunst, Akademie der Künste, Berlin. Photo: Arwid Lagenpusch.

of a historical situation. Both rely on folkloristic circle forms, yet Bausch breaks out of such forms more consistently than Schilling, who maintains the circle even when the group moves as a cluster around the stage. Schilling's focus on geometrical forms and archetypal embodiments enabled a generalization from the concrete historical situation at the beginning of the Peasants' War to the essence of religious oppression and class exploitation. This generalization seemed to answer socialist realism's call for the depiction of the essence of social developments, yet simultaneously the bodies of the dancers and the choreography became the material for a demonstration of formal dance elements like body postures and spatial configurations and their formalist potential as key elements of dance.

It is especially in strong relationships between a mass and a leader that Schilling's prologue references his teacher Mary Wigman's early modernist choreographies and more generally *Ausdruckstanz*'s investigation of group-leader constellations after World War I. In their stiff movements at the beginning, the masked men also recall Kurt Jooss's *The Green Table*. Echoing *Ausdruckstanz*'s reaction to the trauma of World War I, the prologue remains abstract, ritualistic, and mystical, which are surprising qualities for an East German choreography of that time.[114] Still, Schilling was bound by socialist realism's rejection of *Ausdruckstanz* and the favoring of folk and ballet forms, whereas Bausch was free to explore the modernism of Stravinsky's score as well as her earlier training in *Ausdruckstanz* at Kurt Jooss's Folkwang School and modern dance in New York. It is also obvious that Bausch's dancers were much better equipped to dance her choreography. Due to East Germany's rejection of *Ausdruckstanz*, most of Schilling's dancers visibly lacked training in how to work their torsos; they were much more effective in their execution of the folkloric earthbound movements. Only the young dancer Arila Siegert stood out in Schilling's work. As I discuss in the following chapter, Siegert trained at the Palucca School, the only school still offering *Ausdruckstanz* at that point.

In addition to emphatic differences in how Schilling's *Schwarze Vögel* and Bausch's *Le sacre du printemps* utilize *Ausdruckstanz* and folk vocabulary, they also have very different goals and outcomes. By tapping into her training at the Folkwang School and in modern dance in New York City, Bausch creates a compelling version of *Le sacre du printemps* that has an investigation of gender relationships at its core. Schilling's *Schwarze Vögel* is an effective amalgam of different vocabularies that relate a narrative both abstract and rooted in a recognizable historical situation. This choreographic solution served as a protection from censorship and guaranteed official support for his work. The content and topic of *Schwarze Vögel* adhered to socialist realist requirements, but Schilling's use of modern dance vocabulary, essential types over character development, and abstract choreographic patterns incorporated modernist qualities into the socialist realist choreography.[115] His approach also demonstrates that socialist realism was not an unchanging, unyielding category; in practice, artists and theorists constantly adjusted their approaches based on the artistic impulses and political developments of the day.

Schwarze Vögel was considered a success and stayed in the repertoire of the Tanztheater der Komischen Oper Berlin for more than a decade. In his subsequent choreographies, Schilling continued to explore different forms and vocabularies in at least one production per year. Often, he choreographed shorter pieces and combined several of them into one evening's worth of dance, among them choreographies exploring *Kammertanz* (chamber music), which was very important to *Ausdruckstanz*. Noteworthy examples were *Abendliche Tänze* (*Evening Dances* [1979]) and *Der Lebenskreis* (*Circle of Life* [1982]).[116] He rechoreographed classics such as *Schwanensee* (*Swan Lake* [1978]), *Romeo und Julia* (*Romeo and Juliet* [1983]), and Jacques Offenbach's *Les contes de Hoffmann* (*The Tales of Hoffmann* [1986]), in which he attempted to restore the intention of the original score or update the narrative to make it relevant to socialist East German reality. He also focused his efforts on the creation of new works, among them a ballet based on Johann Wolfgang Goethe's *Wahlverwandtschaften* (*Elective Affinities* [1986]), which became one of his most popular works.

Even though increasingly younger choreographers were allowed to assign pieces to the ensemble of the Tanztheater der Komischen Oper Berlin, Schilling remained the main choreographer. Oddly, he believes his work was unaffected by censorship, which of course is impossible given the constant surveillance of all cultural production in East Germany.[117] However, he was very privileged and potentially able to deal with any censorship or problems at the higher levels of the socialist power structure. For instance, he was able to continue to work and tour abroad, even when dancers repeatedly defected: two dancers left the company while on tour in Yugoslavia and eleven more on a tour in Helsinki in 1971.[118]

Köllinger labeled Schilling's *Schwarze Vögel* an exemplary model for future choreographers as well as the embodiment of contemporary ballet's required poetic and aesthetic qualities. In his opinion, it had the same "exemplary importance as the best work by Brecht and Felsenstein, who created something new and at the same time something lasting in the cultural tradition of our country."[119] While I would not place him in the same category as Brecht or even Felsenstein, Schilling produced interesting and important work as a result of his unique training and privileged position at the Komische Oper Berlin. I would also not simply dismiss him with the label "socialist realist," because he—like many other artists in East Germany—produced unique work *within* the constraints of socialist realism and by doing so effectively changed the form. In reaction to these changes embodied in dance, socialist realist rhetoric had to adjust as well, which in turn permitted even further experimentation.

After his 1986 *Wahlverwandtschaften*, Schilling was never able to create a similarly successful work. Toward the end of the 1980s, a new generation of choreographers appeared on the stage of East German dance, a generation willing to rethink Schilling's vocabulary, his traditional gendering, and even East German theatrical structures. A year prior to the fall of the Berlin Wall, Schilling choreographed *Orpheus-Stationen* for the Ballett der Deutschen Oper in West Berlin. This production was panned by critics and audiences. This, and his waning importance in the 1980s East German dance culture, made it difficult for him to deal with the changes in the East German cultural landscape after the reunification in 1990. In 1993 he retired, and choreographers from the West took over the Tanztheater. Beginning with its 2004–5 season, the Komische Oper Berlin terminated dance as one of its performance disciplines, and thus a remarkable nearly forty-year history of influential dance productions at this institution came to an end.

At the last congress of the association of artists of the GDR in 1988, socialist realism was officially eliminated as an artistic category in East Germany and the term "art in socialism" was adopted.[120] Even with all the adjustments to the category of socialist realism, art in East Germany had outgrown and emancipated itself from the term. This was mostly enabled by changes in the political structure, the economic downfall of the state, and increasing exchange with international art. As Goeschen suggests, "while art up to the end of the 1960s is characterized by its relation to the classical Modern of the first two decades of the twentieth century, from the 1970s onwards artists were working increasingly with contemporary Western art."[121] My account of Schilling's choreography and of developments in socialist realist dance rhetoric is intended to undermine dominant histories of modernism in dance. As I demonstrate in the following chapter, the 1980s brought a broadening of such engagement with modernism and eventually postmodernism, mostly in the form of movements resistant to the state doctrine. Artists changed institutions, invented new forms, and inverted existing structures to create a uniquely East German movement.

3

Resistive Motions in the East

Rechoreographing Opposition
(1980s)

There it was—that blank stare, that look, the erasure. I had encountered it many times before; it was, in fact, an all-too familiar experience.

We were all sitting around a conference table, international scholars sharing our work and giving comments on each other's writing. One European scholar mentioned a recent reconstruction of Mary Wigman's choreographies by the Ecuadorian dancer Fabián Barba. Barba devotedly reconstructed Wigman's work, including dances from the cycle *Swinging Landscapes*, even performing it at Hellerau, where Wigman began her dance training with Jaques-Dalcroze. The dancer effectively embodied Wigman's angular style of moving with its strong lines and powerful movement initiations. Even Barba's male body did not interfere with his loyal reconstruction; rather he managed to emphasize Wigman's unique approach to femininity and gender.[1] The scholar referred to Barba's performance as a specific approach to reconstruction, one that restaged the original.[2] To point to a contrasting approach, another scholar mentioned Martin Nachbar's reconstruction of Dore Hoyer's *Afectos Humanos* (*Human Affections*), in which Nachbar brought out his own struggle with Hoyer's choreography through a lecture-performance.[3] As these two scholars started to argue the pros and cons of each approach, it became clear that only a few of the non-European academics in the room had heard of either work. Several knew nothing about Dore Hoyer or about Nachbar's performances.

In response to the flurry of questions, a very established dance scholar from West Germany began to explain Nachbar's 2006 reconstruction of Hoyer's work. She described how Nachbar made his inability to dance the *Ausdruckstanz* vocabulary—and thus to faithfully reconstruct the dances—a part of the final performance. Nachbar was trained in release-based techniques and was not able to perform the strong shapes and lines of Hoyer's distinct vocabulary. The scholar welcomed Nachbar's approach as contributing to a productive discourse on reconstruction. Yet in her celebration of Nachbar's aesthetic and dance theoretical accomplishments, she was unaware that a political problematization of German contemporary dance history in relation to modernism and *Ausdruckstanz* was missing from her account and his reconstruction. The West German scholar went on to discuss the history of the original choreography and explained that there was an earlier reconstruction in 1988 by Susanne Linke, a Wigman pupil working in West Germany.[4]

I waited, hoping that she would eventually mention Arila Siegert's reconstruction of *Afectos Humanos* that same year in East Germany.[5] But she didn't. I finally addressed her, saying: "Well, it is kind of interesting and important for a discussion of reconstruction and historization of Hoyer's work that there was also a reconstruction by Siegert." A blank stare ensued. It was finally broken when the West German scholar said that she hadn't mentioned Siegert's work because Nachbar was only referencing Linke's reconstruction. "That is exactly my point," I said. I am not sure she understood. Or to be more precise, I am sure she didn't grasp the politics of my insistence.

This chapter attempts to make my point clear by insisting on the politics of such diverse concepts as reconstruction, choreography, and pedestrian performance and examining them as embodied resistance in East German dance. These concepts are central to dance studies and have been explored in relation to aesthetic concerns, yet their political dimension has not always been at the forefront of our field's discourse. By reading reconstruction, choreography, and pedestrian performance as resistive acts against cultural indoctrination, I re-politicize each concept and contribute to producing a more balanced debate. I provide three unique case studies of East German movement culture, which went mostly unnoticed by, or at least are no longer part of, the official unified German discourse on dance and movement. Each of these examples of East German movement demonstrate a resistance to the socialist state in which they were performed and to the movement culture they reference. However, they are very distinct in their approach.

Central to Siegert's reconstructive and institutional resistance is her distinct engagement with *Ausdruckstanz* and the founding of her own dance company. Looking at Siegert's work, I highlight how dancers and choreographers in East Germany began to work more openly with modernism, which had been re-pressed by the demand the artists adhere to socialist realism. Siegert's work also permits a discussion of choreographic reconstruction as political and dance historical labor. At the same time that dancers were playing "catch up" with modernism, a younger generation of artists started to move into postmodern aesthetics, drastically rethinking the aesthetic and political functions of dance. My second example, Fine Kwiatkowski, broadened the category of dance by performing outside all institutional structures in East Germany. She was not part of a state-sponsored dance company, nor did she participate in the vast amateur dance scene. Utilizing improvisation and interdisciplinary collaboration with sculptors and musicians, Kwiatkowski not only challenged the definition of dance and choreography in East Germany but also avoided a fixed artistic identity by constantly evolving her performance structure and approach to movement. Through this tactic, she undermined censorship and helped create a new category of artistry in East Germany, comparable to what was considered postmodern choreography in the West. Charlotte von Mahlsdorf, an East German transvestite, challenged fixed identities through her performance of gender and sexuality. Von Mahlsdorf also utilized the arbitrary relationship between spoken language and movement to challenge censorship. I highlight her pedestrian performance in front of the Stasi in order to provide an example of an easily missed performance of resistance.

These case studies move from the fairly visible and documented choreographies of Arila Siegert to the barely known work of Fine Kwiatkowski to the completely lost moment of resistance in Charlotte von Mahlsdorf's performative gesture. Each case necessitates distinct methodologies: whereas Siegert's work allows for a more traditional dance historical and choreographic analysis that situates her work in a larger dance studies perspective, Kwiatkowski's requires a theorizing of refusal—refusal as a choreographic approach and refusal in relation to archival practice—and a comparison with other interdisciplinary art. Although I researched and interviewed both artists, I am able to provide more dance historical material on Siegert than on Kwiatkowski. Yet given that I am more interested in analyzing the politics of their choreographic choices than in installing these artists in a dance historical narrative, Kwiatkowski's nonvisibility becomes an important indicator of her opposition. To examine von Mahlsdorf's resistive performances of gender and sexuality outside the traditional artistic realm requires a combination of methods from dance and queer studies. Moving across multiple methods within dance studies as well as in neighboring disciplines, this chapter thus reveals a wide variety of forms of resistance to East German doctrinaire structures performed by dance and movement artists.

Resistance in East Germany

As discussed in chapters 1 and 2, East Germany experienced a short period of relative artistic freedom and tolerance during the early 1970s. Erich Honecker, the first secretary of the SED Central Committee, famously exclaimed at the committee's fourth assembly that "if one assumes the stable position of socialism, there cannot be—in my opinion—any taboos in art and literature."[6] In the wake of this statement, formerly banned literary works were published, theater companies staged new plays, rock and jazz music became official, youth clubs opened all over the country, and smaller galleries and movie clubs started to develop inside existing cultural institutions. Western hippie, punk, communal-living, and other alternative cultures appeared in larger cities. New models for artistic production outside the official artistic landscape were established. Most importantly, socialist reality became material for a critical discourse distinct from socialist realism's reflections of socialist ideals.

This burgeoning artistic production and discourse all came to a sudden standstill when on November 16, 1976, GDR officials expelled songwriter and poet Wolf Biermann from his adopted home country. Biermann was born in 1936 in what became West Germany after World War II and moved to East Germany in 1953, where he saw his politics as a communist affirmed. Only ten years later, he became an open critic of the socialist system in his songs and poems, and after a concert in Cologne, which was broadcast on West German TV, GDR officials revoked his East German citizenship. Biermann's exile catalyzed the largest response from the East German art scene in the history of the GDR. Twelve prominent writers and one sculptor started a petition that was soon signed by over a hundred artists from all different fields.[7] GDR officials did not reverse their decision; in the wake of Biermann's expulsion, numerous artists who expressed their solidarity with him were prohibited from producing their art, imprisoned, and exiled. These measures put a halt to the more open dissident scene in East Germany and pushed opposition back into the underground. Biermann's expulsion also opened, or at least made visible, a rift between older critical artists and younger alternative artists.

To understand this rift, it is important to situate nonofficial artistic culture in relation to broader artistic production and the citizens of East Germany in general. The GDR was a country with a tightly controlled media. All theater, opera, concert, and dance productions in the official theaters and on the amateur scene were censored. Moreover, there was no access to printing and copy machines. Hans Magnus Enzensberger explains how the Soviet Union artificially restricted access to technology.[8] It refused to give access to copy machines, he explains, because such machines could transform anyone into a printer. The copy machine was thus connected to economic and political power, and the state feared it would lose control over the media and information. In East Germany, this anxiety about media extended into film and television. The GDR provided Soviet 8mm home-movie systems, but the cameras had to be manually wound up and only provided thirty seconds of filming. There were only two TV stations in East Germany, one of them broadcasting Soviet programming once a week. All programming concluded before midnight so as to ensure that socialist workers obtained sufficient sleep.[9]

As a result, information—including art and information about it—was disseminated only through official channels, making it nearly impossible to establish alternatives. Everyone could attend official theater productions, read endorsed books, and see movies, but very few had access to oppositional culture. There were of course exceptions to these restrictions. Rock groups, such as Renft with its critical lyrics and Western rock music, were very popular and their concerts were sought after.[10] Yet few East German citizens knew who Biermann was before he was expelled because only the West German TV channels that could be received in parts of East Germany reported on him. Not surprisingly, the alternative art scene in general flew under the radar of most East German media. Even though there were alternative arts activities in most towns, the major oppositional networks were concentrated in larger cities. Unless you were a member of these networks, lived in one of the larger cities, or actively sought out oppositional culture, you would barely have known about it or experienced it.

Not only was the visibility and influence of the oppositional scene limited, but there was no unified community of artists. Artists of Biermann's generation had been a part of the GDR since the beginning, and despite their critical position toward East German socialism, they generally supported it. The next generation of artists, who were born in the 1960s, did not identify with the GDR in the same way and turned away from its political doctrine.[11] The older generation often completely dismissed the younger generation as self-centered. For instance, Biermann retrospectively condemned the generation of opposition artists who lived and worked in the 1980s as "spätdadaistische Gartenzwerge mit Bleistift und Pinsel im Schrebergarten der Stasi" ("late Dadaist gnomes with brush and pencil in the garden of the Stasi").[12]

In German, the term "Gartenzwerg" ("garden gnome") connotes a petit bourgeois, narrow-minded individual and a conservative lifestyle. Both the literal and metaphorical gnomes mostly gather around little artificial lakes and engage in a variety of leisurely activities or in labor that relates to the building of small houses or gardens, their little bodies of childlike proportions exuding a happy dullness. Their smiling facial expressions seem disconnected from the strenuous and unexciting activities in which they engage. In addition, these gnomes seem indifferent to the fact that they belong to an exclusively male society. Very rarely does one see any female gnomes on display. The contradictions in human society contribute to the artificiality of the gnomes' world. This artificiality and the abundant reproduction of gnomes have led to their construction as icons of middle-class kitsch in Germany. People displaying gnomes in their houses and gardens in Germany seem to be concerned only about their own private domains and do not care to understand their influence on society and vice versa. Biermann's quip thus points to several issues important for an understanding of the oppositional art scene in 1980s East Germany: the socialist versus capitalist definition of public and private space, gender inequality, the extent to which artists worked around or in collaboration with the Stasi, and the lack of understanding and even general visibility of the oppositional art scene.

German philosopher Jürgen Habermas's theorization of the development of the public sphere in bourgeois society in his *Structural Transformation of the Public Sphere* proves helpful for understanding the socialist context, even though his work has since been challenged for its universalizing tendency and exclusion of marginalized groups.[13] Drastic changes to public discourse as a result of information technology also need to be taken account of; nonetheless Habermas's work offers a way in to the different constructions of public spheres in capitalist and socialist societies. Habermas postulates that *Öffentlichkeit,* which in English is translated as "public sphere," a much narrower concept than the German *Öffentlichkeit,* emerged out of literary and cultural public gatherings in eighteenth-century German bourgeois society. Because access to public discourse in such societies was limited to property-owning and educated citizens, this practice has been critiqued by contemporary scholars for its exclusion of female citizens, members of the developing proletariat, and non-propertied minority groups. *Öffentlichkeit* functioned as a regulatory and "self-articulation" mechanism for policy-making governmental structures.[14] As such, private people met to discuss public matters, independently of governmental and church institutions, which previously had held a monopoly over public discourse. Toward the end of the nineteenth century, when *Öffentlichkeit* was at its height, there were, according to Habermas, strict separations between state and society as well as public and private spheres. For instance, the family structure was private and regulated by private law, such as inheritance laws, that ensured control over property.

With the ongoing development of capitalism thereafter and the concentration of wealth in a few hands, these separations between public and private were increasingly weakened. As a result, public discourse came to be influenced by the wealthy, who manipulated it to serve their personal interests and to assert control over industrial and financial institutions. Media became an important aspect of this shift, and formerly private citizens lost power over their privacy because family structures changed as well. In particular, bourgeois

families were stripped of their important function as a regulating structure for
private ownership and became more and more defined by public law. Habermas
theorizes that as public laws begin to control the private sphere more, private
arenas get reduced to "the purely 'personal' ones of their [private people's]
noncommittal use of leisure time."[15]

If one applies Habermas's theorization of the developments of the public
sphere to dance, dance would then seem to have to be understood as undergoing
a transformation from a representational power tool in feudalism to a predominantly female leisure activity constituting entertainment for men in bourgeois
society at the turn of the twentieth century.[16] Linda Tomko, Janice Ross, and
others complicate this simplistic understanding of division of public and private
labor along gender lines. Both Tomko and Ross describe how dance went
beyond being merely a form of family leisure and increasingly became an influential part of *Öffentlichkeit* with the dawn of modern dance.[17] As a result of
women's push into the public sphere, dance was no longer just a pastime but
came to play an important role in the reconstruction of the public sphere. A
similar analysis of dance in relation to the public and private spheres is necessary for our understanding of socialist society.

The role of dance artists in socialist East Germany needs to be read in relation to the discrepancy between the ideal and the actuality: the ideal envisioned
truly separate public and private spheres and the disappearance of gender as
a hegemonic structure, while the actuality was the largest secret service system
in the world and a traditional heteronormative family structure. In socialism,
private ownership does not exist and thus ownership as a prerequisite for participation in *Öffentlichkeit* is no longer possible. Also, *Öffentlichkeit* no longer has
to function as a societal regulator of the state because the state is controlled by
the majority, the proletariat. Thus, in the Marxist view, the state in socialism
has only administrative functions and is no longer used to enforce policies in
the interest of a minority and no longer serves as a means by which one class
may oppress another. Ultimately, the distinction between state and society dis-
appears; people motivated by the desire to protect their private ownership no
longer need to engage in public discourse to critique and regulate state action.
Instead, public discourse is conducted by private citizens who are truly private,
free from public economic determination. Family structures change as well,
because men no longer have economic control over women. For the first time
in history, families become truly private and no longer require to be regulated
by the law.[18] Consequently, dance in East Germany should have strictly occurred
in the public sphere under socialism, determined by proletarian interests.[19] Of
course East German society looked quite different from this Marxist utopia,
and a reading of resistive dance practices can help us understand the socialist

reality that emerged. Resistance in East Germany needs to be read in relation to the discrepancy between the never realized ideal of a separation between the public and private spheres that would truly equalize women and thus erase gender as a social structure on one side and the East Germany's traditional heteronormative family structures and all-intrusive secret service system on the other side.

In theory, women were equal to men in socialism. However, this equalization was apparent mostly only in relation to public labor. The socialist East German state attempted to include women in the production process fully and thus made them independent from men. The inclusion of women was made possible by a well-developed support network for all tasks related to family life.[20] For instance, the GDR was famous for its child-care system. Approximately 85 percent of children attended nurseries, kindergarten, and after-school care. Thanks to this system of care, 91 percent of working-age women participated in the labor market before the fall of the Berlin Wall in 1989. Socialist ideology was, of course, only one reason for the high employment rate of women in the GDR. Another major cause was the rapid growth of production and the resulting shortage of work force in all socialist countries.[21]

However, even though the original East German constitution not only called for the equality of women in society in article 7 but also inside the family in article 30, women were still responsible for home, family, and children, just like many women in capitalist societies.[22] Most men did not participate equally in those domains. For men, family provided recreation more than additional demanding work. Furthermore, female public labor was restricted mostly to the traditional areas of female employment, such as retail, child care, lower-level medical professions, education, assembly-line labor, and laboratory work. Still, their participation in the public workforce provided women with access to socialist citizenship.

The foundation of citizenship in labor in East Germany reduced very complex issues to a simplified materialist ideological stance.[23] Identity, nationality, and citizenship collapsed into the single category of labor. As a result of East Germany's conflation of distinct categories into labor, the female body became reduced to the standards of the male laboring body and thus deprivatized and degendered. Even though the female body was defined as essential and emancipated in socialist ideology, it was deprived of its unique sexuality, pleasures, and desires because it had to function as equal to the male body.[24] Women in East Germany experienced patriarchy in very different ways from woman in capitalist societies and thus had a different take on feminism and gender politics. In this chapter, I have chosen to discuss exclusively female resistance to highlight distinct forms of gender politics in East Germany in relation to dance. I also want to demonstrate that there was no unified approach among female artists to a rethinking of female embodiment. Siegert, Kwiatkowski, and von Mahlsdorf each approach female gendering and labor in very different ways, providing challenges to traditional gendering through institutional, choreographic, and performative tactics.

Contravening Marx's and Engels's vision of a separation between public and private domains, the socialist East German state regulated even the supposedly private space of family. The 1965 *Familiengesetzbuch* (code of family law) provided explicit guidelines for the construction of a socialist family and the raising of children as "active builders of socialism."[25] The family was defined as the "smallest building block of society" and thus was transformed into a part of the public sphere.[26] Similarly, the supposedly defunct distinction between state and society in socialism took a rather macabre shape in East Germany. Habermas critiques Marx's and Engels's theories about the interlocking of state and society by claiming that the public sphere loses its mediating position between state and society. Already in developed bourgeois society, special interest organizations that arose from the private sphere and parties that originated in the public sphere had begun indoctrinating society in the interest of the state. Lenin knew that, of necessity, multiple parties and organizations form, and so he developed his theory that the communist party must be the leading organ in a socialist state. However, for Habermas, Lenin simply "replaced the 'smashed' Tsarist state apparatus with the incomparable more powerful one of the Central Committee."[27] The communist party merges with the state apparatus. Thus, public opinion is still generated from above, and *Öffentlichkeit* as critical debate exists but is repressed. According to Habermas, this kind of domination in a socialist society manipulated the public, perpetually legitimated itself before it, and extended state power into all realms of society.[28] The Stasi became the most important tool for the repression of *Öffentlichkeit* and extension of state power into the private sphere in East Germany.

The GDR seemed to have outdone Franz Kafka's imagination in the anonymous violation and surveillance of humankind by an unknown state power. The Stasi left six million files to the united Germany; four million of these are on citizens of the GDR and two million are on citizens of the Federal Republic of Germany. The files contain among other materials the following: at least 18 kilometers (11.2 miles) of dossiers, 7 kilometers (4.3 miles) of court files, and 11 kilometers (6.9 miles) of files on *operative Vorgänge* (operative processes). These files contain reports on the immediate observation of persons. An additional 1.5 kilometers (1 mile) of index cards contains the real names of all persons who observed and who were observed. The archive holds 122,000 bundles of files, 1,600 bundles of index cards, 755 bundles of form sheets, 13 tons (8,125 lbs.) of unused form sheets, and 158 file cabinets. There are also 936 bags with partly shredded files, 1,122 unopened packages and boxes, 195 suitcases, 500 bags with X-ray slides, and 195 paper bags. This list describes only part of the archive in Berlin. There are other archives in former district capitals, like Leipzig, Dresden, and Chemnitz (the former Karl-Marx-Stadt). The archive in Leipzig possesses, for instance, such bizarre materials as a collection of personal clothes in jars that served as a file of scents.

Even though the world was only at the dawn of the information age at the time of the fall of the Berlin Wall—the first megabyte chip was produced in 1986—the Stasi was connected to an electronic data association of the members of the Warsaw Pact known as SOUD.[29] However, most of the data collected in the archives of the Stasi were still processed as physical and not digital memory. Mark Poster theorizes the digital database as a superpanopticon. Foucault's panopticon constructs the observed person as a subject. In contrast, Poster's superpanopticon objectifies the individual. As a result the superpanopticon produces "individuals with dispersed identities, identities of which the individuals might not even be aware."[30] The East German secret service can be described in terms of both models. The whole observational apparatus of the Stasi still relied on physical data and the process of subjectification. As I show, the Stasi could only act when the individual was singled out of the abstract mass body of the proper citizen by an act of subjectification. The mass body was the socialist state's own creation, but the individual body was valued over the ideological construct of the mass body as the material site of truth. Even though socialist individuals were objectified by the state into a mass body, they were also individualized in order to be observed.[31] The main difference between the way Poster's digital database works and the Stasi's functioned is the level of subjectification. However, there are some similarities in the constructions of these apparatuses. The author of the written Stasi files was mostly unknown to the observed object, as is the case with the creator of Poster's digital database. There are also similarities in the self-generated reproduction of both databases. Poster illuminates how one database generates the next one.[32] Similarly, the Stasi produced files on the observer, and no one was exempt from the observational chain.

This unimaginable quantity of files led to a qualitative change in the structure of the archive without the use of advanced technology. In reference to the electronic database, Poster writes, "the populace has been disciplined to surveillance and to participating in the process."[33] As it turned out, family members spied on each other, lovers reported on lovers, and many members of the new oppositional generation of artists were informants of the Stasi. Even though most members of oppositional groups were not aware of surveillance by their peers, they, like the general population, knew about the constant presence of the Stasi. Yet for the artists this awareness also became an important artistic principle. It yielded the practice of performing or creating in spaces that undermined surveillance and censorship because of the location's obscurity. Through these practices artists also contributed to the redefinition of the relationship between public and private space. Happenings were staged in private apartments that were turned into galleries, and elaborate dinners with friends were transformed into performance art events.

Despite East German officials' employment of the state apparatus in an unprecedented way to reinforce their ideological and political power, opposition existed at all levels of society. The oppositional forces differed from each other in their goals, approach, results, and degree of appeal. Nevertheless, all forms of resistance in East Germany engaged in the effort to challenge the state's attempt to naturalize its position of power. Pointing to the presence of "commonsense" as a prerequisite of any domination, Pierre Bourdieu argues that power structures need the appearance of naturalness to assure their power.[34] This naturalization of governing structures allows the state to claim commonsense as the underlying principle of and as the objective reason for its dominant position. Even though Bourdieu limits his observations primarily to class structures, the notion of commonsense as a principle of power operates similarly in regard to other identity constructs, such as race, gender, ethnicity, nationality, age, and sexuality.

Bourdieu's understanding of society challenges a simple division of the social into dominating and dominated forces. It returns agency to the dominated parts of a social order by allowing that the dominated need not only comply with the dominating power but can also resist it through challenging the naturalness of the order. This notion proves especially valuable because it broadens the definition of resistance to include acts that are not always primarily and intentionally structured as resistance to political structures—or that are not readable from the outside as such—but that nevertheless do ultimately create oppositional structures. Focusing on the intention in resistance, Tim Cresswell distinguishes between resistance, transgression, and deviance.[35] For Cresswell, resistance is a function of the intention of performer and transgression is a function of the results and the reaction to the transgression, whereas deviance is only defined by its effect. Resistance implies a purposeful action with the intention of changing the given order or at least challenging it. A transgression crosses an imaginary line that should not have been crossed. In doing so, transgression elicits a response from the powers that established those lines. Unlike resistance, an act of transgression can lack intention on the part of the transgressor. Cresswell observes that resistance and transgression are not mutually exclusive. A transgression can be intentional and an act of resistance can yield a reaction from powers that maintain the status quo. Deviance is an act that breaks from an established norm and becomes visible through the response that it creates.

As much as such careful distinctions between resistance, transgression, and deviance are intriguing, I choose to use just the term "resistance" in this chapter because intention is always difficult to guess. Movement is rarely unintentional and it always results in a change, even though these changes might not seem to break with established norms. James Scott's work on the resistance of subaltern people in *Domination and the Arts of Resistance* questions the total consent to domination that Gramsci's notion of hegemony, in which the repressed's consent enables the repressor's power, implies by investigating the difference between seeming compliance in the public arena and resistance in hidden areas of society.[36] His notion of the constantly present yet invisible resistance is productive.[37] An analysis of corporeal reactions to domination provides a way of making visible resistances inside the system that might go by unnoticed by an outside observer. Or as Foster puts it, "A blank stare does not mean the same thing for all bodies in all contexts."[38]

A close reading of movement in conjunction with a discussion of symbols, norms, and ideological forms that they rely on reveals not only hidden oppositional forces but also illuminates the normative structures in society. Often norms and models in a society are only apparent when transgressed. Descriptions of the East German oppositional movement in publications have repeatedly been reduced to the more visible oppositional groups and to individual intellectuals and artists. So-called *Bürgerrechtler* (civil rights persons) ranged from individuals such as Biermann to oppositional groups inside the Protestant church, exemplified by the Friedens- und Umweltkreis der Zionsgemeinde in Berlin, a peace and environmental justice group sponsored by the Protestant Church. These individuals and groups had an important impact on the existing socialist system and in shaping the *Wende* (the turn of events surrounding the fall of the Berlin Wall) and reunification. I attempt to enrich this history with less visible examples of people who make use of the body and choreography as a site of resistance—and as Biermann's statement suggests, these artists may not have been legible at all to East Germans. In studying the ways in which hegemonies are contested even in the smallest way, we begin to understand the impact of domination on the body.[39]

The socialist state aggressively regulated and attempted to choreograph every moment of public and private life. In the face of this coercion, citizens responded with a highly developed awareness of performance and choreography on all levels, ranging from collaboration to resistance, often at the same time. Knowing about the state's extensive surveillance, GDR citizens had to create a set of behaviors that they could perform properly for state officials. Because East German citizenry were forced into highly structured behavior, they were always conscious of the performative and choreographed structure and did not perceive their behaviors as natural. This awareness enabled the East German resistance to carefully balance its performance of the cooperating citizen with its resistance inside the socialist system. In other words, there was resistance in people's obedience to the state. Arila Siegert's career and choreographic practice is a vivid example of this balancing act. Her work could indeed be read as a privileged individual endeavor, yet a closer look at her engagement with modernism and her strategy of reconstructing *Ausdruckstanz* repertoire reveals an ongoing negotiation with the strictures of the East German state. And it allows a more nuanced evaluation and a reappraisal of one of East Germany's most remarkable dancers and choreographers.

Arila Siegert: Reconstruction as Resistive Modernism

Arila Siegert was born in 1953, in a small town near Dresden, and joined the Palucca School as a child. Improvisation classes with Gret Palucca and Eva Winkler, a Marianne Vogelsang pupil, were most influential for Siegert's career. However, it was her classical ballet training with Nina Ulanova, a pupil of Agrippina Vaganova, that provided Siegert with the technique required to win a job in one of the best companies in the country. Tom Schilling saw Siegert dancing the *Prélude* from *Les sylphides* at an annual East German ballet competition and, taken by her sincere interpretation, hired her in 1971 when she was eighteen.[40] Coming from the Palucca School, where individual expression and creativity were valued, she had a hard time adjusting to Schilling's choreographic process in which dancers were treated as instruments.[41] Yet she was fully aware at the time that she was performing for one of the most important dance companies in East Germany and that she needed to grow *inside* the company if she wanted to continue working as an artist in the GDR. "I always tried to battle with the conditions that were provided and to make that battle into my philosophy. I never had the opportunity to reject anything and to say, I don't want this and just leave and go somewhere else."[42] With such an approach, it isn't surprising that only five years after joining the Komische Oper Berlin, Siegert advanced to soloist, dancing main roles created for her and performing in Italy, the Soviet Union, India, Australia, and China with the company.[43] When she finally decided to leave Schilling's company at the Komische Oper, she made the highly unusual move to become a prima ballerina in Dresden at the Staatsoper. Berlin received much more funding and attention than Dresden and was seen as the epicenter of official artistic production in East Germany. But an important factor for Siegert and other artists was that Dresden had a strong tradition of modern dance. Jaques-Dalcroze had worked outside Dresden at Hellerau; Mary Wigman's famous school had made Dresden the center of modern dance before World War II; and the still-existing Palucca School struggled to continue that tradition in East Germany. Though it was perceived as provincial by people of the more cosmopolitan cities of Berlin and Leipzig, 1980s Dresden began to foster a unique alternative dance and art milieu that allowed for new models and expressions to develop.[44] Thus, Dresden allowed Siegert not only to focus on her dancing but also to develop her choreographic ambitions.

Siegert had always been interested in choreography. While studying at the Palucca School in 1970, she choreographed a piece, and she continued to choreograph while dancing at the Komische Oper Berlin, which staged her work in 1976 as a part of a program of shorter choreographies. Soon after she moved to Dresden—and while dancing major roles in *Giselle*, *The Green Table*, *Orpheus*, and *Swan Lake*—Siegert intensified her choreographic work, creating at least one choreography a year, including *Progreß* (*Progress* [1981]), *Klänge der Macht* (*Sound of Power* [1982]), and *Windungen* (*Turns* [1983]). She received the first prize in choreography at the national choreography competition in 1981 for *Progreß*.[45] Her first solo evening, *Gesichte* (*Faces*), in 1985 was composed of her own choreographies and a reconstruction of Marianne Vogelsang's *Fünf Präludien* (*Five Preludes*).

Siegert saw herself as continuing the lineage of *Ausdruckstanz* in Dresden established by Jaques-Dalcroze, Laban, Wigman, Palucca, and Vogelsang.[46] Her choice of Vogelsang's material speaks to this understanding of her position. Like most leading *Ausdruckstanz* figures, Vogelsang, one of the first students who graduated from the Palucca School in 1934, danced, taught, and choreographed throughout her entire career. She danced with Palucca and taught at Laban's Deutsche Tanzbühne, at the Folkwang School in Essen, at several classical dance schools in Berlin, and after the war at the College of Music in Rostock and the Mary Wigman Studio in Berlin. Vogelsang founded her own school in the eastern part of Berlin, which eventually became part of one of the three state dance conservatories in East Germany, and she continued to teach at that school until 1958, at which point the growing hostility against *Ausdruckstanz* forced her to quit. She continued to dance in theater and opera productions, though she never gained the status that she deserved. Marion Kant calls Vogelsang the "most gifted young German modern dancer" in her evaluation of post–World War II developments in modern dance in Germany. Kant points out that, unlike Palucca and Wigman, Vogelsang reflected critically on

Germany's Nazi past and *Ausdruckstanz*'s collaboration with the Nazis. With the exceptions of Laban and Jooss, Vogelsang was also the only German modern dancer to undertake a systematic investigation of vocabulary and pedagogy in relation to social developments.[47] *Fünf Präludien*, choreographed to Johann Sebastian Bach's *Wohltemperierte Klavier* (*The Well-Tempered Clavier*), was Vogelsang's last piece (1972–73). She set it on her pupil Ernst Schnelle a few weeks before her death in 1973.[48] It was from Schnelle that Siegert learned the choreography. Siegert's commitment to *Ausdruckstanz* began well before her 1985 reconstruction; however, it was the first time that Siegert made clear that she was not only dedicated to a utilization of principles and vocabulary from *Ausdruckstanz* in her own work but also that she saw the reconstruction of original works as valuable for new generations.

Making Vogelsang's work visible again was an act of opposition on Siegert's part because she was both celebrating modernist choreography and staging the nearly forgotten work of an artist who was not able to continue her work in East Germany due to the repression of *Ausdruckstanz*. Siegert emphasized her transgression when she left the institutional structures of the Staatsoper and founded a *Tanztheater* at the Staatsschauspiel Dresden (the main theater company in Dresden), stating that her goal was "to take up the *Ausdruckstanz* tradition again and . . . to develop it by making the technique usable through an incorporation of contemporary contents and aesthetics."[49] Siegert's first choreography for her new company was *Herzschläge* (*Heartbeats* [1987]), followed by a reconstruction of Dore Hoyer's *Afectos Humanos* (1989) and reconstructions of Mary Wigman's dances (1991), among them the famous *Hexentanz* (*Witch Dance*). Despite many attempts to reconstruct Palucca's work, Siegert never got her mentor to agree to a reconstruction, because Palucca firmly believed that her work should die with her.[50]

In all of Siegert's reconstructions, she treated the original choreography as an important source for present reevaluation. Often she performed them in concert with her own choreographies, thus gesturing at the historical and the living archive simultaneously. To understand such an approach as a political act, it is necessary to evaluate Siegert's work in relation to other reconstructions of *Ausdruckstanz* material. We must also consider a theorization of reconstruction in dance studies. By performing the gap between the past and the present, reconstructions of dances always pose more questions than they provide answers. These questions revolve around issues of authenticity, authorship, copy, copyright, and the value of repetition.[51] Gerald Siegmund adds "modern dance" to this list, noting that reconstruction is a common and unquestioned practice in ballet but not in modern dance. Did modern dance choreographers, who were commonly both choreographers and interpreters of their works, see their choreographies as genuinely original creations? And how can we continue to perform this inheritance after the creator's death if the movement is so tightly connected to his or her own body? Stirred by these questions, Siegmund concludes that an engagement with history is not simply a labor of preservation but also raises questions about ethnic, cultural, and gender identities.[52]

Still the issue of preservation is important and literally haunts dance because of the fetishization of disappearance and ephemerality.[53] In a melancholic imagining of dance's ontology, in which its disappearance at the moment of performance seems inevitable, reconstruction becomes a ray of hope. The reconstructive effort is to perpetually work against dance's disappearance, but for this effort to be valued, dances need to evoke institutional power structures.[54] Therefore ballet, with its unquestioned heritable value, built on strong technical, educational, and theatrical institutionalization, becomes an ideal arena for reconstruction. Dance can also have a function in national, ethnographic, and archival institutions. Given its strong ties to theatrical and pedagogical institutions, *Ausdruckstanz* also seems predestined to be reconstructed. Nearly all *Ausdruckstanz* principals had their own companies at one point or performed solos on stages. All of them taught, and many opened schools. As both Kant and Manning illustrate, *Ausdruckstanz* also became tightly connected to the national interest at the end of the Weimar Republic and the beginning of Nazi Germany. Yet *Ausdruckstanz* was not able to retain that national importance after World War II in either part of Germany and was replaced with a revival of ballet and emphasis on folk. It survived only as a pedagogical and choreographic instrument at the Folkwang School in the West and at the Palucca School in the East. *Ausdruckstanz* therefore lost its value for reconstruction with its loss of stature in the official hierarchy of dance. Hoyer's biography vividly speaks to this devaluation of *Ausdruckstanz*.

Though she was hailed as one of the most important solo dancers of the *Ausdruckstanz* tradition, Hoyer never achieved the stardom of Mary Wigman or Rudolf Laban, nor the artistic longevity of Gret Palucca. Born in 1911 in Dresden, she trained mostly in rhythmics and gymnastics and studied for one year in 1930 at the Palucca School. Upon graduation she was hired as a soloist by a city theater in the smaller town of Plauen. By 1933, Hoyer had danced her first critically acclaimed solo evening in Dresden. Even though she received several awards for her choreographic work, the last honor given just days before her untimely death in 1967, Hoyer had to self-finance all of her solo evenings throughout her career. In addition to performing solos, Hoyer performed for short periods in Wigman's company and also in the Nazi-sponsored Deutsche Tanzbühne. After the war, she appeared in Wigman's critically acclaimed stage productions of *Le sacre du printemps* and also took over the Wigman School

Dore Hoyer in *Ehre/Eitelkeit*
from *Afectos Humanos*, 1962.
Deutsches Tanzarchiv Köln.
Photo: Siegfried Enkelmann.
© 2012 Artists Rights Society
(ARS), New York / VG
Bild-Kunst, Bonn.

in Dresden and eventually choreographed *Tänze für Käthe Kollwitz*, which she dedicated to the Communist Party. Her 1947 formalist choreography *Der große Gesang* (*The Great Hymn*) made her a target in the rising socialist realism debate, so she left East Germany in 1948 for the West, where she worked as a director and choreographer in theater and opera. She toured very successfully through Latin America in the 1950s and visited the American Dance Festival in 1957, where she saw José Limón, whose work and technique very much impressed her. She choreographed *Afectos Humanos* in 1962. After putting on many unsuccessful performances of new solo works and coming to the realization that she might not be able to dance ever again due to an injured knee, Hoyer committed suicide on New Year's Eve 1967.[55]

Afectos Humanos is based on Baruch de Spinoza's *Ethics*. Hoyer choreographed *Eitelkeit* (*Vanity*), *Begierde* (*Craving*), *Hass* (*Hate*), *Angst* (*Fear*), and *Liebe* (*Love*) to music composed by her longtime collaborator Dimitri Viatovitsch. Hoyer was a very tense and controlled dancer, and she often initiated movement in the center of the body, which gave it much power. Isolations provided her with the ability to perform several physical discourses at once. Despite the abstract nature of the pieces, each is recognizable as a thoughtful pondering on an aspect of the human condition. The strongest piece in terms of controlled vocabulary and execution is probably *Hass*, as tension is visible in every part of Hoyer's body, especially in her large hands. *Liebe* and *Eitelkeit* play more with gestures. For instance in *Liebe*, Hoyer's hands become two independent lyrical beings that frequently unite. Both execution and vocabulary are deeply modern. The careful exploration of phrases, gestures, space, and choreographic principles establish the modernist self-referential investigation of form. Hoyer's distinct, grounded style, spatial awareness, and dramatic depth clearly situate her work in an *Ausdruckstanz* tradition. Her choreography and interpretation remain absolutely fascinating to me because of her complete commitment to physical shape and spatial molding.[56]

Susanne Linke, who together with Pina Bausch, Reinhild Hoffmann, Gerhard Bohner, and Johann Kresnik is seen as one of the main figures in *Tanztheater* in West Germany, reconstructed Hoyer's *Afectos Humanos* in 1987 as part of her *Hommage à Dore Hoyer*. In 1988, she integrated the material into her own choreography with her partner Urs Dietrich for *Hommage à Dore Hoyer II*. Linke did not attempt to reconstruct the original by presenting a faithful copy. As Simone Willeit notes, Linke was able to replicate the tension characteristic of Hoyer's movement because she was familiar with Wigman and Jooss's techniques, but, significantly, she chose to keep her own much softer execution, making the difference between her physical style and Hoyer's visible.[57] Linke also changed her costumes onstage between her interpretation of the different affects, making apparent the distinction between her own dancing body and the historical choreographic text.

Martin Nachbar utilizes a different strategy for a similar outcome. Nachbar trained at the School for New Dance Development in Amsterdam and Performing Arts Research and Training Studios (P.A.R.T.S.) in Brussels and danced with important contemporary companies and choreographers, such as Les ballets C de la B, Sasha Waltz, Vera Mantero, Meg Stuart, Thomas Lehmen, and Joachim Schlömer. His reconstruction highlights the distinction between his movement approach and Hoyer's execution even more.[58] Nachbar reconstructed three of the five affects in 2000 with the dance collective BDC, which he cofounded, and finished the entire cycle for his lecture-performance *Urheben Aufheben* (2008).[59] In both efforts, he received the help of Waltraud Luley, a friend of Hoyer, who manages her estate. Nachbar presented various versions of his struggle with the reconstruction, each of them more in the format of a lecture-performance rather than a traditional stage dance. In his presentations, he lectured first and then danced, illustrated his points with an affect, or showed an excerpt on video. For instance, in a now famous presentation of *Urheben Aufheben* in 2004, Nachbar discussed how Luley, in guiding him on *Hass*, had explained that the whole body needed to be tense. Nachbar, who had learned the dance from a 1967 video of Hoyer performing *Afectos Humanos*, then demonstrated for the audience his version, which he had shown Luley. In response, Luley merely pointed out the lack of tension in Nachbar's little fingers. In his demonstration, Nachbar returned to the stage to show the pose again, this time with tension in the little fingers.[60] Thus, Nachbar made what was undoubtedly an intense process more easily digestible for the audience by turning it into a slight joke.[61]

Nachbar's reconstruction is part of a larger cultural phenomenon in dance. The late 1990s and early 2000s saw a sudden rise in performances that engaged with historical material. Most famously, Sylvie Guillem worked with material from Wigman's *Hexentanz* and *Sommerlicher Tanz* (*Summery Dance*) in 1998. Since 1996, Cesc Gelabert has been dancing Gerhard Bohner's *Im (Goldenen) Schnitt* (*In the (Golden) Section*).[62] Betsy Fisher also reconstructed *Afectos Humanos* along with other works belonging to—as she calls it—the German lineage of contemporary dance.[63] And in 2009, as I have mentioned, Fabián Barba reconstructed dances from Mary Wigman's cycle *Schwingende Landschaften* (*Swinging Landscapes*).[64] But as Siegmund and Willeit argue, Nachbar's approach is among the most challenging in recent years. Siegmund detects in Nachbar's reconstruction a third entity that is neither Nachbar's body, which changes in the engagement with Hoyer's dance, nor Hoyer's body, which simply can't be there, because it is gone. This third entity, which points toward the process of the reconstruction, is only present for the duration of the performance because it is the difference between the historical body of Hoyer and Nachbar's present body.[65] Similarly, Willeit argues that there is a productive distance between Nachbar's body and reconstruction, on the one hand, and Hoyer's original dance, on the other. She celebrates Nachbar's approach, which makes Hoyer's choreography visible yet at the same time comments on the practice of reconstruction.

Both analyses are fascinating in their thorough investigation of aesthetic and methodological concerns. Even though Siegmund does point to social structures, mentioning ethnic, cultural, and gender issues as important for any historical investigation, he does not raise the issue of gender when discussing Nachbar's reconstruction. And Willeit remains strictly inside the realm of aesthetics in her analysis. When Willeit presented her analysis at a conference I also was presenting at, I asked her about this decision.[66] She replied that an incorporation of social structures was not necessary at that stage of her analysis and was not her concern at this time. I respect her and Siegmund's decision to focus on an aesthetic and methodology. However, understanding the value of Siegert's reconstruction of Hoyer's choreography requires going beyond their analytic frame.

Of all the reconstructors, Siegert—with her long limbs, elongated body, and strong facial features—is probably the one who resembles Hoyer the most onstage. In addition, Siegert wears a costume that replicates Hoyer's costume. She even wears the tight cap that made Hoyer's appearance so distinct in these dances. Siegert leaves the stage after each affect and returns for the next one. Siegert's approach to Hoyer's dance, according to Willeit, is to seize control of the material yet not of the isolations that are important in the original dance. She also mentions Siegert's overly ornamental and extremely expressive interpretation. Siegert emphasizes the expressive qualities with her face, whereas Hoyer allowed no expression to play across her face. Siegert embodies a "formalized emotion" that Mark Franko defines as a unifying feeling, an approach to emotion that originated in the political dance tradition of the 1930s in America, which in turn developed in exchange with the Soviet socialist realist dance tradition.[67] Thus, Siegert introduces an East German socialist realist approach to expression into her reconstruction of a modernist *Ausdruckstanz*. In addition, Siegert's ballet training seems to be visible in some of her movement initiations and postures; for example, certain of her movements seem light as compared to Hoyer's movement, which seems consistently grounded. While I am able to parse and examine aspects of Siegert's approach to Hoyer's vocabulary now, when I saw Siegert perform her reconstruction in East Germany in 1989, I was too overwhelmed to analyze. It was one of the most important dance events I had ever attended. I saw something I had only heard of but had never seen onstage before. I was awed by the modernist abstraction, the rigor of the choreographic investigation, the movement vocabulary, the isolation, the sophisticated attention to space, the groundedness, and by the fact that Arila Siegert enabled me to finally see an *Ausdruckstanz* work.[68]

As I was living in East Germany at the time, I could not see Linke's 1987 reconstruction of *Afectos Humanos*. It is an important work for West German *Tanztheater*, yet it is not surprising that only a year later Linke would incorporate *Afectos Humanos* into her own choreography to make the distance between her work and Hoyer's work even more visible. At that point, *Tanztheater* had reached its zenith. Pina Bausch had choreographed her iconic pieces, including *Café Müller* (1978), *Kontakthof (Contact Zone* [1978]), and *1980—Ein Stück von Pina Bausch (1980—A Piece by Pina Bausch* [1984]), and had just begun producing pieces in collaboration with institutions in foreign locations, an approach that would become the trademark of her later career.[69] Reinhild Hoffmann had staged her large-scale works, such as *Könige und Königinnen (Kings and Queens*

Arila Siegert in her reconstruction of Dore Hoyer's *Afectos Humanos*, 1988. Photo: Hans Ludwig Böhme.

[1982]) and *Callas* (1983), in Bremen. Johann Kresnik presented *Schwanensee AG* (*Swan Lake Inc.* [1971]) and *Sylvia Plath* (1985). By 1977, Gerhard Bohner had already reconstructed several Bauhaus dances, among them Oscar Schlemmer's *Das triadische Ballett* (*The Triadic Ballet*).[70] Linke herself had become famous with her *Im Bade wannen* (*Bathtubbing* [1980]) and the autobiographical *Schritte verfolgen* (*Following Steps* [1985]). All of these choreographers were known to the audiences as students in the tradition of or artists engaging with *Ausdruckstanz*. These West German choreographers also publicly struggled against *their* traditions, but at the same time, they had critical and popular success. They each made their commitment to the tradition visible and partly shifted the West German orientation in dance from ballet to modern dance. Even ballet companies, such as John Neumeier's Hamburger Ballett, John Cranko's Stuttgarter Ballett (which had been led since 1976 by Márcia Haydée), and William Forsythe's Frankfurter Ballett (still existing at that point), had to engage with the strong modern dance presence in West Germany. *Ausdruckstanz* became a valuable tradition and marketable technique.

West Germany had gone through a period that Jameson labels high modernism, and by the mid-1970s, it had begun to shift to a postmodern paradigm
that would question the universalizing and coherent gesture of modernism.
Linke's reconstruction of *Afectos Humanos*, with its visualized differences, breaks,
and other choreographic incongruities, is part of that process of questioning
modernism. Yet it still relies on affect, as Hoyer had in her original performance,
and celebrates the historical modernist artifact. Nachbar's approach stands as
the logical next step after Linke's reconstruction; for his generation, *Ausdruckstanz* material was no longer valid as an expressive tool but it was still used as a
technique.[71] Siegmund has provided three reasons for the renewed interest of
Nachbar's generation in historical choreographies: the desire to negate the
concept of originality so important to modernism, to reflect on the position of
the dancer in a media-dominated society, and to make relevant the ephemeral
art of dance and Nachbar's generation's own careers.[72] The first two points
speak to a postmodern questioning of modernist principles. I address postmodernism in my subsequent discussion of Fine Kwiatkowski's work. Here I
want to highlight Nachbar's tactics: he questions the objective truth of the material he works with and questions his own approach through ironic distancing,
challenges the binary of Hoyer's body and his own, inquires into the attempt at
universality of Hoyer's affects, negates the idea of a linear progression between
Hoyer's and his own execution, and quotes her material in a fragmented, postmodern way.

Nachbar's lecture-performances are a poststructuralist dance scholar's
dream (or nightmare) because they hit all the right marks in current academic
discourses that focus inward on disciplinary issues and aesthetics. I don't think
Nachbar and his contemporary reconstructors' works are produced as an
"empty culture-effect, which is for the sake of gesture alone," as Franko says.[73]
These reconstructions frequently use quotation—of historical dance material—
owing to the influence of media and nearly unlimited access to information
from the Western world. Investigating the recent application of concepts from
the open-source movement to choreographic practices, Lena Hammergren
asks if reconstructors are aware of their practices' relationship to the social
structure. As Hammergren states, "It seems as if politics are considered imma-
nent to the practice of dancing itself."[74]

I had tried to say something similar to the West German scholar who
pointed out that Siegert's reconstruction was not relevant to Nachbar's reconstruction since he doesn't refer to her work. Yes, Nachbar's work *is* an
important disciplinary and artistic investigation. Yes, he labors through his
failure to take on the *Ausdruckstanz* technique with his release-trained body, and

he problematizes the process in an interesting way. He most likely also was aware of Arila Siegert's reconstructions, but as the West German dance scholar said, he only references Susanne Linke in his work. He cannot reference Arila Siegert for a simple reason: it would force him to leave the confines of his own aesthetic and his notion of dance history, because Siegert does not appear in it. Siegert seemingly fails on an aesthetic level and does not exist in historical terms. As Hammergren points out, the current generation of reconstructors predominantly situates the political in an aesthetic investigation. Contrary to this practice, Siegert's reconstruction is political, yet it is not always possible to read this resistive political potential without a consideration of the surrounding social structures. A historization and theorization of Siegert's work is thus a neglected and necessary contribution to the larger German dance studies discourse.

Siegert had neither Linke's nor Nachbar's degree of access to *Ausdruckstanz*. Siegert reconstructed *Afectos Humanos* from a tape that was smuggled into the GDR for her.[75] *Ausdruckstanz* choreographies were not performed at all because the GDR dance culture had not officially worked through the interrupted modernism of the prewar era; Siegert enabled this discourse. She didn't have to demonstrate the gap between her reconstruction and the original because she was so well known in the small GDR dance scene and even smaller Dresden scene that every single audience member was familiar with her work and saw that she was laboring at the dance and not just taking on a role. It wasn't Siegert becoming Hoyer, because East Germans had no reference for Hoyer; rather it was Siegert working through a specific *Ausdruckstanz* as part of a larger project. She underscored this in the program notes, writing, "I reconstruct the Hoyer dances not for technical or historical reasons, but because I want to transport the useable content into the present, to be able to learn from the coherent shapes."[76] Hence the visible effort and the dramatic interpretation in Siegert's performance. Palucca's training and her emphasis on improvised scenes, as well as on jumps and swings—and thus on lightness and the peripheral—was all Siegert knew about the *Ausdruckstanz* tradition at that point, and that knowledge had not fully prepared her to dance Hoyer's technique: "I am a different person with different life experiences than Dore Hoyer. But she molded her content into such a clear form, that it can withstand modification."[77]

If aesthetics are not divorced from politics, then Siegert's accomplishment merits her inclusion in the larger dance historical project. She single-handedly helped GDR dance culture reapproach modernism as an East German tradition. As mentioned in chapter 2, in 1987 the GDR government was still insisting on the paradigm of socialist realism, as indicated by its emphasizing it at the eleventh convention of the SED in Berlin.[78] Even though the East German state no longer repressed endeavors such as Siegert's, hers was still a resistance against the stagnation of East German official dance.

When Siegert founded her *Tanztheater* in Dresden in 1987, it received much attention. The step was unusual for a prima ballerina, yet the structure of the whole endeavor was even more unusual because Arila Siegert's *Tanztheater* company had only one member: Arila Siegert. All other participants in her productions worked with her on a project basis. As common as such a structure might be in today's dance world, East German official dance had never seen it before. Siegert's *Tanztheater* created a new paradigm for dance in the GDR in which dance was located neither in a big, state-funded opera nor in the amateur scene. It is worth stressing the point that an alternative dance scene hardly existed at that point. Dance, like every other part of East German society, was meticulously planned and controlled. The three state schools in Berlin, Leipzig, and Dresden always enrolled and graduated exactly the number of dancers that were needed in the professional companies of the country. Thus, there was no dancer without a job needing to make a living outside the state-sponsored dance sphere. In addition, all dancers received a pension after fifteen years of work. Leaving the official dance company would have meant the loss of this unusual security. There was also no training, no performance spaces, and no sound and lighting for any kind of dance outside the amateur and official theater scenes. So to work in an alternative way did not just mean dancing outside established theatrical structures but meant radically rethinking what dance could be and the dancer's relation to the art form. No dancer with training from a state school had done that until Siegert.[79]

Thus, when Siegert founded her *Tanztheater*, she had no model to copy. The company only provided her with the space she needed to concentrate fully on her choreography. Yet she did not have to worry about financial support because she was part of the theatrical structure of the Dresdner Staatsschauspiel. It was the first time in East Germany that a woman managed a company, choreographed all the work, and danced in all the pieces. Even though such an undertaking seemed to be in alignment with the more emancipated role of women under socialism, it in fact modeled the traditional structure of *Ausdruckstanz*. Wigman, Vogelsang, Hoyer, and Palucca had all done the same.[80] Thus, Siegert was not only referring back to *Ausdruckstanz* with the work she reconstructed and the choreographic principles that informed her work but was also re-creating the institutional structures of the *Ausdruckstanz* tradition. These structures contrasted with the centrally planned and collective dance culture of the amateur and state theaters because they stressed individualism in all areas of dance. As such, Siegert's replication of these structures constituted a resistive gesture that challenged the role of the dancer in a socialist market economy.

In her aesthetic, Siegert reinserted modernism into East German dance in three ways: through reconstructions of a modernist repertoire, through her own choreographic work informed by her training with Palucca, and through institutional structures that replicated the institutional model of *Ausdruckstanz*. She also was among the initiators of two conferences on *Ausdruckstanz* in 1987 and 1988 in Dresden. The Dresdner Tanzsymposium in these two years brought practitioners, dance scholars, and administrators from both Germanies together for the first time. Participants reflected on the *Ausdruckstanz* tradition, on the different developments in West and East after World War II, and even on the influences of *Ausdruckstanz* on other forms, such as butoh.[81] Such critical reflection added to Siegert's choreographic and institutional contribution to a change in East German dance.

Having complete control over all areas of her dance creation proved fruitful for Siegert. She received much attention for her choreographies. For instance, her solo *Die Maske (The Mask)* received the Special Jury Award at the International Choreography Competition in Lyon in 1986.[82] In her solo work, she collaborated with musicians, singers, and painters, and often emphasized the collaborative aspect of her work by incorporating improvisation as a dialogue with these other artistic expressions into the final product. The already mentioned *Gesichte* was a collaboration with the singer Annette Jahns. In *Herzschläge* Siegert brought Jahns back and added the jazz trombone player Conrad Bauer. *Afectos Humanos* combined the reconstruction of Hoyer's dance with her own choreography, titled *Affekte*, and was choreographed to Gerald Humel's musical work *Die Folterung der Beatrice Cenci (The Torturing of Beatrice Cenci)*. Siegert's dance *Fluchtlinien (Flight Lines* [1991]) was performed with Siegert's reconstructions of Wigman's *Hexentanz* and *Abschied und Dank (Farewell and Thank You* [1942]). Concurrently, Siegert started to choreograph for other companies. She created *Othello und Desdemona* (1988) and *Undine* (1991) for the Tanztheater der Komischen Oper Berlin. In 1992, she choreographed *Medea Landschaften (Medea Landscapes)* for the Leipziger Ballett. The West German reviewer Jochen Schmidt, usually critical of East German dance, retrospectively called *Othello und Desdemona* "a piece that even prior to the *Wende* evoked a hopeful future for GDR *Tanztheater*."[83]

The fall of the wall had naturally had an impact on Siegert's career. She had to close her *Tanztheater* company in Dresden in 1992. Subsequently, she accepted a position at the Anhaltisches Theater in Dessau. In 1996, she became the artistic advisor for the stage at the Bauhaus in Dessau. Although she continued choreographing her own work and for other companies, she increasingly focused on directing operas. Already in 1986, Siegert had assisted former Palucca pupil and opera director Ruth Berghaus in Berghaus's production of

Hans Werner Henze's *Orpheus* at the Vienna Opera. This collaboration impressed Siegert and prepared her for her subsequent productions for opera companies throughout Germany. As an independent artist, she broadened her work into musicals and operettas. She worked with much interest on new or never-performed compositions, such as those of the Soviet composer Sergei Slonimsky. Siegert received major awards, among them the German Critics Award for Dance in 1989 and the Order of Merit of the Federal Republic of Germany in 1993, Germany's highest state decoration. Siegert continues to work as a solo dancer, most recently in her own choreography *Liebe/Bolero* (*Love/Bolero*) in 2005 as part of a German-Arab dance project.[84]

I interviewed Arila Siegert in 2004 about her past work and present projects. I never asked her how she felt about her absence from the unified German dance canon and history. At that point, I was not fully aware of the extent of the erasure of East German dance that had occurred in just fifteen years. Only subsequently, after conducting more research for this book and engaging with the German dance studies community, did I come to realize how little was still known about East German dance, how archival institutions and leading dancers and choreographers increasingly disappear from the official dance historical canon, and, above all, the extent to which the lack of interest is not personal but ideological, especially in Germany. It is not my theorization of Siegert's reconstructive practice that provided the initial resistance; it was her practice itself.

My theorization only attempts to expose the ideology of the empty stare of the West German dance scholar and put it into the context of an erasure of East German culture and art after reunification with the West. Utilizing Siegert's nationally unique approach to reconstruction and modernism, I hope I have gestured toward the necessity of constructing appropriate theoretical and historical frameworks for the evaluation of East Germany's cultural productions. Contemporary German dance studies needs to address their lack in the study of more than forty years of dance in recent German history. Yet often it is not even the approach that misses the point; it is the complete absence of recognition that it is critical to study models of dance that pose alternatives to the Western hegemony over the form. The following part of this chapter explores the unique alternative dance scene in East Germany that is now completely absent from any German dance history. Fine Kwiatkowski became one of the most interesting figures in this small dance community that operated outside of official East German dance culture.

Fine Kwiatkowski: Ostmodern/Postmodern

On May 14, 1986, dancer Fine Kwiatkowski improvised in a multimedia event titled REALFilm, staged by filmmaker and painter Lutz Dammbeck with a

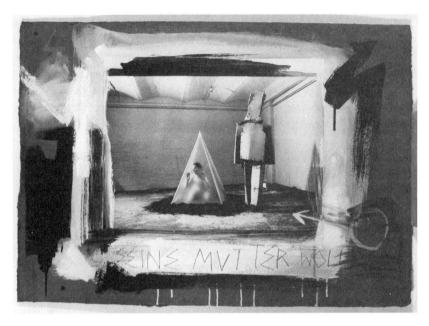

Lutz Dammbeck, *Storyboard Herakles Konzept*, detail. Cardboard, photo, gouache, chalk, 107 × 86 cm, 1984. Fine Kwiatkowski inside an impermanent structure utilized for a storyboard by collaborator Lutz Dammbeck. Photo: Karin Plessing.

musical collaborator Robert Linke at the Haus der Volkskunst in Leipzig.[85] The event was highly unusual for East Germany because it utilized an official performance and event space for a performance that neither engaged with socialist art nor directly opposed it. By presenting something so different from concert dance, the event sidestepped the question of which dance technique or choreographic approach was used and went beyond the dichotomy between state-sanctioned art and subculture. Instead of channeling the different media into a coherent oppositional message, the project utilized rifts, montage, de-montage, simultaneity, erasure, and in the case of movement, improvisation. Kwiatkowski's improvisations cannot be evaluated independently from this postmodern approach that she adopts in a country where modernism had barely been explored. Slowly wiggling her way out of a pyramidal sculpture composed of branches and wax paper, meticulously destroying it in the process, Kwiatkow-ski angles and bends her body in a refusal to acknowledge the audience's gaze or the range of elements expected of dance: a coherent technique, affect, narra-tion, and chronology. Like no other dancer in East Germany, she consequently remained outside of any institutional dance in her technique and improvisational approach. Without having had any exchange with Western dance, and possibly unknowingly, she propelled East German dance into postmodernism.

In order to understand Kwiatkowski's unique contribution to East German dance it is necessary to contextualize her generation's attitude toward their homeland and their beliefs about the function of art. Beginning with the 1980s, a young generation with values very different from the preceding ones emerged in the GDR. These young people, born around the time of the erection of the Berlin Wall, were no longer interested in socialist values and morals defined by labor. Unlike their predecessors, who either supported the socialist regime with varying degrees of critical distance or openly opposed it, these artists "ignored the GDR inside the borders of the GDR."[86] The new generation neither identified with the socialist ideal nor joined underground opposition groups. They refused to function in the state-opposition model. They instead drew from a lexicon of nonsocialist ways of life in an attempt to create their own reality.

Theater director Frank Castorf, who became the head of the Volksbühne in Berlin and who belonged to this generation, described his oppositional past in the GDR in the following way: "[I was oppositional] only up to a certain point. . . . I never participated in dramatic situations. Still, I sometimes got in trouble. . . . But I was able to finish high school and I served my army duty at the border between East and West Germany. I accepted the norms of this society. I rebelled only inside its structures."[87] Many artists at the end of the 1970s and during the 1980s refused to define themselves as an antistate movement. The importance of this artistic subculture derived from the fact that artists challenged the structures of the socialist system individually. These artists still used state resources, but only to enable their decadent lifestyle, which stood in contrast to the socialist ideal.[88] A major component of this lifestyle was artists' unwillingness to function as a part of the socialist collective. The artists of the 1970s and 1980s developed their art foremost by problematizing individuality in relationship to socialist collectivity. This individuality made it difficult to analyze the art subculture during that time as representing a coherent vision. However, these artists' shared refusal to become a part of neither the official state culture nor the opposition demands an interrogation into their specific form of resistance to the socialist state. This kind of resistance in the areas of fine art, theater, and music has begun to be explored yet still awaits its analysis in dance.[89]

These various artistic groups often gathered loosely around a more prominent artist or created collectives in collaboration with different artists. Due to the increasing discrepancy between socialist rhetoric and the reality of East German society, as well as the loosening of censorship around art, groups utilized different forms of art. Fine arts and jazz music were often an artistic starting point for these groups. Amid the notorious shortage of living space in East Germany, fine artists received dilapidated large apartments that included working spaces. These private spaces functioned as unofficial places for meetings and exhibitions. Due to the predominantly individualized nature of the fine arts, collaboration was limited and occurred mostly around exhibitions and performance-related events. This was also true for literature, which was the dominant interest of these groups at the beginning of the 1980s. This focus shifted, however, as a growing number of people illegally occupied empty and abandoned apartments, yielding more space for performances. From the early 1980s on, theater, concerts, and performances became central activities in these artists' lives.

To understand the context these artists worked in, it is helpful to consider the housing situation, as well as how they negotiated access to space in East Germany. The housing program was centrally controlled by the government and held a key position in the state's five-year plans over several decades.[90] In the plan for 1981 through 1985, the tenth SED convention recommended the building and renovation of 930,000–950,000 apartments for 2.8 million people. Of those apartments, 600,000 were supposed to have been newly built. The plan stated that the new apartments would be offered first to working-class families, families with several children, and young couples.[91] This preference was only one example of the elaborate rules governing the distribution of apartments. Large cities such as Berlin, Dresden, and Leipzig, for example, had quotas that needed to be kept to avoid overconcentration of population. Therefore, only people who could prove they were employed in the city they wanted to live in could ask for living space. At the same time, employment in the city was dependent on an address in the city. This catch-22 could only be resolved by sharing an apartment with a friend or relative in order to establish an address.

The next step involved a months-long or even years-long struggle with housing officials who followed a strict hierarchy for the distribution of apartments. At the top of the list were people in houses that threatened to tumble down from decay or that needed to be evacuated for house-building projects.[92] This group was followed by families with children, young couples, and single mothers with children. At the bottom of the list were young single citizens. The artists' groups consisted mostly of such single citizens. They had no legal possibility of obtaining living space, not to mention space large enough to gather in groups. At the beginning of the 1980s, however, government agencies responsible for distributing housing increasingly lost control over the decaying housing market. As a result, it was possible to occupy apartments and live in them for years before being found out by officials. Young artists took advantage of this situation and occupied large apartments that could accommodate their life and art. Since rents in East Germany were state-sponsored and extremely low, many even paid rent in the name of a person who had abandoned the property to avoid being found out.

Despite the fact that life in East Germany was relatively cheap, this new generation learned to earn money in abundance by tackling the socialist market. This market suffered from a shortage of a variety of consumer goods, with fashion and clothes being in especially high demand. The state-sponsored production of these goods was too slow and inefficient to keep up with fashion demands, which were increasingly influenced by West German TV. Thus, the sewing machine became one of the most important tools for achieving and maintaining an artist's lifestyle. The machine could not only produce clothes to dress artists—and distinguish them from the proletarian masses—but it also allowed them to produce a surplus of fashion, which they sold at markets and through an elaborate distribution network. Their products were mostly simple T-shirts, dresses made out of cotton bed sheets, and leather clothes of any kind.[93] Selling these products, a single person could earn more on a weekend than a university professor earned in a month. Other artists had jobs related to their creative lives; since there were plenty of jobs due to East Germany's labor shortages, artists were able to adjust their schedules to their needs. These approaches to work and labor permitted artists to operate outside the norms and principles of the socialist system. Older artists such as Biermann saw this existence as apolitical and did not understand that the younger generation consciously avoided the artist versus state binary. The poet Barbara Köhler described their approach as seeking the "chance to avoid an oppositional position that produced only negative repercussions. The main mission was to avoid getting pressured into contrariety."[94] Yet Castorf, who was part of this nonoppositional generation and whose plays were constantly threatened with state censorship, perceived this situation as indicating that the overarching socialist initiative had failed. Dropping out of society thus became a way of making a mass disappearance from socialism's official structures.[95] As history demonstrated, this approach was much more effective in the long run.

The arts became not only an essential outlet and niche for this generation; they also developed into aesthetic resistance. The new generation's awareness of the important link between art and resistance received a new stimulus when Peter Weiss's *Die Ästhetik des Widerstands* (*The Aesthetic of Resistance*) was published in East Germany in 1983. Weiss's three-volume fictitious history of antifascist resistance centers on the role of art in political resistance against doctrinarian regimes. Weiss uses montage as a narrative device to reveal opposing positions but avoids taking a coherent stance on art and politics and so manages to discuss the possibility of political change through aesthetic means explicitly. Even though the novel was published in a very small print run and was only distributed to academics, retyped copies soon surfaced everywhere in the artistic world. Instigated by the book and their own experience of artistic resistance to socialist mandates, young people increasingly problematized the contradiction between official discourse and socialist reality through art. However, they chose to perform such awareness through an investigation of the artistic medium and contents rather than through oppositional art.

Part of that process was a "catching up" with proletkult, expressionism, surrealism, and other modernist experiments in the 1970s. Simultaneously in the 1980s performing artists questioned structures of society by breaking with the institutions and conventions that had defined Western European performance for two hundred years. Texts, characters, narratives, the use of space, concepts of time, and the barrier between stage and audience were questioned.[96] Consequently, some younger directors started to challenge the division between different artistic practices. Jo Fabian, for example, created entirely alternative spaces to socialist reality and the dominant theatrical paradigm via a very slow movement, a self-referential iconography, the destruction of texts, and the dislocation of time and space. I discuss his work further in the following chapter, because it not only instigated a change in theatrical representation but also survived and reflected on the fall of the Berlin Wall.

Even though dance, like visual art and music, distanced itself from socialist demands, it took longer for dance to initiate this process of questioning. As described, Siegert began exploring modernist practices and theorizations in the 1980s. Just as she rethought the *Ausdruckstanz* tradition, other dancers challenged the institutional structures of dance and what dance meant in East Germany. Dresden had a specific relationship to dance because of the city's *Ausdruckstanz* tradition, and the presence of Émile Jaques-Dalcroze, the Palucca School, the ballet at the Dresden Oper (which was renamed the Semperoper in 1985), and Siegert. Susanne Ladopoulos maintains that improvisation was an intrinsic part of Dresden's dance culture.[97] At the Bildungsanstalt Jaques-Dalcroze in Hellerau, improvisation was an important tool for developing expression. Jaques-Dalcroze used both musical and movement improvisation as a central part of his teaching. Wigman, who never improvised in public, did employ improvisation in her choreographic process. Her belief in dance as an expression of a chosen artist's view of the world and in the singularity of the dancer's individual expression forced her to carefully purge dance of any unnecessary elements. This creative process might start with improvisation, but the instinctual artistic impulse needed to be overcome through the disciplined labor of choreography. Palucca, Wigman's student, utilized improvisation in every aspect of her work: at all stages of the creative process, in performances, and in her pedagogy.

Influenced by the history of improvisation in Dresden and by Palucca's approach, several graduates of Palucca's school started an improvisation evening in 1980 in Dresden. By this point, improvisation had become an important tool of corporeal resistance to socialist realist stagings. These public improvisations were initiated by pianist Peter Jarchow (a long-term musician at the Palucca School) and by dancers Siegert and Thomas Hartmann. Hanne Wandtke, a former student and later pedagogue at the Palucca School who embraced Palucca's concepts in her own teaching more deeply than other of Palucca's students, curated the evening mostly with alumni of the Palucca School. Even though the local press criticized the first evening as being too much like an improvisation class, audiences attended these performances with interest. They became a regular event once or twice a year.[98] As a result, dance audiences in Dresden were exposed anew to improvisation. Increasingly, the participants changed the setup by using more and different kinds of musicians, by changing the organizational structure, and by inviting actors and singers to take part. Initially, the group designated a leader who would set tasks for the improvisation and communicate with the audience. Ladopoulos, who witnessed most of the evenings, states that the programs changed radically when the group eliminated the leader role. Tasks and goals were then negotiated by the group and set beforehand. Through this process, participants not only investigated dance as structure, method, and material but also incorporated outside sources and critical views on East Germany.

The one artist who is completely absent from Ladopoulos's investigation into the role of improvisation in Dresden is Fine Kwiatkowski. Kwiatkowski is also just about missing from histories of dance, and in fact, of art in East Germany altogether.[99] This seems startling because she was active from the early 1980s, collaborating with many artists from diverse disciplines, working not just in Dresden but throughout the country, and drastically rethinking dance in East Germany. Kwiatkowski was entirely self-taught. Born in 1956, she engaged mostly in sports in her childhood and was a member of the Pantomimentheater Prenzlauer Berg in Berlin (now Mime Centrum Berlin) for three years beginning in 1978. Even though the Pantomimentheater was an important center for the investigation of a variety of nonverbal theatrical movement systems in the GDR, Kwiatkowski left the center to focus on improvisation and her solo work. She founded the improvisation collective Fine with the musicians Lothar Fiedler (electronic guitar), Dietmar Diesner (saxophone), and Christoph Winkel (bass). Simultaneously she pursued several other collaborations with, for example, multimedia artist Lutz Dammbeck and filmmaker Christine Schlegel. In 1988, she presented her first evening-length choreography at a theater in Frankfurt/Oder in collaboration with director Andreas Kriegenburg. After the fall of the Berlin Wall, Kwiatkowski worked predominantly inside institutional theater structures. She spent three years at the Freie Kammerspiele in Magdeburg, and since leaving Freie Kammerspiele, she has continued her collaborations mostly with musicians and media artists, on a project basis.

This would not be a surprising biography for an independent dance artist in a Western country, but it is highly unusual for an East German dancer. Even dancers in the amateur dance scene needed to obtain an official evaluation called an *Einstufung* (classification) to be able to perform in public places and to receive payment. The amount of compensation was clearly determined by the skill level of the artist, which was evaluated by commissions that would observe the dancers. Usually only solo dancers were evaluated individually; group dancers were evaluated as part of the entire ensemble.[100] The criteria for these evaluations were not made public but presumably were in line with the technical and ideological focus of East German dance more generally. Because of her unusual and abstract vocabulary and because she lacked any official training or affiliation with a group, Kwiatkowski was not able to obtain any *Einstufung*. As a result, she performed in private apartments or in public spaces, such as youth clubs, lobbies of cinemas, or restaurants that were able to pay her a minimal fee through their general budget. Often, too, she was paid through the musicians she collaborated with. Even in the affordable GDR, Kwiatkowski was not able to live from her dancing and had to work as an assistant at a theater in Frankfurt/Oder.[101]

Whereas her earlier works were improvisations in response to the music of her collaborators—predominantly free jazz and contemporary atonal music—the projects with Dammbeck and Schlegel were more conceptual. Dammbeck was one of the major filmmakers and multimedia artists of the underground GDR scene. His film *Hommage à La Sarraz* offers one of the most poignant depictions of the 1980s artist scene and its view of the rest of East German society. It is also exemplary of the kinds of works that were created by these artists, including Kwiatkowski. The most important characteristic of such artistic productions was their strong interdisciplinarity. The artists did not just paint pictures, make films, dance, or perform but combined all of these creative acts. They filmed paintings. They also filmed performances that were staged in front of film projections. Or they filmed painted bodies, crawling out of paper structures or glass boxes, destroying these structures in the process. Then these artists took the films, painted over them, and scratched them and then showed them in private screenings in yet another performative context with live music. Borders between artistic practices and products—as well as of bodies—were not just challenged or questioned but were radically destroyed, and then these acts, objects, and bodies were reconstructed only to be destroyed again. The results were extremely fluid, without definable centers and distinct identities. Archival material, especially films and photos, became an important raw

Lutz Dammbeck, *Mediencollage REALFilm*. Still, 1986. Fine Kwiatkowski moving with her own projection, partly projected onto her body. Photo: Karin Plessing.

material. These materials were cut and live-edited and shown next to contemporary or more archival material—never to create a coherent message or narrative but instead to expose differences and similarities. Most importantly, such utilization of archival material did not turn the work into a problematization of historical texts and forms, or a living archive. Rather, it was the destruction of history and its documentation that figured prominently in these performances.

In the middle of all this, Kwiatkowski performed with her shaved head and delicate yet strong physique. She coiled her body around sculptures, making her way hesitantly through debris, slowly twisting with bent arms and knees, changing her facial expression from surprise to the unreadable. There were no clear lines, distinguishable poses, comprehensible affect, no technical brilliance, no surfaces or transparent references. Her improvisation did not engage with the *Ausdruckstanz* tradition of improvisation because it didn't concern itself with universal themes, imagery, or investigations of space. It also did not react to rhythmic and musical structures or follow tasks common to the improvisation scene in Dresden. Kwiatkowski did not investigate the weight of objects or other bodies in the way that contact improvisation did. Although her dance language was from time to time reminiscent of butoh, it was also distinct from the Japanese movement's internalized attention and inward- and downward-focused movement quality. Her body did not constitute a single unit; rather it seemed to be in constant exchange with her surroundings, the music, the sculptures, the films, the paintings, and itself. As one critic described it, "Fine's hands [are] searching for her legs, her feet, touching the body and face like a foreign object that needs to be discovered."[102] The effort of this discovery was visible, and there was never an attempt to disguise or please, to settle into a phrase or shape, or to conclude. As a result of this constant shifting, Kwiatkowski fragmented reality and her own body, opening it up to its surroundings, refusing any coherent choreographic investigation, destroying history.

East German society had a clear goal: to travel the Marxist-Leninist path from a capitalist past to a socialist present toward the communist future. Its socialist realist artistic doctrine aimed to control and utilize the power of the arts in the service of this national goal. In this state-choreographed environment, Kwiatkowski shifted her body across multiple spaces and temporalities of performance. She explored without attempting to fully comprehend the stage space or what lay beyond it, thrilled to find opportunities for movement through time, challenging the fetish of the present of performance by reaching simultaneously back to a past that her society had not worked through and toward the future that no longer shined ahead. Improvisation became not a vehicle of exploration or the object of elitist investigation but the only possible and simultaneous transgression of the borders of dance, her country, and presence. By moving anywhere and anytime, Kwiatkowski's improvisations disengaged from the importance of the present and tested the notion that performance becomes itself through disappearance.[103]

Kwiatkowski radically changed what dance was in East Germany. She did not work in any existing paradigm of the form or its function in society. Even though many artists, including her collaborators Dammbeck and Schlegel, attest to Kwiatkowski's influence on their work, she does not appear in any dance historical narrative. Shards of her presence and her improvisations are in Schlegel and Dammbeck's films and in images depicting various 1980s art events. Kwiatkowski's image is painted over or scratched or her body is used as a canvas for projections during filmed performances. Even after I interviewed her in 2004, I still didn't know enough about her aims and her improvisations to be able to fully analyze either. They defy both categorization and the standard definitions of a dance event. No matter how many snippets of her work we see, how closely we watch her, Kwiatkowski's improvisations will never be reducible to the stills or films of her work or to the live act of her performance. She did not strive to catch up with developments in the West but instead created a specifically East German corporeal engagement with social structures. In retrospect, the obvious label for this kind of dance might be postmodern.[104] Yet Kwiatkowski did not react against modernism at all, which is often assumed to be the impetus for postmodern dance. She stood completely outside such Western-dominated periodization and systematization. The few authors, such as Melzwig, Schmidt, and Cramer, who have written about 1980s East German dance evaluate the East German case using West Germany as the standard.[105] As a result, they conclude that East German dance never reached the level of choreographic exploration of the West. This colonial view prevents them from fully understanding the unique milieu in the GDR and Kwiatkowski in particular. There was no artist like her in West Germany, because there was no *need* for anyone like her.[106]

Charlotte von Mahlsdorf: The Invisible Resistance of the Everyday

It is hard for an outsider to see, analyze, and comprehend everyday resistance in East Germany. Here I provide an example of such pedestrian resistance by working through an oppositional choreography even more removed from the canonical dance history notion of performance. I want to demonstrate that in order to understand the sophistication of such resistance a careful analysis and the appropriate methodological approach—in this case, gay and lesbian studies—is necessary. There is a growing amount of scholarship on German gay and lesbian identity in both East and West Germany. In this part of the chapter, I add to this literature by charting significant developments in East German gay and lesbian culture through the example of transvestite Charlotte von Mahlsdorf. To do this it is also necessary to discuss East German approaches to the politics of sexual minority identification in relation to hegemonic North American queer identity and theorization. This comparison enables an analysis of nationally specific developments in sexual identification and resistance and drives my analysis of Charlotte's work. Despite a history of limited access to the rights of citizenship for minorities, the United States displays a remarkably unified nationalism and strong allegiance to the idea of America. Because a potent emphasis on individualism supports this nationalism, minority resistance to national systems of state power in the United States has tended to lead to the creation of and reliance on strong community identifications, such as civil rights or gay and lesbian movements. In contrast, East Germans experienced a serious abuse of national identity and community in Nazi Germany and under the socialist regime. These experiences made East Germans suspicious of group identification and led them to put an emphasis on individuality in the context of acts of resistance. Von Mahlsdorf's performance throughout her life illustrates one approach to minority resistance that suggests alternative tactics to those associated with the increasingly corporate export of North American queerness as a dominant model for nonnormative sexual identification and resistance.

Von Mahlsdorf's unusual life story seems to mirror German twentieth-century gay history.[107] Born male as Lothar Berfelde in 1928, her abusive father tried to raise his son according to Prussian and fascist male standards.[108] Von Mahlsdorf rebelled against him, and she also refused to join the Hitler Youth. Motivated by a lesbian aunt (who caught von Mahlsdorf dressed in her clothes), von Mahlsdorf read Magnus Hirschfeld's book *The Transvestites* at the age of fifteen. This encounter with Hirschfeld's writing encouraged von Mahlsdorf to consciously resist society's demand for stable and binary gender definitions. While working in a secondhand furniture store in Berlin at the beginning of World War II, von Mahlsdorf started to buy and wear exclusively female clothes. She was once caught cross-dressing but escaped imprisonment in a concentration camp because the police judged her act to be a young boy's joke. In February 1944, von Mahlsdorf allegedly killed her violent father, when he threatened to shoot his "dysfunctional" son along with the rest of the family.[109] During her resulting imprisonment, von Mahlsdorf was kept under observation and given a psychiatric evaluation. She was set free in April 1945 because the Soviet soldiers were marching into Berlin. During these last days of the war, members of the SS were hunting and shooting any men who were out on the street and not serving in the German army. Von Mahlsdorf was caught by the SS and survived that fate only because the approaching Red Army bombed the very spot she and the SS were standing on.

After the war, von Mahlsdorf had to negotiate another set of discriminations in the newly Soviet-occupied eastern part of Germany. In an article on sexual identity during the Cold War, Katrin Sieg explains that the socialist stance toward homosexuality was based on prewar and World War II politics. Sieg points to communists' employment of homophobia as a political tool to defame opponents.[110] East Germany inherited this tradition by defining itself as antifascist and as a successor to the oppositional communist Left of the Weimar Republic and fascist Germany. As Sieg rightly points out, the GDR's ideology was also influenced by the Soviet Union. After a short period of sexual liberation following the October Revolution in 1917, the Soviet Union repressed any sexual experiments that challenged the heterosexual family.[111] That repression resulted from Marxism-Leninism's neglect of sexuality as a driving political force. The reduction of sexuality to a private and exclusively physical act frames sexual identity as private and corporeal, removing it from more abstracted group and class interests that powerfully underwrite the Marxist-Leninist concept of class struggle.

It is thus not surprising that upon its founding in 1949, the GDR adopted the original 1871 version of Paragraph 175 of the Constitution of the German Empire, which punished male homosexual acts with imprisonment and possible loss of citizenship.[112] The notorious Paragraph 175 was replaced in 1968 by Paragraph 151, which lowered the age of consent but still included a provision prohibiting same-sex sexual activities with minors under the age of eighteen. Still, any fight for equal rights by East Germany's gay men and lesbian women was read by government authorities as resistance to socialist norms and values and Marxist-Leninist doctrine. As a result, gays and lesbians in East Germany had to develop unique strategies to become visible in a state that refused to acknowledge their sexual practices and their sexual identity. Although a few gay bars existed (mostly in East Berlin), East German gay and lesbian social and political life was rarely visible in public places before the 1980s.[113] As with other resistance efforts against the East German government, all political meetings had to be disguised as private parties or excursions if the organizers were to avoid punishment by the state. For instance, the first important social and activist gatherings of gays and lesbians in East Germany were held at one of von Mahlsdorf's private museums on the edge of East Berlin. Von Mahlsdorf began collecting furniture from the design period Gründerzeit (1870–1900) at the beginning of World War II and eventually reconstructed an old mansion and founded a private Gründerzeit museum to house her impressive collection.[114] Beginning in 1974, she offered this semipublic space free of charge for political meetings and social gatherings of gays and lesbians. But von Mahlsdorf had to defend her museum many times against the East German government because private museums were not supposed to exist in the GDR, and they were seen as a threat to the central control of cultural heritage. The government wanted to sell von Mahlsdorf's antiques for hard currency, but most importantly it wanted to shut it down as a meeting place. Government officials finally prohibited these meetings in 1978.[115]

After this ban, the struggle for meeting places for activist gay and lesbian groups then led paradoxically to the Protestant Church, which provided not just the physical space but also the necessary legal protection against the socialist government.[116] The first working group on gay and lesbian issues under the protection of the church was founded in Leipzig in 1982 and was soon followed by more groups in Berlin and other cities throughout the republic. This was, of course, controversial for the socialist government, but it was also problematic for the Protestant Church. Though the church saw any homosexual as a person in need, it remained ambivalent about homosexuality itself. Moreover, the church did not want to become the catalyst for a gay movement, which it

Charlotte von Mahlsdorf in her Gründerzeit museum. Photo: Erwin Bode.

eventually did. It is important to note that even though these groups met under the protection of the church, they were not antisocialist: their members still saw themselves as gays and lesbians fighting for an equal place in East German socialist society. Only a few gay men and lesbians in East Germany extended the critique of the socialist state's homophobia into a general critique of socialism's Marxist-Leninist ideology.[117] Yet the majority of gays and lesbians agreed in the critique of the East German Stalinized adaptation of this ideology.

When the growing number of gay and lesbian working groups in the church threatened to develop into an independent political movement, East German officials had to rethink their attitudes toward homosexuality. Additional pressure came from atheist gays and lesbians who did not want to utilize the church spaces and who pointed to the church's historical employment of antihomosexual rhetoric. These gays and lesbians searched for meeting places that were not just tolerated but sanctioned and supported by the socialist government. These efforts were not in vain, because, reacting to activists' demands, the government finally legitimized meetings for gays and lesbians in the mid-1980s. The GDR government's eventual acknowledgment of sexuality as a defining identity category was consistent with a general emphasis on individuality in socialist rhetoric and politics in the 1980s. The eleventh convention of the SED in 1986 demonstrated a much more developed concern with the needs of the individual citizen than the tenth convention had five years earlier.[118] This emphasis on individual citizens permitted the East German government to perceive gays and lesbians as *individuals* with specific needs and desires in socialist society rather than as communities defined by homosexuality.

With this changed focus on citizens as individuals at the end of the 1980s, a gay and lesbian culture with support groups, as well as a public club and bar scene, started to emerge in larger cities.[119] In 1988, East German law finally dispensed with Paragraph 151 and did not replace it.[120] This step obliterated any differences between homosexual and heterosexual citizens under the law with regard to sexual conduct. It also affirmed the GDR (again in legal terms) as the most progressive state among the socialist Eastern Bloc countries in curtailing discrimination based on sexual orientation; it was even less discriminatory than its West German neighbor. Despite these progressive changes, the GDR still did not recognize gay or lesbian partners in regards to marital rights, tax laws, inheritance issues, adoption, and hospitalization visitation rights.

Still, a changing attitude toward homosexuality in East Germany was also notable in popular culture and the media. For instance, programs on the extremely popular youth radio station DT 64 featured talk sessions on homosexuality, inviting young gays and lesbians as guests in the studio. These guests answered listeners' questions with confidence and an occasional irony that established homosexuality as a possibility rather than a fixed identification.[121] This understanding of sexual identity strategically defined it as fixed only for the purpose of gaining access to social structures. This view on the utility and temporality of identity categories might seem reactionary when compared to the notion that sexual identity empowers communities as forces for social change. Yet given that East German ideology firmly established communal identification as the official socialist identity, any emphasis on individual choice tended to be perceived as powerful resistance to socialist norms. In North American society, on the other hand, individual rights tend to be regarded as the building blocks of national identity. In that context, community identification, such as queer identity, can provide a strong oppositional force to discrimination with the national power structure.

The distinctive East German approach to identity was also evident in the events that led to the fall of the Berlin Wall. When large peaceful demonstrations swept through all major cities in East Germany demanding a transformation of Stalinist government structures, freedom of expression, and liberty to travel, gay and lesbian activists joined these popular uprisings without emphasizing gay and lesbian issues. Retrospectively, this approach has been questioned by queer activists and scholars.[122] Yet a comprehension of the unique functions of community and the individual in East German society might enable a reevaluation of the choices gays and lesbians made during the last days of socialist society.

As a paradigm for individual choice over group identification, Charlotte von Mahlsdorf had become something of a celebrity in East German gay and lesbian circles by the end of the 1980s. Von Mahlsdorf had provided her furniture as props for many East German period movies and had been an extra in several of them. She became one of the subjects of a documentary on gay life (*Die andere Liebe* [1988]) and also a character in the first and only East German gay movie. November 9, 1989, the night of the fall of the Berlin Wall, coincided with the premiere of Heiner Carow's movie *Coming Out*, in which von Mahlsdorf played a barmaid at a gay bar. Appropriately, the character recounts iconic parts of German gay history in telling her own biography.

In 1992, after the reunification of both Germanies, von Mahlsdorf received one of the German government's most prestigious decorations, the Bundesverdienstkreuz, in recognition of her unique contribution to German culture and for her preservation of cultural artifacts.[123] In the same year, von Mahlsdorf published her autobiography, *Ich bin meine eigene Frau* (*I Am My Own Woman*), and starred in Rosa von Praunheim's movie version of her life. Yet shortly thereafter, the media accused her of voluntary collaboration with the East German secret service.[124] The negative publicity and increasing financial difficulties prompted her to leave Germany in April 1997 for Porlabrunn, Sweden, where she opened a new Gründerzeit museum. She died in 2002 during a promotional tour for her autobiography in Germany.

In *I Am My Own Woman*, von Mahlsdorf describes a 1988 encounter with the Stasi on the doorsteps of her second museum near Berlin:

> Two "gentlemen" approached my house in unison steps, as I was cleaning the main entrance stairs and the doormat. Without any greeting, both of them pulled out their identification badges.
>
> "Is this the private museum?"
>
> "Yes."
>
> "We are looking for the male citizen Berfelde; don't tell us that you are him."
>
> I stood, looking like a cleaning woman on the stairs, wearing an apron and holding a broom and dustpan in my hands.
>
> "Yes, that's me. I collected everything from childhood on and the museum has been open to the public without entrance fee since August 1960."

The one in the trench coat yelled, "You are an undesirable person for us, remember that."

"It is very kind of you to tell me that, so now I know it, gentlemen," I replied while curtsying.[125]

Von Mahlsdorf vividly describes her own choreographic response to the police intimidation, exemplifying a subtle yet significant form of resistance against East German state discipline. What I find extraordinary in this scene as recounted by von Mahlsdorf is that her obedient body seems superficially to move in alignment with the choreography of the East German ideological system. The socialist state stipulated that individual bodies should be configured as a constituent of a mass working-class body. Von Mahlsdorf aligns herself with this working-class body because the police discover her at work—sweeping the stairs leading to her porch. At the same time, she also mocks her own staging of the cooperative citizen by disruptively inserting feminine movement vocabulary—curtsying and even the fact that she is obsessively sweeping—into her performance for state officials. The curtsy is not at all a part of the socialist movement vocabulary, because this movement is one of the best-known emblems of a noble and correspondingly bourgeois society, which, in theory, should have long been overcome by the socialist GDR. Consequently, through the curtsy, the supposedly servile von Mahlsdorf withdraws from the class of proletariat and stages her body as a part of a petit bourgeois tableau. The museum with the turn-of-the-century furniture collection provides a perfect backdrop for her resistive performance.

With this slight yet eminently subversive gesture von Mahlsdorf avoids the state official's systematization by refusing any categorization. She challenges class distinctions through her excessive performance of the wrong kind of feminine labor. And she functions in neither the gay/straight nor the female/male binary.[126] It is also not possible to categorize von Mahlsdorf in terms of passing or visibly crossing gender or sexual identities.[127] Her choreographic response to the secret service agents, moving as a woman, sweeping, and curtsying, provides us with a potent example of an intervention in the nation's system of normalized gender and sexual representation prior to the fall of the Berlin Wall.

In her description of the 1988 encounter with state security, von Mahlsdorf justifies her model citizenship by stressing her hard labor throughout her entire life and by defining her museum as a public space. By casting her body in the role of a laboring body, a cleaning woman, she assimilates her body into the mass working-class body of all socialist citizens. This abstractable body integrates two major ideological constructions: Marxist philosophy and bourgeois citizenship. In her essay "National Brands/National Body: Imitation of Life," Lauren

Berlant explains that proper citizenship in a bourgeois state requires a dialectic between an abstraction from individual corporeality and the embodiment of a standard body of the state. Standardization of this dialectic allows the state to assemble its individual citizens into a mass body that constitutes the foundation for any public discourse. This standard body is figured by the state as male, white, heterosexual, and middle class. Thus not all citizens can abstract from their own corporeality to constitute this mass body. Citizens who differ from the standard body never completely disembody themselves and therefore never participate in the mass body to the same degree as their more "standard" fellow citizens.

What I find so interesting in von Mahlsdorf's story of the encounter with the Stasi is that, when superficially analyzed, her body seems the only real body. The secret service agents are present more as metaphorical constructions than as real bodies. They belong to the abstracted standard body and thus to the even more abstract mass body. Yet these bodies are performing not in a bourgeois society but in a socialist system. Thus Berlant's definitions need to be modified to take account of the category of labor as defined in Marxist philosophy. A female body in socialist society could accomplish a similar abstraction to that of male citizens by relating itself through labor to the standard body. Only then would a female body be able to become a part of the socialist mass body. As much as the East German state incorporated female bodies into state choreographies, the mass working-class body remained a male one. The male body symbolized the industrial working class in any public depiction, while the female body was restricted to a portrayal of agriculture with its connotations of nature and the natural. Still, the emancipatory movement of East Germany attempted to equate women to men. Women were supposed to function in the same realms as men, and the state transferred traditional female work from the private sphere of the household to public domains such as day care and public kitchens. By professionalizing women's work, it could be dissolved into the labor of the masculine mass body. Through labor, then, women's bodies figured as part of the standard body needed to create the mass body.

The state could control this mass body only to a certain extent. To be able to monitor and regulate its citizens, the state needed to differentiate among individual citizens. Only a singled-out, individual body can be held accountable for its actions. Therefore the state had to recover a citizen's individual body to observe and eventually discipline it. As a result, the state summoned up images of a mass body and at the same time divided the mass body into individual bodies to control them. Any resistance in the GDR arose in reaction to this double movement, the state's creation and deconstruction of a mass body. These specific conditions for resistance explain the unique employment of individual over community identifications by minority groups.

Von Mahlsdorf is an interesting example because she resisted socialist corporeal standards in so many different ways. Her resistance operated as both mimicry and mockery of the socialist standard body as well as its movements.[128] Homi K. Bhabha defines mimicry as an important part of colonial discourse. For Bhabha, the object of colonization performs mimicry to adapt to the colonial power. This mimicry relies on the colonized's observation of the appropriate body and movements that are performed and imposed by the colonizer. This observation allows the colonized to mimic the colonizer's postures or movements, going beyond a simple imitation. The objects of colonization incorporate the observed movements and behaviors into their own behaviors. Their mimicry does not assume the same position as the colonizer's or, as Bhabha calls it, "the place of power," because the action of the colonized "is almost the same, but not quite."[129] This lack or dissonance ensures that the colonized objects who perform mimicry can never take the place of the colonizer. The performed movement of the colonized, who mimics the colonizer, might look the same as the colonizers' movement, but it is never exactly the same, because it lacks the appropriate body. Still, the ability of the colonized to perform the proper movement unveils the constructed nature of that movement. In other words, when someone is able, through mimicry, to imitate a given movement, it reveals that movement as not "naturally" arising but learnable and performable. Consequently, mimicry allows the colonized to expose the construction of colonial power and thus enables a critical perspective on both "normalized" knowledges and disciplinary powers.

Von Mahlsdorf employed an approach similar to the mimicry of the colonized. She observed the movement of the normative socialist body, which included her observers. She realized that she needed to perform the laboring body to be able to pass as a standard socialist body. She reenacted the observed movement, in her case the labor of cleaning and sweeping. Judged from her movement, von Mahlsdorf seemed to perform in alignment with the standard body and was thus able to be incorporated into the mass body. Her cross-dressed body permitted this incorporation only to a certain extent; still von Mahlsdorf's ability to perform the proper movement, even though she lacked the appropriate body, revealed to the members of the secret service the artificial construction of the standard body. Such an exposure of power structures is crucial for an understanding of von Mahlsdorf's resistance, because it returned agency to the individual citizen. Because of mimicry's ambivalence and seemingly cooperative nature, outside observers often overlooked its power.

Von Mahlsdorf also evaded the disciplining of the state in the way she was wearing female-connoted clothes. She never had surgery, nor did she attempt to pass as a woman. "I never wear make up, I don't dye my hair, and to adorn myself with flashy jewelry is not my cup of tea. I am what I am. Mostly, I wear an apron and a bandanna and I am satisfied being a housemaid."[130] While von Mahlsdorf defined her body as part of a petit bourgeois mise-en-scène by performing as a housemaid, she nevertheless rejected any extravagant female additions or alterations to her body. This rejection is more vividly apparent in the fact that von Mahlsdorf refused to label herself a transsexual.[131] She never intended to have surgery and repeatedly stated that unlike other transgendered women, she was not at odds with her penis. Even though she reiterated the phrase about being woman living in a male body, she titled her autobiography *I Am My Own Woman.* The title suggested that von Mahlsdorf was not suppressing one or the other side of her corporeal identity. Rather, she created an identity that included male as well as female elements of her corporeality. Von Mahlsdorf embodied all parts of her corporeal identity and conjoined them with her simultaneous employment of diverse class and sexual identities. Von Mahlsdorf also rejected an illusion of totality by performing various identities that interacted with each other and informed each other. She deliberately exposed the gaps between these different identities. Rather than presenting a consolidated or seamless body, she choreographed an interplay between the disparate components of her identity.

An outside viewer might not have been able to recognize von Mahlsdorf's resisting curtsy. For such a viewer it could have been just a scene between state officials and a woman at the staircase in front of her house. But an analysis of von Mahlsdorf's body and movement allows us to comprehend the tactical resistance to the dominant socialist strategy. I am employing here a distinction made by Michel de Certeau.[132] In his brilliant analysis of the production of seemingly simple cultural appearances, de Certeau defines strategy as an action of power that creates a stable and proper place. Tactic, on the other hand, inserts itself into the site of the strategy without stabilizing itself there. It never conquers this place; rather, it creates a mobile, shifting space defined by movement. However, tactics are not chaotic. They playfully reveal the power relations through which the strategic takes place. De Certeau does not grant tactics a clearly defined goal or the potential to lead an organized revolution against the strategic place. Still, the nimble performance of tactics interrupts the production of strategic power, and though this kind of disturbance in the GDR might have lasted only a short amount of time and might have gone by unnoticed, East Germans were alert to its potential.

There was no audience present at the moment of von Mahlsdorf's encounter with the secret service officials. Yet the two Stasi officers saw the curtsy; they knew who von Mahlsdorf was and how she had resisted state officials throughout her life. Her resisting acts can be understood in relation to the proper place of the dominant doctrine. Through her movement, von Mahlsdorf generated inhabitable spaces inside an otherwise uninhabitable place. In doing so, she revealed the constructedness of socialist power and questioned the state's normalized right to this power. This embodiment was neither essentially transgressive nor essentially retrograde. I am not suggesting that von Mahlsdorf was a chic phenomenon of gender performativity. Rather, her body and her everyday movements emphasized flexible individual identifications, an approach she developed in response to state domination and socialist society's focus on community identity. Von Mahlsdorf consciously performed resistance to the demand for established group identifications.

Having lived under two political systems that had severely abused the notion of community, von Mahlsdorf did not position her critique in communal identity politics. Rather, she emphasized the shift from one individual interpretation of an identity category to the next. This emphasis did not provide the power of communal forces, yet it challenged the dominant group categorization that she experienced. Her approach was not more or less commendable than the North American approaches to identity politics. But it shows another way of envisioning differences in minority discourse that is not solely informed by the globalized notion of proper community imported with the commercialized queer identity and academia from North America.

Each nation, locality, culture, and so forth has its own histories and definitions of minority identities. Yet, with the globalization of the American concept of queer, which is always primarily economic and secondarily cultural, those histories and identities get restructured in line with the imported commodity queer. It is important for us to create genealogies of other nationally specific developments of gay and lesbian identities in order to understand the intrinsic relationship between national and sexual identities. I have attempted here to contribute to one of these genealogies by highlighting a specific approach to gay and lesbian identity in East Germany, a national system that disappeared and now exists only in representations.

Von Mahlsdorf's sexual resistance in combination with Siegert's institutional and reconstructive resistance and Kwiatkowski's improvisational refusal allow a glimpse of the nearly invisible oppositional culture in East Germany. Only through an exploration of such diverse resistances and the hope for a utopia that they create can we start to understand how people survive any doctrinarian regimes.

4

Border Crossings and Intranational Trespasses

The Fall of the Berlin Wall (1989–2009)

2009

The last place I ever expected to watch the Berlin Wall fall was Brooklyn. But there I was, twenty years after the real thing, in the Mark Morris studio space, a sign for the Brooklyn Academy of Music rotating in my peripheral view as if to remind me of the incongruity of my whereabouts. Watching rehearsals for *The Berlin Wall Project*, a new dance piece by Nejla Y. Yatkin, I realized these young dancers were performing an event that I participated in twenty years before when I was their age—and that many of the dancers might not even have heard of the Berlin Wall prior to engaging with this piece.

I was endeavoring to understand how the choreographer and the dancers were approaching the representation of the fall of the wall and East Germany (GDR), the country that built the wall and influenced international politics for many decades and that suddenly disappeared from the map of the world. Yatkin is a Turkish German choreographer from West Berlin, who has been living and working in the United States since the mid-1990s—nearly as long as I have been. Like me, she grew up with the wall, only on the other side, the West. Both of us started our dance careers performing folk dance techniques—East German folk dance for me in the 1980s, Turkish dances for her in the late 1970s.

Yatkin observed her dancers with attention, ever so slightly marking some of the movements. As the dancers walked in a group in the small studio, one of them suddenly stumbled and fell to the ground. The group kept walking as if

131

Nejla Y. Yatkin in rehearsal of her choreography for *The Berlin Wall Project*, Brooklyn, NY, 2009. Photo: Astrid Riecken, NY2Dance.

nothing had happened, and the dancer slowly got up and joined the group. The dancers started to stomp and exhale on each forceful step in a motion that contracted their upper bodies. Yatkin stopped the run-through and explained that she wanted the exhaling to look more like frustration. The dancers tried several times and interestingly enough, the movement shifted away from a Graham-esque contraction and began to recall a more resigned collapse. Yatkin had given subtle guidance throughout the rehearsal; she ended the day by explaining how the dancers were not just performing a dance routine or executing a movement but were performing something that their characters had experienced as a group.

1989

Twenty years ago, on November 10, 1989, when we walked toward the wall dividing East and West Berlin, we already knew how to walk for a cause, how to walk for change, after months of participating in demonstrations throughout Leipzig and other East German cities. This walking was never a stroll, nor was it Walter Benjamin's flaneuring.[1] It was also not a resolute hike toward a clearly demarcated goal. But the walk had power, power that arose from the impact it had on the space in which it occurred. This walk was a forceful attempt to gain new space, yet we did not know if the border guards would put a stop to our walk once we arrived at the checkpoint.[2] This uncertainty made us hyperaware of our spatial choices as well as the choreography of our body postures while walking toward the wall. This awareness differed from our daily consciousness of surveillance by the East German secret service.[3] Still, the choreographic tactics that we had learned as a result of being surveilled over the years informed our movements that day.

An elderly woman passed me. She seemed determined to make it to the other side. She probably remembered her childhood when she had been able to visit her relatives who lived there, before it became "the other side." The woman's long, striking steps belied her age. She knew that she had to make it across that border or she might never have the chance again. A short man next to me seemed hesitant in his approach and lowered his gaze when I looked at him. His leather jacket and polyester bag made it very likely he was associated with the Stasi.[4] Why was he going? Wasn't he supposed to prevent the very movement in which he was participating? Had he been sent to report on the citizens' movement toward the border?

We looked at each other and realized the collective power created through our walking. Yet we also sensed the individual choreographic choices in that pattern. This walk did not expand our movement vocabulary; rather it made us experience familiar movement anew. As we moved up to the checkpoint, fear made us almost begin to march. We attempted to conquer rising emotional responses to the unknown with more confident body language. We took more ground with our steps and lifted our knees higher. We put more weight on our feet as they hit the ground, and we rolled through our feet, exerting more pressure over the pavement. As we arrived at the line in front of the checkpoint, we straightened our backs, held our heads up slightly higher. Thus, when the gaze of the border guard who checked our documents hit us, we appeared confident and in control of the situation.

Gradually walking onto the bridge after he gave us the necessary stamps in our papers, we felt swept away by the movement around us.[5] Yet, slowed down by the masses in front, no one was able to rush to the other side of the bridge that connected us with the western part of Berlin. Deliberately putting one foot in front of the other, I walked in astonishment over that bridge. The actual crossing was unbelievable—outside of the realm of any imagined possibility. I started to see myself as though from an outside perspective. How did my body look in this space and moment, which later became the focus of worldwide news, the subject of movies and books? I saw myself looking at people and at the machinery that protected the border. I felt the slight push from the bodies behind me, the tension of my neighbors, and the pull of anticipation of the bodies in front of me. I watched myself consciously incorporating my observations of my body's movement and the movement of the surrounding walkers into my own. This awareness of my corporeal senses, even as I visualized myself among the other walking bodies, created my sense of spatial and historical significance. As I later learned, many of my fellow walkers shared that apprehension. The conscious reflection on the double perspective of that walk on the bridge—the outside view of the body and the sensations inside the body—created the historical moment.

Pedestrian Choreography as Epistemology

This re-creation of the choreography of a pedestrian movement provides a social, political, and methodological underpinning for this chapter in which I relate three dance productions to the aforementioned social movement. All three choreographies take stances on the political situation in East Germany during and after the opening of the Berlin Wall in 1989, though from different national perspectives and through different choreographic approaches. Our walk across the border ultimately informed these dance productions, both thematically and choreographically. Examining the dialectic relationship between bodies' conscious movements during a historic walk across the border, on the one hand, and diverse contemporary choreographies as interrogations of such movements, on the other, exposes shared choreographic and social mechanisms. In other words, an interrogation of the interdependence of the artistic exploration and its seemingly vanished cultural and corporeal referent enables a theorization of bodies and their embodiment of a society's past, present, and even future structures.

This approach is inspired by Mark Franko, who argues in his article *Mimique* for a related rethinking of performance, and specifically of dance, through the terms "presence" and "disappearance." Franko works against the common notion of dance's ephemerality that has glorified but also trivialized and marginalized dance and consequently the body. The widely used phrase "the disappearing body" casts bodies as only temporarily appearing in space and time, therefore reducing them to an essence that exists outside all cultural systems. This approach to bodies and performance removes the performing subject (and here again especially the dancing subject) from cultural and political issues.

Franko questions this notion, moving corporeality back into culture by investing movement with a capacity to be performed again. The movement and performance would be able to produce not only the past and a present but also a future. Therefore not only does the sociocultural system produce certain bodies and movements; bodies and embodiment themselves produce far more than just memory. Bodies thus have to be analyzed as cultural constructs. Likewise, culture is created through embodiment.[6] Using this notion of corporeal agency that acknowledges bodies' capacity to create social systems, I want to look at the corporeal practices of both theatrically staged dances and pedestrian movements.

My introductory description of such a pedestrian movement provides the set up to the exploration of the dynamic between the staging of East German identity by Sasha Waltz, a West German, and by Jo Fabian, an East German choreographer—which is complicated by Yatkin's choreographic response to the event twenty years later. The walk across the border (a discursive as well as a literal one) bridged two distinct national identities, and that bridging informed the choreographers' view on East German corporealities and movements.[7] Even though Waltz, Fabian, and Yatkin all depict East German identity around the reunification and the fall of the wall, their distinct approaches and training produce dramatically different choreographies. Yet I do not mean to ground my analysis of the choreographers' work primarily in their origin on either side of the Berlin Wall. Rather, my critique of their disparate views on the East German sociopolitical system relies on an analysis of their dances and choreographic processes. Often discourses on societies' structures refer to bodies as symptomatic corporeal sites. Only over the last two decades have scholars and choreographers started to understand bodies and their movements as creators of social systems.[8] Readings of corporealities and choreographies on and off stage are among the techniques that return agency to bodies as the main protagonists of historical movements.[9]

It is precisely the differing location of agency in their choreography that becomes most essential for the subsequent comparison of Waltz's and Fabian's productions, particularly in relation to the historical walk across the Berlin border. This walk amalgamated the double perspective of an internalized awareness of a social referentiality of movements with the outer experience of that movement's historical significance. Michel de Certeau's analysis of walking through Manhattan provides the ground for charging the walk across the bridge with such potential. By defining "walking as a space of enunciation" he affirms that walking creates more than just a one-dimensional choreographic pattern in a geographical or architectural structure. For de Certeau, walking contracts, extends, inverts, and invents space by appropriating and embodying the space through which it moves. Walking also creates relationships with other geographical, social, and discursive spaces by connecting them and by erasing the distances between them. Yet most importantly, walking always moves with an entire "tree of gestures" through space, thus multiplying meaning.[10] Walking produces a relationship with the authorial space but also recalls memory and, with it, the influences that structured the space and the walk.

Even though de Certeau is mostly interested in pedestrian enunciations that resist disciplinary structures, he still positions them inside an administrative, ideological, and panoptical space without the power to overthrow these disciplinary structures. In addition, the readings of a walk's inherent meaning and agency are only possible from an elevated and voyeuristic position. For de Certeau, the people walking through space are not capable of grasping their complex corporeal practice, let alone of employing this understanding to dramatically change the structures in which they move.[11] Yet, as the walk across the bridge demonstrates, the position of the elevated observer and the involved participant can be integrated, and in turn this can lead to a complete transformation of the space in which the walking occurs.

As I demonstrate, Fabian understands this integrative double perspective not only as necessary for the creation of a new social order but also as clearly assigning agency to the body. He is able to communicate his awareness to the audience by translating it into a compelling choreography that explores in multidimensional tableaus how citizens adjusted their moving bodies to the collapse and subsequent re-creation of societal structures. Even though Sasha Waltz has explored corporeal agency in many of her works, she chose not to fully investigate the connection between movements and their social referent or the role that bodies play in the creation of social systems in her choreography *Allee der Kosmonauten*. The following comparison of both choreographers' training and choreographic approaches for their pieces illuminates how I arrived at such different evaluations of Fabian and Waltz.

Two Choreographic Trajectories

Sasha Waltz is currently Germany's most sought-after theatrical export. Her invitations to perform abroad have even exceeded those extended to Pina Bausch's world-famous Tanztheater Wuppertal. At the beginning of her career, Waltz studied dance in Karlsruhe with Waltraud Kornhaas, a pupil of Mary Wigman.[12] Wigman's legacy of a nonnarrative approach to choreography, her abstraction and individuality, and her preference for performing a set choreography continues to exert an influence on Waltz's choreographic style. Following her studies with Kornhaas, Waltz attended the School of New Dance Development in Amsterdam. The school is internationally known for its focus on contact improvisation.[13] Contact improvisation has long been important to Waltz's creative process, serving as a major tool by which she reevaluates movement vocabulary both for her dancers and her choreographies. Yet Waltz's dancers rarely improvise onstage owing to her earlier Wigman-influenced training and its attachment to established stage choreography. Rather, much of Waltz's movement vocabulary material builds on contact improvisation's negotiation of weight and encounter as a choreographic component. After studying in Amsterdam, Waltz went to New York City, where she exposed herself to yet another, more interdisciplinary approach to dance that relied on collaboration among different art forms, such as the fine arts and contemporary music.

Returning to Germany, she founded Sasha Waltz & Guests in 1993.[14] Waltz's first piece with this new company, *Twenty to Eight*, the initial part of her *Travelogue* trilogy, earned her the prize for choreography at the International Choreographers Competition in Groningen. In 1996, Waltz opened the Sophiensäle, a performance space in East Berlin. *Allee der Kosmonauten*, her first work performed there, established Waltz's current fame and is still toured extensively by her company. In 1997 Waltz was invited to perform *Allee der Kosmonauten* at the annual German theater festival Theatertreffen in Berlin. During the following year, Waltz adapted *Allee der Kosmonauten* for film in collaboration with the two government-sponsored TV stations. The original choreography on which the film was based won the prestigious Adolf Grimme Award for Outstanding Individual Achievement for writing, directing, and producing in 2000. *Allee der Kosmonauten* was restaged in 2009 at the Sophiensäle.

Waltz's work has never been exclusively about choreographing dances; she is also a remarkable organizer and initiator. For instance, from 1999 to 2004, she was the artistic codirector of the prestigious Schaubühne am Lehniner Platz in Berlin, together with the dramaturges Jochen Sandig and Jens Hillje, and the playwright and theater director Thomas Ostermeier, a position that allowed her to focus on her interdisciplinary approach to choreography and her artistic vision of dance in relationship to theater. At the Schaubühne she choreographed now-famous pieces, such as *Körper*, *S*, and *noBody*. *Körper*, which opened the Schaubühne under its new leadership, has become one of Waltz's most toured pieces. With its focus on the social construction of embodiment and movement through a careful investigation of the choreographic possibilities of diverse bodies, it can also be seen as emblematizing her choreographic approach.

Waltz frequently initiates her investigation of social relations through an exploration of physical encounters between bodies and different environments. *Körper* accomplishes this in one memorable scene in which various nearly naked bodies are crammed into a glass box. Pressed against each other and the translucent surfaces, the dancers shift against and with each other in their struggle for space. Architectural attention toward simple movement situations defines many of Waltz's key scenes, and she juxtaposes these scenes with more character-driven stagings of her dancers.

Since 2005, Waltz has managed the interdisciplinary center for training and production—Radialsystem V—which she founded in Berlin. The center provides one of the stages for her company Sasha Waltz & Guests' many productions and also serves as a platform for experimental choreographic inventions by young international choreographers. Waltz has shifted her own choreographic work into the world of opera with her versions of Henry Purcell's *Dido and Aeneas* and Hector Berlioz's *Roméo et Juliette*. Her company performs around one hundred productions a year worldwide and is one of the most successful international cultural enterprises.[15]

Compared to Waltz, Jo Fabian works much more at the periphery of major funding streams. Trained as an actor in the early 1980s, Fabian is a member of the generation that no longer engaged with the socialist system in East Germany. As described in chapter 3, this new group of artists enacted a specific form of resistance to that system. Fabian joined the movement, leaving an established career in state theater and working in the margins of government-sponsored theater from 1984 until 1989. This marginalization from government sponsorship enabled him to produce work that departed in style, content, and focus from the official theatrical discourse in East Germany that was dominated by the traditions of Bertolt Brecht, socialist realism, and Heiner Müller's apocalyptic historicism.

Even though his interests were shared by other East German directors, Fabian found his unique voice and style by focusing on the body and movement in his dance theater pieces.[16] Tableau-like pictures, repetition of sequences, slowed-down movements, and various kinds of projections led Fabian to be labeled—and even dismissed—as the "East German Robert Wilson" by West German critics after the fall of the Berlin Wall. However, they hastily reversed their opinion, declaring him the rising star of the off-theater scene after he was invited to the 1994 Theatertreffen.[17] Fabian's work was the only off-theater production performed at this important German theater festival that year. Thus, Fabian is unique in that he, unlike other choreographers, was able to move his work from the periphery of state-sponsored East German theater to the more visible Berlin off-theater scene after the reunification. In 1999, significant theaters in Germany jointly awarded him the prestigious German Producers' Prize for Choreography. Following that, Fabian received funding from the Berlin Senate and continued to produce controversial new work in collaboration with major off-theaters in Berlin and other cities in Germany.

This secure funding structure provided Fabian with the time and space to pursue very diverse projects, such as developing a new movement system based on the translation of words into movement called Alphasystem, releasing a CD-ROM titled *no fish, no cheese*, and creating a method for the connection of seemingly unrelated thoughts, ideas, memories called *Spektralsurrealismus*. All of these endeavors approach dance and performance through a highly critical and ironic stance. For instance, even though Fabian explored and developed Alphasystem through several new choreographies, he stated from the beginning that a translation of spoken or written language into movement is bound to fail.

In 2003, he reconstructed his highly acclaimed 1994 choreography *Whisky & Flags* with its original cast. After its premiere, the piece received numerous awards for its witty and poignant critique of the German reunification process and for its refusal to accept the marginal place East German citizens' history had been assigned in the united Germany. The whisky referenced in the work's title appear as a row of Johnny Walker Red Label bottles at the back of the stage, and flags line both sides of the stage. As Fabian explains in interviews, the title refers to the drugs that were readily available after the fall of the wall and to pre-fall ideological indoctrination.

Framed by these ironic symbols of capitalism and socialism, four female dancers and two male actors fight for space on the stage, accuse each other of lacking technique, comment on their own importance in the theatrical process, explain and demonstrate their craft, and even simply drink from the whisky bottles. These activities seem unrelated to a critique of the concrete historical processes after the fall of the wall. Yet every gesture and every word in this complex piece work on more than one level to inform and comment: gestures are established through repetition and then connected with more and more words; also gesture and word combinations are repeated excessively in multiple situations. This choreographic strategy not only exposes the arbitrary relationship between spoken language and movement vocabulary but at the same time points to the cultural connotation of movement and language—in this case the East German connotation. With this strategy, Fabian focuses on the internal conflicts and aesthetics of theater as an institution and a medium. He thus creates dance theater that regains the political potentiality of theater.

Fabian's 2003 reconstruction of his original *Whisky & Flags* raises questions about choreography's changed function in the reunited Germany. At the time of the original production, Fabian himself saw the piece as more than just a depiction of a specific moment in German history and as a comment on a time-bound political situation. He also considered its value for the future by suggesting that "if performed every ten years with the same cast, this piece could possibly multiply its impact in East Germany's fight for a place in the future."[18] As much as the tasks of excavation and repetition have been the historical functions of theater, it is still unusual to empower a dance theater piece by projecting it into the future. Fabian's vision demands a comprehension of history that differs in its Foucaultian genealogical structure from the chronology and progression of the dominant history of united Germany. By making this difference a main topic of his theater, Fabian points vividly to the politics at play in the constructing of history.[19]

Due to major funding cuts in all areas in Germany, the 2003 reconstruction of *Whisky & Flags* seemed to mark Fabian's departure from Berlin's off-theater scene.[20] Yet collaborations with other funding bodies and theatrical institutions enabled Fabian to continue his work. He has produced numerous theater and dance productions since then, among them *Independent Swan* (2009) and *PI morphosen* (2010). Fabian also shifted his work away from dance into explorations of multimedia work, virtual reality, and installation. Since Fabian has always explored dance and choreography as an element of *Gesamtkunstwerk* productions, this shift does not indicate a departure from dance but rather suggests a broadening of his choreographic investigations in relation to other media.

Choreographic Practice as Social Commentary

The title of Sasha Waltz's 1996 *Allee der Kosmonauten* translates as *Avenue of the Cosmonauts,* which is one of the major boulevards leading through a suburb of East Berlin that consists solely of large and identical apartment blocks. The East German government built these suburbs to provide affordable housing for its citizens in an expeditious manner. Often the development of infrastructure and service and cultural facilities could not keep up with the rapid construction of these apartment buildings. As a result, for many Westerners these vast, monotonous suburbs became emblems of anonymous living in the Eastern Bloc. While North American suburbs are largely middle class and upper middle class, populated by privately owned homes constructed to shield their owners from the rigors of city living, the apartments in the East German suburbs were mostly rented and did not fulfill a dream of property ownership.

After the reunification, middle-class citizens left the East German suburbs either to live in the center of the cities or to move even further outside the city, to individual houses. As a result of that migration, only working-class families remained in government housing. Due to the dismantling of East German industries after the reunification, these families were hit hardest with unemployment. Often, an entire family became unemployed, and the younger family members who were still in school had no chance of receiving a job-oriented education. In their desperation and search for meaning in their lives, these disillusioned young men and women sometimes turned toward right-wing, racist, and neo-Nazi organizations. All these developments furthered the reputation of East German suburbs as undesirable areas overrun by lower-class citizens who engaged in violent, meaningless behavior.

For the creation of *Allee der Kosmonauten,* Waltz went to government housing projects in East Berlin and interviewed citizens of the former German Democratic Republic. She crossed the former border from the west to the east after the wall had come down to investigate East Germans' lives in the newly unified Germany. As Waltz repeatedly reports, she went to the East Berlin projects and simply knocked on doors.[21] Raised in West Germany, she wanted to explore a life that she knew nothing about. As Waltz recounts, the people in the projects were at first reluctant to open their doors and lives to her.[22] Waltz seems to be surprised about that reluctance. Yet this reluctance is understandable in a former dictatorship; under surveillance by the Stasi, citizens had to evaluate every step they took, and they learned to be cautious toward strangers knocking at their doors.[23] In 1996, while Waltz was working on her piece, the German media reported new revelations daily about the depth of reach of the Stasi. The majority of these reports depicted former socialist citizens as cooperative or as silent onlookers. East Germans' paranoia and mistrust toward West Germans were furthered by these reports. Not only did former East German citizens learn over forty years to be careful with strangers owing to the distinct possibility that they might be involved with the Stasi but they also might not have wanted to open up to a West German because of a legitimate fear of uninformed and generalizing judgment by one of their Western co-citizens.

Given that Waltz seemed neither fully aware of these fears nor of the reality of life under a dictatorship, it is worth asking how much her representation was able to capture East German identity. Even though the piece only set out to represent a specific kind of family in the East German projects along the Allee der Kosmonauten, the choreography's extensive international touring inevitably established it as a very visible general representation of East German identity. What promised through its title to be the depiction of a particular social situation can certainly be read as a universalized investigation of East German dysfunctional family structures.[24]

Waltz's methodology for the creation of her piece recalls highly critiqued early anthropological studies that did not problematize the hierarchy created between the observer and the native informant (the observed). Scholars such as Edward W. Said and Gayatri Chakravorty Spivak have shown this model of anthropological studies to be complicit in the West's creation of an oppressed and exoticized other.[25] Surprisingly unaware of her impact on the referent of her piece as well as the limitations of her point of view, Waltz stated in a 2001 Irvine Barclay Theatre press release that "for me the most important thing about the work was to paint a transparent view of the communal life of a family,

without judging, sympathetic and ironic, loving and cruel." With this declaration Waltz demonstrated that she did not fully grasp the effect of her own
subjectivity on the piece.

Waltz's limited awareness of the power of her position as an artist and
choreographer inside societal structures—or at least her decision to not make
her authorial position visible in *Allee der Kosmonauten*—also informs her other
choreographic and dramaturgical choices in the work. In the opening scene, a
man on a sofa appears reduced to a torso that bumps and rolls around on a
piece of furniture. Gradually, the rest of his body becomes involved in this
acrobatic exercise, and various body parts begin to manipulate each other like
props. At the same time, through movement quality and emphasis, the sofa
becomes an equal player in the interaction between body and furniture; the
sofa bounces the man back in the same way that his own hand pulls him up and
pushes his torso from side to side. Waltz presents with immediacy a spectacularized version of daily gestures—in this case that of sitting and lying on a sofa.
The appeal of her choreography derives from an overdrawing of those gestures
and the surrealistic managing of props. It also equalizes bodies and props and
as a result objectifies bodies.

Waltz often starts with such random collisions of a human body and a
prop and then explores all possibilities catalyzed by the initial encounter. Even
though she also turns to the more private issues of relations between men and
women without ignoring established sociological dimensions of these gender
relations, Waltz seems more interested in the spatial and physical constellations
that occur when various people inhabit confined rooms. She explores places as
well as the way bodies inhabit them. She sometimes begins with an investigation
of how one positions a hand while opening a door or the angle at which someone holds a knee in order to take a step on a stair. Occasionally, an absent-
minded and vigorous petting of a cheek intensifies into hitting; an unexpected
turn of one body toward another one makes the second body shrink back and
results in an elaborate choreography of swings and vacillations. Or, in the
instance of the beginning of *Allee der Kosmonauten*, she looks at all possible—or
even impossible—ways that a body inhabits a sofa or that a sofa engulfs a body.
These variations extend spatially and take over progressively more body parts.
Through this type of abstraction, the movements move further and further
away from their original circumstances and thus from the social situation that
caused them.

These choreographic principles are at the core of *Allee der Kosmonauten*,
which Waltz describes as belonging to her less abstract period.[26] Some of the
dancers are easily recognizable as characters, given their attire and their relationship to each other. An old-fashioned man and a woman clad in a housedress

Bodies as props in Sasha Waltz's *Allee der Kosmonauten*, 1996. Photo: Thomas Aurin.

seem to be the mother and father of a family. A girl and a boy are dressed in children's clothes and their movement quality can be read as more childlike than that of the other characters. An additional couple in tacky adolescent clothing could be another son and his girlfriend.[27] These probable relationships are challenged by scenes in which apparent siblings play out sexual interactions. Of course, Waltz might be indicating an incestuous situation, as these situations often become vigorous in her choreography. Most members of the audience, initially amused and entertained by the actions onstage, turn quiet and shift uncomfortably in their seats during these eruptions of energy.[28] Yet soon they are preoccupied again by the next athletic movement sequence.

Such an acrobatic encounter occurs halfway into *Allee der Kosmonauten* when all characters except the father, who accompanies them with his accordion, join in a dance. The older son initiates this abstract dance by slowly turning while holding a board on his shoulder. In order to avoid getting hit by the board, the other son, daughter, and girlfriend, who had previously positioned themselves next to the older son, have to bend forward or backward, depending on the direction of the board's rotation. Gradually, this movement gains momentum, travels to the lower parts of their bodies, extends spatially, and even takes over the mother at the other side of the stage. The initial ducking movement transforms progressively into rotations and turns of the dancers, who have aligned themselves into a formation. Finally, walking stiffly on their heels, the dancers perform sudden swirls and turns as if participating in some folk or social dance. Yet they swing their arms independently from the rest of the body, thus making their arms seem attached to their bodies without any capacity to initiate movement. This sequence is the only part of *Allee der Kosmonauten* where the dancers move in an obviously choreographed formation across the floor. However, they challenge the employment of more traditional dance movements with their exaggerated execution, the swinging of the apparently uninvolved arms, and the awkward walking on heels. The movement quality and the contradictory control of torsos and limbs invite a comparison with marionettes not in control of their own movement.

Fabian has similarly focused on movement exploration in his choreographies, but his interest is in the critical evaluation of social situations that initiate movement. Fabian's utilization of slow motion in many of his early pieces distanced his choreographies from their original source in everyday movement. Audiences observing this temporally extended variation of pedestrian movement are forced to reevaluate their preconceptions of it. This reevaluation removes the dancers' bodies from any immediate reference to the world outside the theater. A North American audience might be familiar with this employment of slow motion as an aspect of postmodern dancers' investigation of bodies, movement, and social space.[29] Yet Fabian's use of slow motion was quite distinct in the historical context of the GDR, since no other East German choreographer at that time utilized movement as consciously as Fabian had for a critique of predominant socialist theater practices.

In Fabian's work, slow-moving bodies create their own reality inside the socialist system. In conjunction with the individualization, this approach illustrates the disengagement of Fabian and his generation from the East German socialist system. Correspondingly, Fabian destroyed, or at least questioned, the hierarchy of modes of representation in socialist theater at that time. This theater was constructed on the principles of socialist realism and favored the vocalizing actor's body as the main theatrical tool. As I establish in chapter 2, this preference had its roots in the distinct construction and function of socialist realism. East German officials favored text-based art forms because in their theory they depicted socialist reality as well as the laws that created this reality in a seemingly unambiguous way. Thus, second only to literature, the vocalizing actor became the main artistic tool of socialist realism. Enmeshed in a complex collectivist society, actors illuminated the historic significance of their social and political circumstances, ideally to further the development of a socialist reality.

This is where Fabian refused to collaborate with socialist theater conventions—and for that matter, mainstream theater conventions as well. By nearly eliminating speech or disconnecting it from the actors' and dancers' bodies, Fabian failed to comply with the demanding socialist theatrical tradition. He shared this resistance to narrative with other East German directors, actors, choreographers, and dancers, who worked outside or at the margins of state- and city-sponsored theaters. This new brand of East German theater no longer attempted to reveal supposed driving forces beneath an ostensibly objective reality. Instead, this theater simultaneously emphasized its autonomy from theater and attempted to break down the division between theater and reality. The new generation of artists achieved this goal by emancipating theater from text as well as from its function as a political and moral institution. Consequently, the new theater initially received a strong and negative reaction from the government, often through official censorship. But growing attention from East German audiences and theater experts enabled its survival and even earned occasional endorsement by state officials.

Throughout his work, Fabian stages bodies to elucidate their intentional construction as both objects and agents of history.[30] Fabian's view of the body as the main protagonist of historical movement returns agency to the body and creates space for resistance. Thus, his dance theater explores not only how the government forced a citizen's body into norms of movement through surveillance but also how a body performs resistance to those norms. *Pax Germania* (1997) also locates itself in relation to a concrete political situation. Fabian reveals how the transformation from a socialist Germany to a united capitalist Germany was induced by the construction of collective and individual identities and the friction between them. Fabian's piece symbolizes the history of forty years of the German Democratic Republic, the fall of the wall, and the time since the reunification on October 3, 1990.

Choreographing Agency

Since 1996, Waltz restaged *Allee der Kosmonauten* at the Sophiensäle, where it premiered, and thus reconnected the piece to its referent in the housing projects of East Berlin. Such restaging also raises anew some of my concerns with Waltz's representational choices in the piece. As an East German, I am thrilled to see my national history reflected in a dance production. But as an East German, I am also disappointed by Waltz's lack of engagement with its complexity and her employment of familiar stereotypes.

In his fascinating study of the representation of East German identity since unification, Paul Cooke draws on postcolonial studies to understand the relationship of the unified Germany to its eastern constituent. Citing "the destruction of indigenous economic structure, the exploitation of available economic resources, the social liquidation of not only the political elite but also the intellectuals of the country, along with the destruction of . . . a population's identity," Cooke defines the unification as a neocolonial takeover.[31] Postcolonial studies has established that any representation of a colonial subject's identity is another means of keeping colonial hierarchies stable. As such, these representations need to be viewed carefully. Similarly, any representation of East German identity by a West German has to be critically evaluated. To contextualize my own reaction for a non-German readership, I would refer to the example of blackface minstrelsy or yellowface minstrelsy in early twentieth-century film. Even though it originally allowed nonwhite identity access to media representation, a contemporary employment of the vocabulary would require an extremely careful evaluation of the suitability of the form for today's understanding of African American or Asian American identity.

Waltz's choreographic representation of an East German family, as well as the global distribution of her depiction through the extensive touring, must likewise be critically appraised. In particular, Waltz's choice to represent agency outside the dancers' bodies perpetuates stereotypes of East Germans as passive recipients of government indoctrination. Waltz's employment and location of movement vocabulary emphasizes the bodies' complete absorption into a highly acrobatic situation without illuminating the social reasons for these situations and without contextualizing the initiation of movement from the bodies themselves. Whereas the walkers who crossed the border in Berlin incorporated their self-observation into the choreography of their walk by consciously reflecting on their movement vocabulary, spatiality, and choreographic choices, Waltz's dancers are moved by an unidentified external force. The exclusive focus on movement variations without exploration of cause, motivation, or solution provides an entertaining affirmation of the present moment, but it does so by sacrificing past embodiments and bodies' capacity to choreograph the future.

The final scene of *Allee der Kosmonauten* confirms this analysis. The dancers unite again for the end of the production, fighting viciously with each other around the sofa that is now surrounded by relatively few props. The fight is continually interrupted as the music abruptly stops and the family members fall into a sudden sleep. After a number of repetitions of this externally initiated action-sleep sequence, the ensemble members all suddenly freeze mid-movement. They resume and freeze several times. These unexpected moments of stillness do not provide a calming atmosphere on the stage: rather, their bodies appear to surrender to exhaustion. More importantly, the tableaux depict the bodies in mid-fight or engaged in a situation that depicts boredom and unhappiness. Finally, a blackout ends the piece during one of these tableaux.

Colliding bodies in Sasha Waltz's *Allee der Kosmonauten*, 1996. Photo: Matthias Zölle.

Over the course of the dance, Waltz stages the passions, the joyless existence, the brutality, and the boredom of a family unit. The dancers move at a high frequency, like comic figures. They fold their entire bodies up only to open themselves up again in a gymnastic fashion. They suddenly fall into a motionless sleep that seems to provide them with the power to burst into yet another fight. As in a cartoon, the dancers' action and mishandling of each other's bodies never leave any lasting impact. With a change of music or an interruption by other characters, the dancers' focus shifts from their current activity and, with seemingly perpetual power, they turn their full attention and physical stamina toward their next action.

Through her work, Waltz constructs the audience members as passive consumers of a spectacle. By terminating the piece with a blackout on one of the arranged tableaux, she suggests that this choreographic interrogation of a dysfunctional family will resume. The family interactions thus stand as a metonym for a much more eternal narrative that could go on long after the audience's departure from the theater. Neither the fragmented structure of the piece nor Waltz's choreographic choices require any audience participation. Rather, the spectacularized movement vocabulary and the repeated interruptions of the depicted family life at the end of the production position the audience as astonished observers.

Waltz also makes the choice to deprive the dancers' bodies of their expressive intelligence by restricting their actions to reactions to collisions and chance encounters that don't elicit antithetical responses or even much resistance; there is never an opportunity that would authorize the dancing bodies to initiate change. As a result, Waltz's movement interrogations don't lead to any solutions or even to the creation of an opportunity that would empower the involved bodies. Waltz's one-dimensional imagination of East German identity and the resulting physicalization in the dancers' and spectators' bodies also fail to grasp the conscious choreography that East Germans were capable of creating and did create in actuality.

Whereas Waltz decided to represent the dancers' bodies as responding objects in her display of East German identity, Fabian re-creates the actual transformation East German citizens underwent through the bodies of the dancers as well as through the audience. In the opening of *Pax Germania* an actor walks confidently, but very slowly, on to the stage, shouldering a red flag on a long pole. His body's movement disguises the fact that he carries the heavy device. After he finds his place at the back of the stage facing out toward the audience, he adjusts himself and the flag, which slowly ripples in an artificial wind. Seven actors follow him reluctantly, one by one. They slowly stroll to the back of the stage until they align themselves next to the flag carrier. Arranged differently from each other, all of their postures appear casual and seem to indicate an unwillingness to perform. Eventually, a head's tilt, a gaze, or a twitch develops into an action.

The almost procrastinating pace of the piece is sustained as a dancer is slapped and tries to return the aggressive gesture but finds he is too short to reach the offender's head. The short dancer's attire—trousers pulled up too high with suspenders, red socks and industrial shoes, and a buttoned down short-sleeved shirt—communicates nerdiness. The offender carries a drum at his waist, but he never plays it. He only raises the drumsticks high above his head with outstretched arms and bangs the sticks against each other as if setting the rhythm for the piece. One woman wears a skirt suit reminiscent of the East German state party's official dress code. A red carnation, the symbol celebrating the working-class struggle, is pinned to her lapel. Constantly smiling as if in embarrassment, she attempts to make contact with the flag carrier. Repeatedly, in an awkward and uncertain motion, she puts her head on his upper arm. Another woman sucks desperately on a cigarette and coughs out the smoke until her body is thrown into her neighbor's arms by the violent coughs. His attempts to ease her coughing with slaps on her back turn increasingly into a violent beating.

Meanwhile, a clock ticks on a projection behind the actors. The digital display counts down the minutes like a time bomb. Projected onto a screen behind the dancers are images of water rippling down and clouds gliding. Slight variations of the slap, cough, drumstick-raise, smile, and beating movements stretch out over the first forty minutes. Constant repetition of these movements in conjunction with the fact that none of the dancers move out of the line at the back of the stage give the appearance of stagnation and perpetual boredom. The audience counts the minutes and starts to get annoyed. Audience members slide uncomfortably back and forth on their seats, coughing and clearing their throats. They comment loudly on the nonevents onstage. More and more spectators leave, bored and angry, slamming doors on their way out. With their casual behavior, they start to participate in the action onstage.[32]

The interplay between the dancers' bodies onstage and the spectators' bodies reenacts forty years of East German corporeal identity. Fabian does not show a one-dimensional critique of the state-enforced, official corporeal identity onstage. Rather, he displays the results of and the resistance to that state disciplining with the dancers' actions and the audience's reactions. He captures vividly the stagnation of East German life by employing reduced and restrained movements. The dancers barely move and remain restricted to their position at the back of the stage in a brilliant depiction of East German citizens' literal and discursive immobility under the restrictive socialist regime.

Like the marchers across the border, East German citizens were always hyperaware of their movement due to the Stasi's constant surveillance. I argue that this awareness resulted in a confined movement vocabulary in public, where excessive movements would have attracted the observers' attention. Such heightened understanding of one's position in a political structure also accounts for the finely tuned awareness of the inner experience juxtaposed with the outer self-observation of the sort that occurred when we walked across the border between East and West Berlin for the first time. Fabian's use of this idea onstage works symbolically, revealing with seemingly innocent movements the influence of socialist state power on its citizens' corporeality. His piece also questions the state's assumption that its right and use of power over its citizens is natural.

Outside the theater, these kinds of restrictions in East Germany led to movements in the late 1980s that resulted in a mass exodus of citizens from the country via the increasingly permeable border between Hungary and Austria. Resistors also began organizing their life outside socialist space and demonstrating throughout the socialist country. East German citizens broke out of the dictated movement pattern and started to express their dissatisfaction

Forty minutes of repetitive movement in Jo Fabian's *Pax Germania*, 1997. Photo: Andreas Stirl.

through individual spontaneous actions and organized demonstrations. Echoing such off-stage breakouts, the audience watching *Pax Germania* engages in a similar resistance: they either leave the general audience body by walking out of the theater and slamming doors or they collectively organize themselves as dissatisfied customers in the artistic market economy. Increasingly, the audience comments on the nonaction onstage and even demands a boost in the minimalist activity.

Thirty minutes, twenty, ten, five—at last the clock displays 0:00:00:00 and stops for a few seconds. A male voice declares, "The Third of October 1990— What a Day." Finally, the clock runs forward. Confused, the actors seem to break out of their routine and interact with each other and even the audience. Still in a line at the back of the stage, a man steps reluctantly forward only to return to the lineup with the other dancers, unsure of his own boldness. Soon afterward, the woman who had been smoking and coughing moves to the front of the stage and starts to reveal parts of her body in a striptease-like display. The man whose comforting slaps on the woman's back had turned into abuse now endeavors unsuccessfully to convince her to stop her exhibitionism and to return to the line. The woman's refusal later turns into overly dramatic regret that shakes her body violently, a movement that seems reminiscent of her coughing earlier in the piece. Finally, she falls down to the ground, shaken by

Reconfigured sameness after the reunification in Jo Fabian's *Pax Germania*, 1997. Photo: Andreas Stirl.

her crying. The short man who was slapped is the next to break out of the line. He even sends the tall man with the drum at his waist—his former accuser—back into the line when the accuser attempts to move forward. The short man now holds a gun in his hand, and his nerdy attire becomes a neofascist uniform. He repeatedly puts the tall man in line, as the tall man enthusiastically attempts to perform the rhythmic claps with the drumsticks above his head. Eventually, the short man makes the tall one collapse in the middle of the stage. Meanwhile the sound system persistently plays the line "the wall fell" from a song, until the meaning of these words turns into background noise, thus losing any connection to a historical event.

The audience now seems to watch with more satisfaction. They are entertained by the semblance of actions onstage. However, they soon realize that the movement style is similar to the one performed before the clock ran down to zero. The action onstage seems to change because the dancers finally leave the line at the back of the stage and move into the formerly unexplored stage space in front of them. But the dancers actually perform and repeat abstractions of the same gestures. Fabian's choreography transforms the connotation of these movements by placing them in different contexts. As soon as this context changes, the meaning changes with it. Performed at another location, in this case away from the line and from the back of the stage, familiar movements become strange and new. This staging forces the audience to participate in this modification of meanings, and in the process of doing so they may come to understand their position to the events onstage and to the actual historical situation in Germany. At the end of the performance, this statement flashes on the screen: "We thank the originators of our history, without whom this evening wouldn't have been necessary." Audience members leave torn between amusement and anger, embarrassment and confusion.

In *Pax Germania*, Fabian combines a collective reminiscence of East German history with more current experiences in the unified Germany. He abstracts stereotypes from both time periods into a series of movements and postures by taking them out of their everyday context. The dancers repeat these movements or stand in their established postures. The audience members are pushed past boredom; unable to watch the monotony any longer, they start to act on their anger. Then Fabian modifies the movement, spacing, and the pace of the choreography, only to fall back into another display of a corresponding same-ness. As a result, he forces the audience members to observe the displayed movement and their own reaction to it more closely. Fabian employs dance theater as a site for an analysis of societal conditioning by manifesting the body's agency in history. Most importantly, he illustrates the significance of the dancing body as a site of resistance by comparing it to the moving body in pedestrian practices. Fabian's seemingly abstract choreography focuses on bodily movements in society and their relation to the dancing body onstage. The audience's resulting awareness of this causal correlation produces a cor-poreal reaction to social, political, and national interests. Their physical reactions to the events onstage also display the ability of bodies and their movements to produce autonomous structures.

Like Fabian in *Pax Germania*, Sasha Waltz appropriates pedestrian move-ment to illuminate social structures in *Allee der Kosmonauten*. Waltz derives her choreography from a concrete social environment. Where Fabian depicts social immobility through minimized and repetitive movement, Waltz questions family dynamics through a paroxysmal choreography of daily gestures and interaction with household items. Waltz does not clarify to whom or what the bodies surrender their authority and agency. Consequently, social power and agency turn into free-floating concepts that are only temporarily connected to the body in Waltz's work and are not grounded in historical experience and structures. Bodies in Waltz's choreography might react to their surroundings, but they never consciously refuse to participate nor do they create their own social situation. Waltz thus loses control of her project by falling back into a formalist study that undermines her point—or maybe it reveals more about her own views than she would like to admit.

Fabian, by contrast, choreographs a history lesson that mobilizes the audience. Moving bodies originated the German reunification, which in turn caused very concrete bodily movement in both Germanies. All this movement serves as a model for the abstraction staged by Fabian. His choreographed performance generates a bodily reaction from the audience. This corporeal process mirrors the creation of history by moving bodies and the influence of that history on bodies. Fabian does not provide any historical facts or individual stories. He turns general movements into a choreography that vividly embodies East German history before, during, and after the reunification. Fabian reveals that bodies are staged in history and shows how they respond to manipulation. But he also shows bodies' capacity to create their own history through movement. The final statement in the piece, "We thank the originators of our history, without whom this evening wouldn't have been necessary," confirms the cultural construction of history. By choreographing the individual's choice not to take action in a historic situation in the first part of the piece, Fabian vividly points to the body's ability to claim—or consciously refuse—agency.

As in Fabian's choreography, East German citizens questioned the socialist state's naturalized claim on collective agency. Eventually, an assemblage of citizens' interdependent intentional acts of resistance led to the overthrow of the East German government and the subsequent fall of the Berlin Wall. The walk across the bridge that connected East and West Berlin serves as a valuable example for the conscious application of choreographic tactics to an everyday situation. According to John Rouse, theatrical re-creations and embodied reflections on such movements are significant in that they are part of "a struggle for control over the way that memory will function."[33] Those who choreograph can materialize a major part of their decision-making processes by being aware both of the inherent power of their position inside social systems and of the agency in their movement choices. In turn, this awareness of memory, choreography, and potentiality can illuminate the role of embodiment in the creation of prospective societal structures.

2009

After the rehearsal, Yatkin and I adjourned to an Austrian café across the street from the studios. I learned that she was born to Turkish parents in West Berlin and raised inside a traditional Turkish immigrant culture. Her eclectic training—which included Turkish folk dancing—and her performance career in West Berlin provided her access to diverse vocabularies, including German modern dance, ballet, Limón, Graham, and butoh. After moving to the United States, Yatkin was further influenced by contributors to African American dance such as Donald McKayle and Cleo Parker Robinson.

Image of Nejla Y. Yatkin's choreography at a remaining part of the Berlin Wall utilized during the performance of *The Berlin Wall Project*. Photo: Astrid Riecken, NY2Dance.

In *The Berlin Wall Project*, Yatkin explores the fall of the Berlin Wall using different media, artistic practices, and means of engagement with audiences. She has choreographed an evening-length dance performance for the stage (*Wallstories*), has choreographed a site-specific dance at the few remaining parts of the Berlin Wall (*Dancing with the Berlin Wall*), and has invited a photographer and a filmmaker to share their vision of the impact of the fall of the wall on today's Germany side by side with her work. Astrid Riecken's photos of the remains of the Berlin Wall and surrounding areas in Berlin were also utilized during discussion sessions with the public on their memories of the fall of the wall. During one of these discussions, the dancers performed parts of the stage choreography and the audience was invited to respond to both the fall of the wall and the choreographic excerpt. Yatkin collected these responses and displayed them on a website that traces *The Berlin Wall Project*'s development. The final performance of the stage choreography was also broadcast live on the Internet and remains there for future viewing.[34] On the twentieth anniversary of the fall of the Berlin Wall, Yatkin reconstructed the walk across the border in a site-specific performance by moving from the Goethe Institute in New York City to another site where Riecken's photos and the film of *Dancing with the Berlin Wall* by Mike Rogers were on display.

Yatkin understands an audience's predominant desire for narrative and coherence. Yet her own identity as someone who has had to negotiate between (and function within) different, yet adjacent, cultures and nations, along with her eclectic artistic development, has instilled in her a more complex approach to narrative. Such a multidimensional corporeal, photographic, and filmic recital of the original event does not provide a coherent narrative that can be easily slotted into one's experiences. In breaking narrative expectations, it instead offers all participants of the performances (and even someone like me who did the original walk across the Berlin Wall) the opportunity to restructure their memory of the event into their own response. Yet, more importantly, none of the different elements are represented as an authentic experience. Rather, the multitude of representations allows an awareness of the arbitrary relationship between the various artistic representations and their seemingly authentic referent of the actual walk across the Berlin Wall.

By emphasizing this multidimensionality rather than a renarration of the actual events of the fall of the Berlin Wall, the historic event of the walk is stripped of its concreteness. As Yatkin described it to me when I interviewed her in September 2009, she was not so much interested in a representation of the fall of the wall as in a rethinking and reconstitution of borders across social structures or inside bodies. Drawing on her own experience of problematizing cultural dividers, Yatkin choreographs the fall of the wall as one initial event among many possible challenges made by culture and politics: she is exploring the impact on embodiment of any border and the potential of physicality to restructure dividers.

Watching her rehearsal and choreography twenty years after I walked across the border between East and West Berlin, I finally understood why Yatkin's and Fabian's choreography interest me even though it has been so many years since the actual event took place. Toward the end of Yatkin's *The Berlin Wall Project*, after narrating her experience of the fall of the Berlin Wall, a woman interviewed and recorded by Yatkin and projected on a screen behind the stage asks the audience not only *what* to remember of this event but *how* to remember it. The construction of memory has always been a complex issue, especially when it comes to events that generate the radical erasure or reorganization of social structures. Writing at the beginning of the twentieth century, psychologist and philosopher Pierre Janet posited people's need to associate such dramatic events with the other events of their lives.[35] Janet postulated that we have not fully assimilated these events "until we have achieved, not merely through our movements, but also an inward reaction through the words we address to ourselves, through the organization of the recital of the event to others and to ourselves, . . . as one of the chapters in our personal history."[36] Hayden White likewise emphasizes this need to structure events and experiences into a coherent narrative for ourselves and an audience.[37]

It is true that a personal memory becomes relevant as a political force once it is retold and makes an impact again. However, if the memory is narrated in a straightforward story, it might allow a certain number of people access—mostly people who share the memory and are able to relate to the specific narrative. Yet if presented as inherently multifaceted, the retelling allows a much larger group access, because it encourages this group to restructure the memory in line with their own narratives. Even people who do not have any memory of the fall of the Berlin Wall—such as the dancers of *The Berlin Wall Project*—not only gain access to the memory but can make it their own by restructuring it. This process allows people who remember it (myself, Yatkin, Fabian) to remember it anew and also shifts agency away from the person who remembers to those who are experiencing it for the first time (the dancers or other younger audiences). These complex layers of remembrance and rememorization and conscious allocation of agency in Fabian and Yatkin's performances have a contemporary political impact that go beyond the literal historical change in Germany more than twenty years ago. And that makes choreographic responses to the fall of the wall still relevant today.

5

Toward a Transnational History of East German Dance

The Choreography of Patricio Bunster (1930s to Present)

Global Mobilities

On August 11, 2006, I was scheduled to fly from London, via New York, to Santiago, Chile, when the UK government uncovered an alleged terrorist plot to simultaneously blow up several US-bound passenger planes flying over the Atlantic Ocean.[1] Heathrow airport became complete chaos. Our baggage was checked and rechecked repeatedly. Flights were canceled; passengers were delayed for hours on end. Finally, we were allowed to board the aircraft without any personal possessions. No laptop, no iPod, no books or pens for a twenty-two-hour flight. The imminent threat effectively challenged all global mobility.

I had originally planned to spend the flight reviewing notes in preparation for my interview with communist Chilean choreographer Patricio Bunster. Bunster had made such international journeys many times, some of them voluntarily as an international dance artist, others of them involuntarily as an emigrant escaping imprisonment, torture, and possible execution. The terrorist threat forced me to situate myself in relation to these differing kinds of migration: the voluntary and involuntary movements across national divides, the adjusting to drastically different cultures, the amending of one's original culture during the process of adaptation, sometimes returning "home" while maybe never feeling truly home anywhere again.

My interview with Bunster would be his last, for he passed away just five weeks after I met him in his home near the Espiral dance center that he and

Joan Turner founded in Santiago after his return from a twelve-year exile in East Germany in 1985. Trained by Kurt Jooss and Sigurd Leeder, Bunster had been one of Chile's leading choreographers prior to his exile. In 1973, after the Pinochet putsch, he sought political asylum in East Germany. He eventually ended up teaching at the Palucca School and successfully choreographed several works. By 1985, when Bunster was finally allowed to return to Chile, he had trained a new generation of dancers and choreographers in East Germany and reintroduced them to a lost part of the *Ausdruckstanz* tradition.

Santiago, August 12, 2006

I am at a café having a café con leche out of a cup, which exudes the fragrance of really nice Western dishwashing liquid with every sip. I am trying to concentrate on my sense of taste and turn off the sense of smell to tune out the discrepancy between the familiar Western smell and the unfamiliar Chilean café atmosphere with its foreign furnishing and excitingly different breakfast items. Listening to French chansons on my iPod, drinking coffee in Santiago, smelling Western dishwashing liquid, comparing my own journey across national divides with Bunster's emigration, I am struck by the multinational experience of this day.

I just called the East German dancer Raymond Hilbert, through whom I was able to make contact with Patricio Bunster. Bunster was utilized by the East German government as an example of the transnational artistic expression of the working class's united international struggle. Yet in his native Chile, he helped establish modern dance education and led both the national dance company and the main dance department at the University of Santiago based on his understanding of *Ausdruckstanz*.

I am going to see Bunster's choreography tonight. I have never seen any of his works live; thus, I am understandably excited. I am especially thrilled because his company will show older choreographies. The main reason that I am interested in Bunster's older work is because I hope to see a manifestation of his earlier attempt to create a pan-American movement vocabulary that would transcend national definitions but still bear traces of regional expressions. Bunster wrote a manifesto in the late 1960s that clearly outlined this endeavor. The movement was supposed to draw from existing movement vocabularies, mostly folk movements and modern dance, but he didn't rule out an exploration of ballet. Bunster empowers this merger of locally demarcated vocabulary with globalized movements— such as modern dance vocabulary derived from German modern dance and ballet—with the potential to restructure existing nationally defined movement in all senses of the word. This utopian understanding of the capacity of movement as a global unifier and transformer seems to recall early modern dance's vision for a changed world through corporeal awareness and choreographed emancipation. I want to retrace Bunster's emigration and homecoming patterns. This will allow me to understand how Bunster's idea of utopia migrated through a complex network of diaspora from Germany via the United Kingdom to Chile, then back to Germany, and finally again to Chile.

This is why I am sitting in a café, drinking out of a fragrant cup and contemplating my ability to—more or less—freely roam the world.

The Diaspora of *Ausdruckstanz*

I trained in the 1980s in the exercise that Bunster, assisted by Susanne Borchers, developed while he was teaching at the Palucca School. The exercise incorporated first a barre and then a center routine. It was characterized by release-based movement sequences that combined Palucca's attention to lines, jumps, and flow with a Jooss-Leeder-inspired focus on dynamics, space, and "stable" versus "off-center" movement qualities. The exercise emphasized spatial awareness and paid careful attention to the potential directionalities of any body part. It schooled dynamics and movement qualities while moving through sequences that felt like part of choreographies. It was a demanding yet enjoyable exercise; it always felt like dancing, not like forcing the body into a rigid system but rather developing it in tune with the body's abilities. In short, we all loved it because it provided us with an improved understanding of our bodies in space and of movement initiation. It was clear that someone who not only knew about dance but also had danced himself and had observed and theorized bodies in all kinds of movement situations must have developed this exercise.

By the time I trained in his exercise, Bunster had already left East Germany and had become a legendary figure in our dance community. His colleagues praised his pedagogy, systematic thinking, and commitment to change through dance. Eva Winkler, who taught at the Palucca School, recalled how she and pianist Peter Jarchow were on the cusp of finally generating a systematic documentation of Palucca's teaching in 1975 when Bunster joined the school and "questioned everything."[2] She later added to this in 1993 that "through his work at the Palucca School, the choreographies for his students, yet most of all through his work with Susanne Borchers and the boys' classes, Bunster built the foundation for an all encompassing comprehension of modern dance's potential. We gained new insights, and most of all the younger generation benefited."[3]

Patricio Bunster in conversation with Gret Palucca at the Palucca School, Dresden, 1982. Photo: Erich Höhne, Deutsche Fotothek.

His students, mostly men, had become visible as a new generation of choreographers and dancers, clearly different from anything we had seen at that point in East Germany. They seemed to explode into movement, accessing a force for their jumps and sudden turns from a well-developed and consciously utilized core. They were more thoughtful in their vocabulary and its references and execution. Space seemed to be something to mold—a partner in dance and choreography. Like many other East German dance professionals, I was intrigued by his students, and I wanted to know more about Bunster and the trajectory that led him to East Germany. I was especially interested in Bunster's international career as a fascinating example of the migration of *Ausdruckstanz* vocabulary and his lifelong affirmation of choreography's political function.

Bunster's biography speaks to such commitment. While finishing his degree in architecture at the University of Chile in the late 1930s, Bunster saw Kurt Jooss's company perform during its Latin American tour. Inspired, Bunster began dancing and training with Ernst Uthoff, Lola Botka, and Rudolf Pescht, all former members of Jooss's company who were offered work in Chile after they were stranded there following a short teaching engagement. These dancers could not leave Chile because, with the outbreak of World War II, no ship would take Germans on board. Jooss's dancers founded a dance department at the University of Chile, where they formed a dance ensemble that later became the Ballet Nacional Chileno. Bunster danced in Uthoff's productions for the dance ensemble and in the national ballet company in modern versions of *Coppelia* and *Don Juan*. Kurt Jooss himself was invited by Uthoff to teach and choreograph in Santiago from 1947 to 1949. Bunster danced major roles in Jooss's most important works: *Der grüne Tisch* (*The Green Table*), *Großstadt* (*Big City*), *Pavane* (*Pavane on the Death of an Infanta*), *Ball in Alt-Wien* (*Ball in Old Vienna*), and *Jugend* (*Youth*), the last specifically created for the ensemble. An invitation was also extended to Sigurd Leeder; he accepted and taught in Santiago from 1959 to 1964.

Jooss and Leeder's teachings furthered some of their mentor Rudolf Laban's investigations of space and movement quality. Unlike the followers of Wigman's absolute dance philosophy that rejected ballet, Jooss and Leeder incorporated the form and integrated characteristics from modern and ballet into a dramatic movement vocabulary. Jooss favored representational choreographic structures with clear references to mostly political and moral issues. In Germany, Jooss and Leeder famously refused to "cleanse" their company of Jewish dancers or to collaborate with the Nazi regime and as a result Jooss had to emigrate overnight in 1933. Both Jooss and Leeder emphasized the investigation of any vocabulary for its dramatic quality. They founded several schools (or influenced existing institutions), most famously the Folkwang School in Essen, Germany, and Dartington Hall in Devon, United Kingdom. The curriculum at their schools included modern, ballet, and folk techniques, eukinetics (an investigation of dynamics and expression), choreutics (the dancers' relations to their immediate surrounding space), improvisation, composition, rhythmic analysis, music, dance history, and Kinetography Laban (the European version of Labanotation). Bunster would later expand on this curriculum in his own teaching by adding an emphasis on everyday vocabulary and Latin American folk. In his choreographies, Bunster responded to Jooss's choreographic focus on group-leader relations because it spoke to Bunster's formal training in architecture, sparking a lifelong attention to spatial configurations.

After Jooss's return to Essen in 1949, Bunster was asked in 1951 to join Jooss's company in West Germany. While on tour in England in 1953, the company was unexpectedly dissolved because the city of Essen cut off the company's financing. Bunster decided to stay in Europe and study with Leeder in London, which led to a deepening in his understanding of Jooss and Leeder's movement system and Laban's theories. Bunster returned to Chile in 1954 and eventually asked Leeder to develop a new curriculum for the dance department of the university emphasizing further the Jooss-Leeder system and thus extending the impact of German *Ausdruckstanz* in Chile. At that point, the department served both as a conservatory for dancers and also as an interdisciplinary institute for research and for the education of choreographers and dance teachers. The institute's research was based on Jooss and Leeder's system of investigating human movement that was not determined by a single dance style but that sought to find the most appropriate vocabulary for a specific choreography. This investigation incorporated a study of pedestrian and labor vocabulary, ballet, Afro-Brazilian dance, and Graham in addition to German *Ausdruckstanz* and Chilean folk movements. In an interview in 1985, Bunster explained the broadening of the curriculum under his and Leeder's leadership: "I wanted to develop all movement potentials of the human body. This is necessary if you presume that life provides the topic for dance. Life is infinitely richer than any tendency or style. Likewise, movement is much more varied than a single— may it be ballet or modern—style."[4]

This statement is indicative of Bunster's philosophy. He not only understood dance as drawing from all aspects of life in its vocabulary but also as an art form that should be able to represent and comment on life. This belief led Bunster to shift the focus of the Chilean national ballet company toward indigenous themes. When Bunster first became the executive director of the Ballet Nacional Chileno, the company predominantly performed work by its director Uthoff and by Jooss. Although the company did not perform any Latin American–influenced choreography, it toured extensively throughout the continent and received much praise. Bunster's first choreography for the company in 1956 did not reflect his Latin American heritage. However, influenced by the poetry of Chilean Nobel Laureate Pablo Neruda, he began to research Chilean and Latin American folk movements and traditions. Bunster's 1959 choreography *Calaucán (Rebellious Bud)* reflected this search for a Latin American identity.[5] Based on Neruda's *Canto general*, it depicted the fight of the indigenous people against the Spanish conquistadores using imagery and movement from Aztec, Mayan, and Inca cultures.

Bunster continued his search for a Latin American—and specifically Chilean—cultural expression through dance in all his subsequent works. For instance in *Catrala desciende (The Descent of Catrala)* from 1969, Bunster depicted a legendary woman from the seventeenth century who allegedly murdered seventy men from all socioeconomic backgrounds with her bare hands after she sexually abused them. Bunster abstracted the story into a highly symbolic and visually arresting dance of one woman with three men—a priest, a slave, and a nobleman—to reflect on sources of cruelty in all classes and in the oligarchy in Chile. The piece exclusively employed abstract female vocals composed by Luciano Berio that together with the surprisingly modern movement vocabulary lent the piece a very contemporary feel.[6] The traditional story also gave an audience unaccustomed to theatrical conventions access to Bunster's choreography, an issue that was very important to Bunster.

With these and other choreographies the Ballet Nacional Chileno toured all areas of Chile, even remote rural provinces. The company always provided an introduction at the beginning of the evening to allow all audiences to understand the dances. They also conducted postperformance discussions on makeshift or open-air stages. Up to two thousand spectators attended these performances at a time. This presentational structure became the template for Bunster's work with the newly founded dance company of the Unidad Popular, the coalition of political parties and groups that helped elect the Socialist Party member Salvador Allende president in 1970. The company, which was led by Bunster's former wife, Joan Turner, literally employed dance as a weapon in class battle.

Together with the communist folk singer Víctor Jara, Bunster created mass dance and theater spectacles in the national stadium in Santiago leading up to Allende's election and during the three years of his presidency. Because of Bunster's earlier encounters with choreographic investigations of mass choirs in the *Ausdruckstanz* tradition, he was able to create works featuring up to one hundred thousand participants, including construction workers, miners, farmers, students, children, and the residents of Santiago's slums. Bunster and Jara even staged the national welcome festivities with seventy thousand people in honor of Pablo Neruda's return to Chile after he won the Nobel Prize in 1971.

Interestingly enough, Bunster and Jara also suggested to the Allende government that dance, theater, music, and writing groups be established to encourage cultural activities in factories, schools, and villages in order to "continually develop and support the creativity of our people."[7] Such structures would have replicated the model of amateur companies that existed in socialist countries, including East Germany. The Pinochet putsch, with the ensuing murder of Jara and Bunster's emigration to East Germany, cut short their endeavor.

Santiago, August 15, 2006

Bunster rested on a couch when I visited him yesterday. He looked frail but was eager to talk to me. I started speaking in English with him, figuring that it might be easier for him than German. I had read that he missed most of the German language courses provided to the Chilean immigrants when they arrived in East Germany because he immediately went to work on a performance. I tried to break the ice by telling him how much I enjoyed seeing his work from such disparate time periods, spanning choreographies from fifty years of his life. Knowing his strong belief in the communicational value of dance and its capacity to reflect on political situations and influence them, I explained that I was impressed by the conviction of the dancers. These young dancers performed his work with a clear understanding of the purpose of every step, and not only that, they were able to convey this purpose. I asked him how he communicated his choreographic intentions to the dancers, who hadn't experienced the time or situation that gave rise to his choreography and who were struggling with a completely different set of issues. Bunster smiled, saying, "I tell stories."

And he had enough stories to fill the entire evening. It became clear to me that Bunster still lived in a time of political strife. He was able to relate to me the imminent problems that still faced Chile, despite the seemingly normal life on the streets of Santiago and the familiar Western consumerism that I had experienced over the past days in the capital. The political past still haunted the country. Bunster talked about the time of his return to Chile in 1985. His friends were deeply worried about him. They all picked him up at the airport to ensure his safe arrival. Even though Bunster was allowed back into the country, his knowledge was not welcomed by the dance department and he wasn't invited back to teach. The Ballet Nacional Chileno eventually asked him to stage a new choreography, but his work faced much resistance from the ballet's leadership and even sabotage (a lighting structure smashed onto the stage on opening night). The choreography was a big success at its premiere, yet Bunster famously decided not to receive the ovations at the end to protest the sabotage and to highlight the still violent political situation. At the same time, the dance studio at the school that he and Joan Turner led was attacked by a firebomb.[8] A politically active actor who was a friend of Bunster had been shot dead only two days after welcoming Bunster at the airport.

Given these circumstances, it seemed inappropriate to ask my prepared questions about national specificity of dance vocabulary and Bunster's approach to teaching and choreographing. Yet it was clear that Bunster told those stories about the political situation only to make me understand the necessity of choreographing the way he did. He had to make dances that reflected on the imminent situation and that allowed him to convey his perspective. Despite the underlying discourse on politics, he always returned eagerly to dance as the subject of our conversation. His views of dance seemed so cosmopolitan and informed by a lifelong passion for dance's revolutionary and civic potential.

I am writing this sitting at the Café Colonia (Spanish for Café Cologne). The coaster says "Tradicion y Calidad Alemana" and wishes "Guten Appetit!" On the way over here, I took a photo of a restaurant named "Brüder." Stereotyped and truncated German culture is visible everywhere in Santiago. It places me in an odd position as a visitor who wants to retrace diasporic patterns. What do I know about these German immigrants? They left traces, but I don't know their relationship to Bunster's work. I understand now that Bunster's teacher Uthoff and even Jooss and Leeder didn't come into a completely alien environment. Chilean culture had been influenced by German immigrants and German culture. Still, these immigrants preserved a very specific version of German culture in Chile. Bunster's work and understanding of choreography was shaped by his mentors' German cultural heritage, but at the same time, he is Chilean. What is the impact of his culture on his work?

The opening dance of *Antología II* is a choreography that Bunster created in 2005. As he pointed out to me, it is supposed to look like a staged folk dance. And it certainly did. Set to music by Víctor Jara, it integrated jumps, arm postures, formations, and gender relations that recall stereotypical folk material. I wasn't able to tell the specificity of the material, but Bunster assured me that he utilized various Chilean and Latin American material. He wanted to combine Jara's music with an affirmation of Chilean folk tradition.

In his 1961 manifesto "Perspectivas de un ballet americano," Bunster called attention to an erasure of Latin American identity through the "ready acceptance of influences from different major cultural hemispheres" and demanded a recovery of indigenous cultural identities.[9] He defined this process as a "fight for cultural wealth" and assigned choreography a major role in this endeavor. For Bunster, choreography was not simply the organization and invention of movement vocabulary in space and time. He believed that choreography should be in service of social development and thus needed to present a potential path toward a better future. To achieve this, he believed that dance vocabularies and techniques should be analyzed for their value and suitability for the revolutionary restructuring of society. Most importantly, the source of revolutionary choreographic material could be found in the study of contemporary "everyday movement as expression."[10] Influenced by Laban's as well as Jooss and Leeder's approaches, Bunster advocated for the observation and utilization of movement found in manual labor, leisure, daily rituals, nature, and the structure of architecture. In Bunster's opinion, all of these sources carried traces of future choreographies that could express a new transnational, (Latin) American, and utopian identity. It was the choreographer in his view who was capable of structuring these elements into potent movement and of demonstrating the meaning of the movement and its revolutionary potential, thus marking the path toward an improved society.

The philosopher Ernst Bloch, one of the foremost theorists of utopia, also saw the present as holding hope and with it the potential for fulfillment.[11] Whereas Marxism defines class consciousness as the driving force that leads to a classless social system, Bloch saw potential and hope in every appearance in the present. Through his philosophical evaluation of being as a state of "not-yet fulfillment," Bloch proposed a reconsideration of artistic production in service of social progress on the grounds that any production already contains the possibility of fulfilling the future. Both Bloch and Bunster saw potential for change and development in all manifestations of the present and thus allowed for the possibility of social progress outside a Marxist understanding of class battle as the driving force for social change. Even though they detected future social progress already in appearances of the present, they both emphasized the necessity of redevelopment and restructuring. Bloch did not see the potential of the present as simply being fulfilled in the future but rather regarded hope in the present as a driving force that will radically restructure the current social systems into a better, yet surprisingly different, tomorrow. Similarly, Bunster spoke out in his manifesto against the simple utilization of existing movement vocabularies and techniques, demanding instead the uncovering of the essence of movement that requires and permits new choreographic choices. Bloch also assigned art a predominant place in the restructuring of present society because art (dance and choreography included) communicates equally through its content and its form.

This understanding of choreography's function is of course not new. Both François Delsarte and Rudolf Laban sought to rediscover corporeal potential in art and everyday life by investigating the body's capability. Jooss and Leeder developed a training system that prepared the dancer's body for such a complex task. They valued the expressive potential of dance and rejected a strictly formal approach. Bunster saw a potential in all of society that could be unearthed, choreographed, and communicated to an audience — if the choreographer was willing, talented, and trained. His choreographies, employing *Ausdruckstanz*'s attention to space and group dynamics and incorporating Latin American folk and everyday movement of the people, took a first step in this direction for him.

In 1973 the fascist putsch (led by General Augusto Pinochet) against the Unidad Popular government of Allende interrupted Bunster's enterprise. The national stadium, which had hosted Bunster's mass choirs, would become a concentration camp where thousands of people suspected of communist and anti-junta leanings would be imprisoned, tortured, and murdered. Bunster, who had denounced the Pinochet regime at the university on the day of the putsch, was forced into exile the same evening. After several shorter stays in other countries, Bunster and many other supporters of Allende found refuge in East Germany, which wanted to solidify the relationship between the East German government and the Chilean Left.

Patricio Bunster rehearsing *Trotz Alledem — Venceremos* with students of the Palucca School, Dresden, 1975. Tanzarchiv Leipzig e.V. Photo: Erich Höhne, Dresden.

Bunster did not immediately gain access to the East German dance scene. At first, he worked for theater productions in his new "hometown" of Rostock and other cities. This led eventually to an invitation from the Palucca School to choreograph for its students in 1975. Shortly after, Bunster started to teach there. It is not completely clear how much pressure was put on Palucca to accept Bunster at her school and to allow with him a second, much more analytical and political interpretation of *Ausdruckstanz*. Bunster, who was only permitted to teach boys at the beginning of his tenure, introduced his own interpretation of the *Ausdruckstanz* tradition as filtered through Jooss, Leeder, the Chilean folk, and his belief in the transformative potential of dance. This powerful combination of aesthetics and politics—which was a radically different approach to *Ausdruckstanz* from Palucca's—would influence a new generation of East German dancers and choreographers, most famously the choreographer Stephan Thoss and the dancer and pedagogue Raymond Hilbert. As Susanne Borchers recalls, Bunster's pedagogy was closely linked to choreographic investigation and performance. In contrast to Palucca, who strove to create an expressive dancer, Bunster valued a dancer who would represent a theme as objectively as possible.[12]

Patricio Bunster teaching male students at the Palucca School, Dresden, 1982. Photo: Erich Höhne, Deutsche Fotothek.

While in East Germany, Bunster choreographed works such as *Trotz Alledem—Venceremos* (*Despite Everything* [1975]), *Porque tenemos sólo una vida—Denn wir haben nur ein Leben* (*Because We Only Have One Life* [1984]), and *Leuchten wird mein Schatten* (*My Shadow Will Be Radiant* [1979]), some of which were presented at the Komische Oper Berlin.[13] All of the choreographies displayed Bunster's trademark combination of *Ausdruckstanz* and Chilean folk and carried a didactic political message.[14] They also demonstrated his craft of choreography with their close attention to space and dynamics. Despite his success and growing influence on the East German dance scene, Bunster never felt at home in East Germany, and his English always remained better than his German.

In 1985, Bunster was finally able to return to Chile. Upon his return, he cofounded, with Joan Turner, Espiral, which in 1997 became part of the

Universidad Academia de Humanismo Cristiano, a progressive, nonprofit private university that was established in reaction to the Pinochet regime. As Bunster explained in an interview in 1987, students ranged from amateur to professionals. About 40 percent of them were able to pay tuition, while the rest trained for free. Besides being trained, students worked in choreographies that were shown at community events. The school's company, also called Espiral, performed in slums and at large political events attended by up to forty thousand spectators. The group collaborated with committees in support of the disappeared and murdered Chileans. The school was attacked several times and the teachers, including Bunster, received death threats.[15]

Santiago, August 16, 2006

The studio was really cold when I arrived this morning to observe a class taught by Raymond Hilbert. The students didn't seem to mind. The warm-up had already started. Raymond told me that he would teach a Jooss-Leeder class and that their routines were not so much a technique as a system that built on Laban's understanding of choreutics and eukinetics. The warm-up and the following class definitely affirmed that. All the exercises focused on juxtapositions of various elements of movement. Centrally initiated movement led to peripheral movement vocabulary at the same time that there was a constant back and forth from a stable vertical state to an unstable state leaving the vertical. Dynamics constantly changed. A peripheral bound swing into the diagonal with the arms stretched overhead to one side contracted suddenly back along the vertical into a central squat.

As the students started moving through space, they maintained this simultaneous attention to all elements of movement dynamics, spatiality, and balance. They performed turns that went out of a peripheral vertical upright stable posture into a contracted forward bend and back to an upright position that seemed to be still centrally initiated. Sometimes a movement phrase was done in a straight line through the room with the body facing forward and then a similar phrase was performed in short diagonals with the body facing toward these diagonals. The changes in the directionality of these moves could be initiated centrally or peripherally. Jumps often incorporated a sudden contraction, yet initially they seemed to focus on the bound peripheral.

All movement phrases built on each other. Sometimes an exercise emphasized dynamics and central or peripheral initiation. Yet the same vocabulary was then extended to incorporate the focus on stability and instability. As Raymond stressed afterward, this way the students were made aware of the construction of all the movement phrases and especially why certain movement phrases were created. Here again the focus on cause and effect and reasoning of movement underwrote the pedagogy, which was so typical for Jooss and Leeder and by extension for Bunster.

Raymond also explained to me that the school doesn't always have money for heating and other costs. Many of the students came from poor families and were not able to pay tuition.

Even though Bunster was initially not allowed back into the building of his former company, he eventually was asked to restage *Calaucán* and *Catrala desciende*. Both works were choreographed before the Pinochet putsch and received a new connotation under his dictatorship. Bunster also choreographed a new version of *The Rite of Spring*, *Vindicación de la primavera*, in 1987. He changed the familiar plot to a depiction of the fight between life and death in order to condemn torture in Chile. During that same period, he and seventy other theater artists received new death threats from a fascist organization.

Ausdruckstanz as a Weapon in Class Struggle

My arrival in Santiago in the summer of 2006 coincided with the second retrospective of Bunster's choreography, *Antología II*, featuring five works choreographed between 1969 and 2005, among them *Catrala desciende* and *Vindicación de la primavera*.[16] All of these works were created in Chile except one, *A pesar de todo*, the choreography for the Palucca School from 1975, then titled *Trotz Alledem — Venceremos*. *A pesar de todo* fictionalized Bunster's experience of the Pinochet putsch in 1973; he extended his personal experience onstage by envisioning a successful revolutionary uprising against the fascist regime.[17] East German officials had hailed the work as proof that socialist ideology could take root across national borders, thus demonstrating the relevance and necessity of GDR solidarity with working-class Chileans.[18]

The 2006 restaging of *A pesar de todo* would serve a drastically different purpose in Chile. The work is a historical document available to the generations of Chileans growing up in post-putsch Chile that allows the events to be rewritten back into Chile's national history—events that the Pinochet regime attempted to erase from public memory. Bunster's piece also provided a generation who experienced the putsch with a mechanism for confronting the events of September 11, 1973, and with an opportunity to remember and position themselves in relation to the Pinochet regime more than twenty years after its reign. I was interested in this shift from choreography as an embodiment of a decisively ideological utopia when first performed in East Germany in 1975 to a choreography that functions as a living archive in contemporary Chile.

Trotz Alledem—Venceremos, Palucca School, Dresden, 1975. Palucca Hochschule für Tanz Dresden. Photo: Erich Höhne, Dresden.

Santiago, August 19, 2006

At one of Pablo Neruda's houses in Chile here in Santiago I had a tour guide all to myself because it was early morning. He was a young, hip-looking guy with fashionable "intellectual" glasses. He clearly was passionate about Neruda as a person and a poet. He was fascinated by the fact that I had read *Canto general*, which I had done because the last big dance performance by the dance company of East Germany's armed forces was a choreography of this poem. It is probably one of Neruda's more political works, and I found some of it didactic. But that judgment might have been instigated by the context in which I first encountered the poem.

The tour guide explained how important Neruda still was to the Spanish-speaking world and that his poetry worked across national boundaries. He stressed Neruda's easygoing and fun-loving character as a major contributor to his ongoing popularity. Neruda's lifestyle was easily detectable in the house. The house had more bars than bedrooms. There were absurd collections of glasses and china to be used for the extensive gatherings of guests. The many courtyards were built to accommodate large parties. Despite the evidence of a bohemian lifestyle, the tour guide repeatedly emphasized Neruda's leftist politics and his active involvement in government and social movements. The guide told me that many people in the countryside and slums still have a picture of Neruda next to one of Allende in their house.

This encouraged me to ask more questions about the current situation in Chile and the stance younger people take toward art. My guide explained that there is still an awareness of poetry and other art forms but that Western popular culture is, of course, gaining influence. People still know Chilean folk songs and folk art, but their significance is waning. Class is an important factor; or as the guide put it, the upper class used to long for Paris and longs now for Miami, with its malls and Americanized Latino culture. I find that very interesting. Especially since I have been told by the dancers from Bunster's company how much folklore is still prominent in people's lives here. I am wondering which of the two assessments is true or if it is just a matter of exposure and contact.

The guide knew of Bunster, but I am not sure if he had seen his work. He described him as the most important and famous Chilean choreographer. Yet he also said that his work feels stuck in the 1980s. This brought me to ask him about the significance of art in dealing with the Pinochet era. He found it very important and was horrified by people who didn't want to know about the putsch and the dictatorship, people who disputed Pinochet's atrocities or who believed that government officials didn't know about the events. He made his point by saying that he was only four at the time of the putsch but that he saw the corpses lying on the river's shore and that his mother shielded his eyes, and yet he knew what happened.

After a "no" referendum on the continuation of his presidency in 1988, Pinochet stepped down as president of Chile in 1990. With this, seventeen years of dictatorship in Chile came to an end. He remained as the commander in chief of the army until 1998. In March 2006, the year I visited, Chile elected a new president, Michelle Bachelet, a woman who had been imprisoned and tortured by the Pinochet regime prior to her own exile to East Germany. Bachelet reformed Chilean government and laws. She advocated for invalidation of the amnesty of Pinochet-era crimes, a law that for nearly thirty years exempted members of the former government from prosecution on charges of murder and torture. Despite such far-reaching reforms, Chile was not united in condemning the Pinochet regime. Upper-class citizens supported the amnesty and challenged left-wing revisions of Chilean history. Pinochet died in December 2006 without having been indicted of any serious crimes committed during the putsch and his presidency. Chile still struggles with its recent violent history.

The restaging of *A pesar de todo* at the 2006 retrospective of his work supported Chileans' working through their recent violent past. Bunster employed Latin American folk material and *Ausdruckstanz* vocabulary to tell the story of the putsch. Choreographically, the piece is composed of a series of repeated tableau-like formations that form and dissolve. The spatial tensions between different groups or between groups and individuals recall familiar investigations from *Ausdruckstanz*.

In the opening sequence male and female dancers perform a celebratory dance in a circle around a central male figure who manipulates a large piece of red fabric that initially serves as a poncho and later, at different points in the dance, as a flag and a death shroud. Dressed in simple costumes (the women in skirts and blouses, the men in calf-length trousers and simple collarless shirts), the dancers swirl and jump around the central dancer until the group marches repeatedly toward the audience in a triangular formation. The rhythmically driven music by Víctor Jara utilizes the Peruvian flute, giving the piece an indigenous Latin American mood. Eventually the calm, yet melancholic, music is overlaid with the sound of gunshots and sirens as the dancers move in and out of formations depicting various scenes of violence, bereavement, and resistance through a careful revisiting of material presented in the first half of the choreography. Raised arms with open hands become fists, folkloric arm positions turn into pieta-like body shapes, and the poncho becomes a flag waved in defiance. The violence culminates when the male protagonist is shot and mourned by three women and a man, who then lead the rest of the dancers in a funeral procession across the stage, at which point the flag becomes a shroud. This procession turns into a large group uprising against an invisible oppressor. Finally, the dance ends with all the dancers marching in a line directly toward the audience until they reach the end of the stage, and one of the women takes up the death shroud to wear as a poncho.

East German officials endorsed this work because they saw Bunster's choreography with its raised fists, strong group formations, and utopian narrative as supporting a proletarian uprising in the Marxist sense that would lead to a new socialist Latin America. As a communist Chilean artist seeking refuge in East Germany, GDR officials considered Bunster a poster child for the revolutionary forces in young nation-states (Marxist code for the inhabitants of decolonized African, Asian, and South American countries). East German officials naturalized the revolutionary fervor of his choreography and hailed the work as a triumphant vision of proletarian struggle in a formerly colonized nation, and thus as the victorious extension of the working-class struggle against imperialism. In other words, GDR officials made Bunster's choreography fit the trope of Marxist-Leninist doctrine. When I first saw *Trotz Alledem — Venceremos* in 1985, I also viewed Bunster's choreographies through the lens of agit-prop aesthetics and socialist ideology. Experiencing *A pesar de todo* in Chile and talking to Bunster forced me to rethink my response.

Santiago, August 20, 2006

At the café where I sat was a guy wearing an East German army jacket. It was so familiar yet so out of place. I had to wear those jackets during my own army service in East Germany. They were the part of the tracksuit we had to wear for all the grueling and senseless morning outdoor exercises, where in winter the metal weights froze to our hands. The first time I saw one of these jackets again was 1995 in California at a little mall on the UC Irvine campus. Somehow, it seemed stranger there than here. Why is that? Maybe because so many memorabilia of the former Eastern Bloc have since made it into the fashion stables of the hip and trendy. Socialism as a fashion trend; that is basically what is left of it. That seems to be a much more lived archive than any dead library or collection of East German documents. The question is how much of the context is still attached to those fashion items. The Russian fur hats, the fatigues, the army bags, and the belts with our national emblem have fading referents.

Bunster's restaging of the putsch came at a crucial moment for the Chilean public and inserted an important voice into this national dialogue. In 1975, when Bunster first choreographed it in East Germany, the dance depicted the putsch and its devastating aftermath but also envisioned a successful grassroots uprising in staging a utopian vision of a unified and free world. The restaging of the choreography in 2006 provided an account of history as lived by Chilean citizens and thus added to the living national archive through its corporeal engagement with history. For Bunster, the performance of his thirty-year-old choreography was necessary not only for the generation who lived through the Pinochet era and was still coping with this complex national history but also for the generation that did not experience the putsch. The performances that I attended affirmed Bunster's conviction. Audience members rose up out of their seats during the performance and commented on the actions, as if they too played a part in the narrative presented onstage. Their passionate applause was more than a celebration of the choreography—it was a celebration of the victory depicted onstage. This cathartic impact on the audience elevated the choreography beyond the staging of an unattainable utopia into a tangible living archive that gave dance and choreography the power not only to reflect and imagine reality but also to change it.

Santiago, August 21, 2006

When I arrived at the performance of Bunster's work for the last time on August 19, the theater was packed. Even though the performances have been selling well, I was surprised to find nearly all five hundred seats taken. The audience seemed to be very young; there were many children and even entire families in it. The shy manner in which some of the audience members approached the theater indicated that they might not have attended many performances before. As far as I could tell, a large portion of the audience seemed to be working class.

The audience's possible inexperience with Western theatrical conventions also became audible in the reaction to all the pieces. There was much clapping, responding, and yelling during the entire performance. The audience reacted directly to the events onstage. Pieces were interrupted at times by applause of technical mastery but also at pivotal moments in the dances' narratives. The audience appreciated and honored both the political messages and the techniques. Bold statements, such as the waving of the Chilean flag in the first choreography, earned as much applause as the advanced technical skills of the main dancers. There seemed to be an unmediated enjoyment of the dances not informed by theatrical conventions or previous experience.

I approached Raymond Hilbert about this phenomenon, and he explained that the performances were actually sponsored by the Metro, the subway company in Santiago. As part of this sponsorship, the company provided free or very cheap tickets to the public. The same day I saw an advertisement at several Metro stations that not only announced the event but also mentioned the sponsorship and how many tickets would be made available.

Raymond also explained to me that several of these stations had built-in stages that allowed performances. Espiral had performed several times on those very simple stages. These kinds of performances give an audience that would normally not attend a dance at a theater access to the experience. [Manuela Bunster later clarified that the enthusiastic viewers and the sold out performances were mostly caused by Espiral's extensive outreach to local organizations and nontraditional audiences. To accomplish this, the company performs nearly exclusively in non-theatrical settings, which of course limits the production value of their performances. Yet they work very hard to perform for people who usually don't see dance. When Espiral rents a theater and is able to show their repertoire at its best, they make sure that they still have their usual diverse audience.[19]]

Advertising for *Antología II* in the Metro station announcing free tickets, Santiago, Chile, 2006. Photo: author.

Afterward

After my time with Bunster in Chile, I flew to my current home in New York City. I still find it shocking on a daily basis that as an East German once confronted by the Berlin Wall, I am able to move freely. This sense of moving freely, what in the West is construed as "normalcy," is ruptured in certain moments, moments like the one when I was faced with the threat of a terrorist attack on my outbound flight to Chile. Such ruptures not only expose my privileged mobility but also the global democracy that enables such mobility as a construct. This construct presents itself decisively as nonideological by constituting itself the norm against which every other marginal social utopia—be it regional, religious, or national—is measured.[20] Yet this globalized normalcy is powerfully disturbed and revealed as ideology whenever a terrorist act is committed or violent national struggle unfolds. These disturbances are always regarded negatively and as antiprogressive by the global democracy. Even a choreography such as Bunster's, with its clearly ideological and national function, could not be recognized as progressive in our Western-dominated understanding of democracy and social development. Yet reading it in conjunction with the histories of migration across national divides forces global democracy to juxtapose itself alongside regional territories that do not always register in our economically defined globalization—because they are on the periphery (Chile) or extinct (the GDR). Inevitably, global democracy can then in turn be recognized as ideological.

With such general statements I am attempting to avoid losing sight of the larger political value of Bunster's work through an analysis of specifics of his choreography. As Ahkil Gupta and James Ferguson caution, there is the temptation to focus on disparate examples of cultural production that move from the peripheries to the centers of the culture industry without an understanding of the totalizing effect of global imperialism and thus to repress political problems that come with Western hegemony.[21] Bunster's career—moving between Chile, the United Kingdom, West and East Germany—not only presents a migration of dance vocabulary but also asks for an alternative understanding of dance and globalization by tracking an ideological diaspora—in this case, the movement of *Ausdruckstanz* as informed by revolutionary and socialist ideology.

Notes

Introduction

1. "Ostalgie" is a term made up of the German word "Ost" ("east") and "Nostalgie" ("nostalgia"). As the term suggests, it refers to a nostalgic longing for aspects of East German life. The term has been exploited in selling memorabilia and replicas of East German products and brands, yet it also raises the question of the extent to which the culture of East German citizens has been lost or devalued.

2. The Sportmuseum Leipzig holds all documents relating to the mass choreographies for the opening of each of the East German *Turn- und Sportfestes*. The German Democratic Republic staged eight gymnastics and sports festivals in Leipzig. The first festival in 1954 drew thirty-five thousand participants who competed in familiar Summer Olympic–style events such as race and track, swimming, boxing, biking, gymnastics, soccer, and fencing, as well as more unusual activities such as marching band (Rodekamp, *Sportschau*, 31).

3. By "mass movements," I am referring to an array of mostly synchronized choreographies with hundreds or thousands of participants. These mass movements are an important display of power and control in any dictatorial regime, and they have been staged in both fascist and socialist countries. Famously, Leni Riefenstahl documented the mass movements at the 1934 Nazi Party Congress in Nuremburg in her *Triumph des Willens* (*Triumph of the Will*). The choreographies at the Arirang Mass Games of the Democratic People's Republic of Korea (North Korea) are contemporary examples. Yet mass movements are also an important aspect of international sports events, such as during the opening ceremony of the Olympics.

4. Twenty-five thousand participants performed in nineteen different mass exercises for the one hundred thousand audience members. Traditional sports associations, soldiers, sports students, children, and representatives from various professions, such as postal workers and factory workers, presented these exercises in groups of around five hundred each and united in a final scene of twelve thousand creating geometrical patterns and human pyramids. In addition, twelve thousand citizens in the eastern bleachers (*Osttribüne*) raised and lowered flags in different colors to form propagandistic images and slogans such as "Honor the GDR," "Value Labor," or "Unity and Peace" as a backdrop for all these exercises. The exercise had been executed all over the country in factories, schools, and other institutions in the time leading up to the festival (Rodekamp, *Sportschau*, 32.)

179

5. See Anderson, *Imagined Communities*.

6. See Foster, *Choreographing Empathy*, for the historical development of the concepts of empathy and kinesthesia in relation to choreography.

7. Documentation relating to East German dance is mostly housed in the Tanzarchiv Leipzig, the Sportmuseum Leipzig, and the archive of the Akademie der Künste Berlin. In 2011, the Tanzarchiv Leipzig (the only East German dance archive) was not only threatened with restructuring by being integrated into the library holdings of the University of Leipzig but the head of the library also publicly mentioned that he was considering throwing out material that he deemed not valuable for storage. Such fate was avoided partly due to an international campaign that saw dance scholars from all over the world approaching the Saxonian government, the University of Leipzig, and the leadership of the Tanzarchiv to ask them to rethink their plans. At the time of writing the archive has been moved into the special collection of the University of Leipzig's library as a whole and can be accessed again.

8. For instance, the material on the Erich-Weinert-Ensemble, the dance ensemble of the armed forces, is now located in a warehouse of the Militärarchiv Freiburg, the archive of the West German armed forces. It is neither archived nor catalogued, and it is not even clear what part of the former Erich-Weinert-Ensemble archive is stored there. After many phone calls, I was told by the archivist that in order to view the material, researchers would not only have to be able to cope with the cold temperatures in the climate-controlled warehouse but would also have to be accompanied by a second person, because the lighting turns off automatically and needs to be turned on every few minutes again. I find this state of affairs to be a very good allegory of the general state of the material on East German dance—not illuminated, undesired, carelessly stored, not archived, nonaccessible, and possibly just gone in a few years.

9. Wong, *Choreographing Asian America*, 5.

10. Each chapter's subject matter requires a different level of subjective engagement. For instance, the first chapters cover events that occurred before I became a dancer. Thus, there I adopt a much more academic voice. The more I am part of the described history, the more I am become part of the analytic performance.

11. This approach is influenced by Susan Foster's groundbreaking essay "An Introduction to Moving Bodies."

12. Manning, *Ecstasy and the Demon*; Karina and Kant, *Hitler's Dancers*; Partsch-Bergsohn, *Modern Dance in Germany and the United States*; Partsch-Bergsohn and Bergsohn, *The Makers of Modern Dance in Germany*; Toepfer, *Empire of Ecstasy*.

13. Climenhaga, *Pina Bausch*; Fernandes, *Pina Bausch and the Wuppertal Dance Theater*.

14. Siegmund, *Abwesenheit*; Siegmund, *William Forsythe*; Hardt and Maar, *Tanz, Metropole, Provinz*; Husemann, "Choreographie als kritische Praxis."

15. The only historical overview of dance in East Germany is provided by Ralf Stabel in *Krokodil im Schwanensee*. Other authors provide information on selected appearances or protagonists of East German dance. See, for instance, Heising, Römer, and Klotzsche, *Der Tanz im "künstlerischen Volksschaffen" der DDR*; Weidt and Kant, *Auf der großen Straße*; Winkler, *Der moderne Tanz nach 1945*; Winkler, "Ausdruckstanz in der DDR"; Ladopoulos, "Die künstlerische und pädagogische Arbeit Hanne Wandtkes in der Tradition des Ausdruckstanzes"; Kühl, *Patricio Bunster*; and Stabel, *Tanz, Palucca!* There are hardly any texts in English; for three exceptions, however, see Kant, "Dance in Exile"; Kant, "*Was bleibt?*"; and Cramer, "Warfare over Realism."

16. Foucault, "Nietzsche, Genealogy, History." Foucault offers genealogy as a historicizing methodology that stresses the singularity of events, discontinuity, and neglected parts of history. Rather than unifying historical occurrences into a coherent narrative, genealogy stresses differences and discontinuities and problematizes its own position of historization. Foucault gives the body an important role in genealogy because in his understanding the body is inscribed and destroyed by historic events and even capable of resistance. Despite this insight, he sees physicality mostly as a passive receptacle of events or a surface to be altered and not as a constructive and creative force.

17. Brandenburg, *Der moderne Tanz*; Lammel, *Der moderne Tanz*; Frank Thiess, *Der Tanz als Kunstwerk*.

18. Boehn, *Der Tanz*, 9.

19. Ibid., 25.

20. Ibid., 129–30.

21. Sachs, *World History of the Dance*, 6.

22. Here grace serves as the controlling mechanism that indicates loss through development that can be regained only through a completed cycle of education and the arrival at a higher state in which total knowledge is in harmony with nature and the divine; see Kleist, "Über das Marionettentheater."

23. For recent critiques, see Foster, introduction, 3–4; and Savigliano, "Worlding Dance and Dancing Out There in the World," 171.

24. Foster, *Reading Dancing*.

25. For the most recent and thorough discussion of the development of choreography as a concept and term, see Foster, *Choreographing Empathy*.

26. For an elaborate exploration of the shifts in early choreography see Foster, *Choreography and Narrative*.

27. For a description of this tremendous change, see Tomko, *Dancing Class*; and Daly, *Done into Dance*.

28. Savigliano, O'Shea, and Novack-Bull all elaborate on this influential impact on choreography in their work.

29. See my own critique of choreography as an academic methodology, which is grounded in an analysis of disciplinary genealogy, in "Dance Studies in the International Academy," as well as Savigliano's similar critique in "Worlding Dance and Dancing Out There in the World," which she undertakes by investigating the broadening of dance into anthropological projects.

30. Foster, who is a proponent of the use of choreography as methodology in dance studies, rethought her position partly as a result of Hammergren's, my, and Savigliano's critiques. See Foster, *Choreographing Empathy*, 5.

31. Foster, *Choreography and Narrative*, xvi; Foster, *Choreographing History*.

32. Among many other studies, see those of Daly, Albright, Ness, Foster, Savigliano, and Manning.

33. Giersdorf, "Dance Studies in the International Academy," 23–44.

34. Many scholars from within and from other disciplines misread Foster. For instance, Andrew Hewitt sets Foster against Peggy Phelan's related discussions of disappearance and performance, proposing that Foster does not understand that to postulate dance as a text does not make it equal to a written document (Hewitt, *Social Choreography*, 8–9). Interestingly, Phelan and Foster both understand the differences between dance or performance and written documentation, but writing from different

disciplinary backgrounds, they respond differently to these issues. Phelan, writing from within performance studies and coming from a literary background, provides valuable ways for understanding disappearance and the ontology of the performance event as temporary; the choreographer/dancer/dance scholar Foster, on the other hand, focuses on strategies by which to elevate dance and its study in art and academia. Even though I find Phelan's ontology helpful for my discussion of nationally specific notions of modernity and performance and the issue of traces of nationality, I want to consider the issue of disappearance and its impact on dance and choreographic choices without fetishizing it.

35. I am using the informal "East Germany" throughout this book because I historicize and theorize dance in the Soviet Occupation Zone, the GDR, and the former socialist areas of the reunified Germany.

36. With the loss of socialist state funding when East Germany reunified with West Germany in 1990, most of these dance outlets disappeared. Only a few companies in major theaters were able to survive, albeit performing little of the East German repertoire.

37. The GDR always planned its economy centrally. The first two-year plan was introduced in 1949. The main goal of this plan was to increase industrial production and to supply the citizens with consumer goods. The plan also called for making extensive reparation payments to the USSR. This economic plan was followed by the first five-year plan in 1951. This plan was more far-reaching in its goals. The GDR worked to develop an industrial base in the form of self-produced raw materials like iron, steel, energy, and basic chemical materials, and in the process, the supply of consumer goods suffered enormously. The two following five-year and seven-year plans attempted to remedy this disproportion between basic industrial production and the production of consumer goods.

38. Even though this statistic has been disputed as a propagandistic myth by some scholars, the increase in the GDR's industrial production was remarkable, considering that, unlike West Germany, much of its industry was dismantled in order that it might make reparations to the Soviet Union.

39. The SED was founded at its first *Parteitag* (party convention) in 1946. The fifth *Parteitag* in 1958 issued the "Ten Commandments of Socialist Morality," requiring GDR citizens to live as ideologically conscious socialist individuals, fight for their country, value the heterosexual family, and display solidarity with the developing world. The eighth *Parteitag* in 1971 had the most impact with its declaration of the unity of economic and social development, aligning the production of consumer goods with the other parts of industrial production and endeavoring to raise the living standard in the GDR. The last party convention took place one month after the fall of the Berlin Wall in December 1989. During the 1989 convention, the SED was renamed the Party of Democratic Socialism.

40. Heising, Römer, and Klotzsche, *Der Tanz im "künstlerischen Volksschaffen" der DDR*, 142–53.

41. See Kant, *Hitler's Dancers*, as well as her "*Was bleibt?*"

42. For extensive documentation on Wigman's collaboration with the Nazi government, see Manning, *Ecstasy and the Demon*; and Karina and Kant, *Hitler's Dancers*.

43. Stabel, *Tanz, Palucca!*

44. Müller, Stabel, and Stöckemann, *Krokodil im Schwanensee*, 249.

Chapter 1. Dancing National Identity in Daily Life

1. An analysis of a nationally specific utilization of dance and choreography provides a valuable methodology for exploring a national system in which many different interests compete with each other in an effort to form the general public's identity. Such competition among different interests is not restricted to the GDR or other socialist countries but appears in most national systems. However, this competition appears most visible when a national identity has been vacated or questioned by an invasion, loss in a war, in the wake of colonialism, or at the end of dictatorships. Contemporary examples are the situation in Iraq, the fight between Chechnyan and Russian national forces, and the Kurdish fight for independence. Because of its emphasis on corporeality, the methodology of dance studies allows us to look at such identity-creating forces at the level of the microcultural and to track either their erasure or incorporation into larger, all-encompassing forces.

2. For a similar project, see Anthea Kraut's examination of folk in relationship to African American choreographic practice in *Choreographing the Folk*.

3. Throughout the Renaissance and Enlightenment, Germany was not a single unified state. Rather it was divided into independent states, mostly ruled by nobles but later also by trading guilds. After the Thirty Years' War in 1648, there were around three hundred independent regions. It wasn't until 1871 that Germany united as an industrial and decisively militarist nation, with the Kingdom of Prussia serving as its ruling constituent after the French defeat in the Franco-Prussian War.

4. The German word "Volk" is often translated as "people," but it is a much more complex concept that evokes folk, national identification, connection to the land, and locality.

5. Lepp, Roth, and Vogel, *Der Neue Mensch*, 164.

6. Baxmann, *Mythos*, 236.

7. Boehn, *Der Tanz*, 128. Jaques-Dalcroze taught his method of teaching music through movement at the Hellerau dance school outside of Dresden. The school became an important institution for the development of *Ausdruckstanz* in Germany.

8. Baxmann, *Mythos*, 236.

9. The BDM was founded in 1930 through a merger of several organizations for girls, and in 1931 it was integrated into the Hitler Youth. Girls between the ages of ten and thirteen joined the Jungmädelbund, and those between fourteen and eighteen became part of the BDM proper. Starting in 1938, older young women up to the age of twenty-one could join Glaube und Schönheit. See Jürgens, *Zur Geschichte des BDM (Bund Deutscher Mädel) von 1923 bis 1939*.

    In a 2006 interview with me, Elfriede Wachek, who had to join the BDM as a girl, reported on those twice-weekly rehearsals during her membership with the Jungmädelbund and the BDM. She also mentioned the older girls performing folk dances at the annual harvest festival for Hitler at the Bückeberg. Although the Hitler Youth and its female branch have received a fair amount of scholarly attention, the employment of folk dance in Nazi Germany's cultural and political structure still awaits scholarly analysis.

10. With its connotation of a rural setting and nature, folk was easily positioned into the Nazi ideology of "blood and soil" and thus became an integral part of Nazi propaganda. Lilian Karina and Marion Kant establish that folk dance was incorporated

into dance during the Nazi era but note that it was not the focus of the invention for a truly German stage dance (*Hitler's Dancers*, 87). Still, folk dances were performed regularly and extensively outside theatrical institutions and at the annual harvest festival at the Bückeberg, which had up to one million participants and was the largest recurring festival in Nazi Germany.

11. The Soviet Union undertook its own reevaluation of art—and dance—after the October Revolution in 1917. Russian formalism was repeatedly attacked—beginning with Leon Trotsky's infamous essay "Literature and Revolution" in 1924—and socialist realism was sanctioned as the official method for all artistic expression in the wake of the first Congress of the Soviet Writers' Union in 1934. Putting art into the ideological service of the complex nation-state of the Soviet Union led to an increasing focus on the folk tradition of its many republics.

Igor Moiseyev's dance company became the template for all state folk dance companies in the world. Founded in 1937, it was most famous for its reinterpretation of songs and dances by the Don Cossacks, for its Red Army dance, and for its choir ensemble, later named the Alexandrov Ensemble, which started to perform folk songs and dances as early as 1928 and famously in August 1948 in East Berlin. For an analysis of the company's specific choreographic style and function, see Shay, *Choreographic Politics*. Shay also provides the first overview of a variety of state-sponsored dance companies from different countries. He rightly points out that these companies merge folk and ballet vocabulary for the stage rather than simply restage existing folk dances.

12. Baxmann, "Der Körper als Gedächtnisort," 15.

13. Founded on only a fraction of the German territory, East German state officials had the arduous task of creating a distinct national identity for East Germany that was different from that of West Germany and socialist in nature yet still unmistakably German. An analysis of the endeavor of East German state officials offers a vivid example of how national identity is culturally constructed.

14. Folk dances often directly reference movements from agrarian labor and manufacturing.

15. Expressionism, cubism, surrealism, and most other avant-garde movements were regarded as being at odds with socialist realism. For a more thorough discussion of socialist realism and its noncongruence with Marxist-Leninist philosophy, see my discussion of the subject in chapters 2 and 4.

16. *Material für die Bildungs- und Erziehungsarbeit der Volkskunstgruppen*, 17.

17. This dance belongs to a group of dances called *Wickler* (winder), which is a relatively new form of pair or trio dances that first appeared at the beginning of the nineteenth century in parts of Bavaria, Austria, Slovakia, Saxony, and Silesia. Aenne Goldschmidt, the principal contemporary dance scholar on German folk dances, classifies the *Wickler* as a group of dances that derives from two larger categories of dances called *Laendler* and *Steyrer*, because the *Wickler* shares the spinning and turning part with them yet lacks the integration of courtship in the originals. Specific forms of it were danced in East Germany in Saxony and Lusatia, and the authors of *Material für die Bildungs- und Erziehungsarbeit der Volkskunstgruppen* seemed to have drawn from a variation of these local modifications of the *Spinnradl* (Goldschmidt, *Handbuch des deutschen Volkstanzes*, 154). The Ministry of Culture contracted Goldschmidt to put together an all-encompassing compendium of folk dance. The resulting *Handbuch des deutschen Volkstanzes* (*Handbook of German Folk Dance*) was first published in 1966 and was reissued four times before German reunification in 1990.

18. The Zentralhaus für Laienkunst was later renamed the Zentralhaus für Kultur-arbeit. It published two journals, *Volkskunst* (*Folk Art*), beginning in 1952, and *Volkstanz* (*Folk Dance*), starting in 1958 (Heising and Römer, *Der Tanz im "künstlerischen Volksschaffen" der DDR*, 28). Heising and Römer's history of folk dance and amateur dance in East Germany is the only publication on the subject in German and thus is most valuable. A comprehensive study of the vast amateur dance scene does not exist and is unlikely to be published, because most of the material on amateur dance companies is now scattered into private collections or even lost. For a discussion of amateur and folk dance in Saxony, see Klotzsche and Römer, *Tanz in Sachsen*.

19. Heising and Römer, *Der Tanz im "künstlerischen Volksschaffen" der DDR*, 44.

20. The Fest des deutschen Volkstanzes celebrated amateur and folk dance in Rudolstadt until 1960. The event was replaced by Fest des Liedes und des Tanzes der DDR in 1964, which changed its name to Tanz- und Musikfest der DDR in 1967, finally becoming the Tanzfest der DDR in 1970. It continued until the reunification and then became the still-existing Tanz und FolkFest in 1991. The GDR festivals were held every other year or annually with some gaps increasingly focusing on dance. The Tanz und FolkFest is an annual festival that highlights alternative folk music. Heising and Römer, *Der Tanz im "künstlerischen Volksschaffen" der DDR*, 142–53.

21. Ibid., 37.

22. All these companies underwent several name changes throughout their existence; for instance Staatliches Volkskunstensemble became DDR Tanzensemble, and Staatliches Dorfensemble changed to DDR Volksensemble. Some of these name changes indicated a shift from an exclusive folk emphasis to a broader program that included ballet, modern, and jazz. Yet some of the companies, such as the Staatliches Ensemble für sorbische Volkskunst, which was established to research and perform dances and music from this German minority group, remain folk companies to this day (Heising and Römer, *Der Tanz im "künstlerischen Volksschaffen" der DDR*, 28, 33, 144).

23. For instance, Aenne Goldschmidt and Rosemarie Lettow-Schulz, two of the directors of these professional companies, are trained ethnographers and have published extensively on folk dance.

24. Goldschmidt, Lettow, and Fritsch, *Der Tanz in der Laienkunst*, 51.

25. Ibid., 77.

26. Doerwaldt, *Der Volkstanz*, 49.

27. Lipsia is the Latin name of the first settlements that later would become the city of Leipzig in Saxony. There were other choreographed social dances with names that commemorated locations such as *Berolina* (Berlin) or that were just linguistic creations, such as *Pertutti*.

28. The promenade position is a V-shaped position in which the two dancers face each other, slightly opening the position in the direction that they dance. The front hands are often lifted to chest level or higher, while the man holds the woman in the back. The position can be opened and closed in the front as needed, effectively making the dancers move with their fronts in the direction they dance or making them move sideways.

29. Even in the 1980s during my own social dance lessons, the dance instructions were combined with tutoring on how to behave toward the opposite gender. This is true for social dance classes in other cultures.

30. Interestingly enough, folk dance and folk music was associated with a resistance movement in the middle of the 1970s. Yet these movements were often influenced by

counterculture and Western approaches to folk music, thus countering the state-prescribed folk.

31. *SUPERillu Spezial*, 67. Alo Koll was the leader of a band from Leipzig.

32. Nevertheless, the demonstration of young people in Leipzig led to the decline of the *Lipsi* (*SUPERillu Spezial*, 67).

33. They ask, "Dear Plan, dear Plan, what have you done for us?" The Plan replies, "I brought you shoes and clothes, I turned black bread white, that's what I did" (*Volkstanz-Sammlung*, 8). In two following verses, the young dancers ask what else the Plan has provided for them, and what he will do in the future. The Plan answers these questions by pointing out that he has built schools and houses everywhere and that he will create prosperity at all times for a future as bright as it had never been seen before. The dance concludes with the dancers asking what their part in this project should be. The Plan requests that they learn and that they keep a lookout for peace, because peace makes everyone happy.

34. Goldschmidt, *Handbuch des deutschen Volkstanzes*, 253, 336.

35. Goewe, "Folklore Heute."

36. The company was named after the German communist poet Erich Weinert (1890–1953), who was a leading figure in educational and cultural institutions in East Germany after his return from exile in the Soviet Union in 1946. Weinert fought in the Spanish Civil War and created propaganda material for the Soviet Union that was distributed behind Germany's enemy lines during World War II to encourage German soldiers to desert the National Socialist army.

37. With a combination of folk dances and songs as well as propaganda material, the Alexandrov Ensemble upheld and restored Soviet soldiers' motivation during their battles with German troops during World War II.

38. Landfeld, "Das Profil einer sozialistischen Tänzerpersönlichkeit im Erich-Weinert-Ensemble der NVA," 28–30.

39. "Sozialistische Persönlichkeit ist das sich im Prozeß der gesellschaftlichen Arbeit selbst gestaltende und entwickelnde Individuum, das unter der Führung der marxistisch-leninistischen Partei in Gemeinschaft mit anderen Menschen seinen Lebensprozeß in ständig wachsendem Maße unter Kontrolle nimmt und in diesem Prozeß seine individuellen Fähigkeiten, seine produktiven Kräfte immer allseitiger entfaltet" (Klaus and Buhr, *Philosophisches Wörterbuch*, 922). East German governmental language is very hard to put into English, because it overly defines and loops back on terminologies and, if taken apart, often doesn't say anything of substance or contradicts itself. Here is an attempt of a translation of the above definition: "The socialist personality is a self-shaping and developing individual that is created in the process of social labor. It increasingly controls its life's development under the leadership of the Marxist-Leninist party and in community with other people. In this process of developing, socialist personalities always unfold their individual abilities and productive forces in a multi-faceted way."

40. Like the English term "personality," the German term "Persönlichkeit" origi-nated from the Latin term "persona." The Latin term was used to describe the mask of actors or their part.

41. The so-called *Grundlagenvertrag* from 1972 between East and West Germany established both countries as sovereign states. The contract was ratified in 1973.

42. Heising and Römer, *Der Tanz im "künstlerischen Volksschaffen" der DDR*, 84.

43. The ballet companies at the Staatsoper unter den Linden and the Komische Oper in Berlin, the Semperoper in Dresden, and the Leipzig Opera were the main state-funded dance companies with the best-trained dancers. Yet, with the general draft, the male dancers in these companies also had to serve in the army, giving the Erich-Weinert-Ensemble an advantage at these national competitions.

44. Draeger, "Auf der Suche nach Profil," 74.

45. See chapter 2 for a discussion of East German dance's relationship to modernism.

46. In 1988, another Erich-Weinert-Ensemble choreography received first prize at the ballet competition. Holger Bey's *Zimmer 15 (Room 15)* was a more direct critique of socialist structures. The choreography presented a vignette of a bureaucrat's rapid decline into madness and the subsequent encounter of other characters in an insane asylum. Utilizing a mixture of everyday and modern dance vocabulary to create a theatricalized grotesquery, the choreography seemed to comment on the state of affairs in East Germany at the time by comparing the society to the insane asylum (Draeger, "Auf der Suche nach Profil," 75).

47. Stabel, "Der Tanz in die 'entwickelte sozialistische Gesellschaft,'" 243.

48. I saw *Canto General* on May 13, 1989, at the Palast der Republik in Berlin during the Pfingsttreffen. *Canto General* was only performed twice and never restaged. I base my subsequent analysis on a recording from the archive of the Komische Oper Berlin.

49. Schmidt-Feister, *Canto General*.

50. Jameson, *The Political Unconscious*, 291.

Chapter 2. East German *Tanztheater*

1. Such limited economic and political assessments of modern progress have been critiqued in relation to other noncapitalist countries by postcolonial scholars; see Pence and Betts, introduction, 12.

2. Pence and Betts, introduction, 17.

3. Other counterparts are the primitive, the emotional, the classical, or the political. These counterparts are not exclusive of each other and are even often incorporated to update modernism.

4. Franko, *Dancing Modernism/Performing Politics*, 39; Manning, "Modernist Dogma and Postmodern Rhetoric"; "Letters from Sally Banes and Susan Manning."

5. Franko, *Dancing Modernism/Performing Politics*, 40.

6. Franko, "Some Notes on Yvonne Rainer, Modernism, Politics, Emotion, Performance, and the Aftermath," 290.

7. Jameson, *A Singular Modernity*, 124. Jameson presents a more complex view on the relationship between modernism and realism in his afterword to Bloch et al.'s 1977 *Aesthetics and Politics*, in which he discusses the incorporation of modernist principles into realism and a political modernism (206, 209).

8. The institution of the Tanztheater der Komischen Oper Berlin is congruent with the East German concept of *Tanztheater*.

9. See Lukács, "Critical Realism and Socialist Realism," or any of the East German documents cited in this chapter that support socialist realism and condemn formalism and decadence, both code words for modernism and abstraction. See also Petra Stuber's narration of the debate around socialist realism in post–World War II East Germany in *Spielräume und Grenzen*, and Gay Morris's treatment of the Cold War rhetoric in the United States in *A Game for Dancers*.

10. The theorization of African American dance faces a comparable dilemma. Richard Green in "(Up)Staging the Primitive: Pearl Primus and 'the Negro Problem' in American Dance" and Anthea Kraut in *Choreographing the Folk* both deal with the complex issue of African American modern artistry and the antagonism between a modernist aesthetic and African American identity. Both authors are concerned with the erasure of African American choreographers and dancers from canonical dance history. Yet in their analysis of Pearl Primus and Zora Neale Hurston, respectively, they move beyond Brenda Dixon Gottschild's valuable work in which she reveals the influence of African American artists and through them an Africanist aesthetic on North American dance (*Digging the Africanist Presence in African American Performance*, 11–19). Green supplements Gottschild's project by problematizing the evaluation of African American dancers and choreographers as African American or modern but never as both. Such categorization can help in investigating identitarian issues in their work; at the same time, however, it excludes African American dance artists from any discourse on modern art and thus limits the development of an account of modernism across racial lines. Kraut also points to the ability of white dancers "to construct themselves as innovative artists working with black 'raw material'" (*Choreographing the Folk*, 174). By contrast, the innovation of black dancers is reduced to a cultural expression and not included in the modernist canon. Gay Morris points to the same issue in her exploration of Pearl Primus's and Talley Beatty's insistence on virtuosity as an important expression for African American artists (*A Game for Dancers*, 115–46).

11. Schmidt, *Tanztheater in Deutschland*, 219.

12. Schmidt's refusal to label Schilling's work "Tanztheater" goes hand in hand with his dismissal of East German dance as antimodern. Schmidt elaborates that the term "Tanztheater" had most likely been used for the first time by Kurt Jooss in "Die Sprache des Tanztheaters" ("The Language of Dance Theater") in 1935. However, Jooss's daughter Anna Markard states that Jooss first used the term in a lecture at the second Dancers' Congress in Essen in 1928 (*The Green Table*, 20) and Karl Eric Toepfer provides an article by Laban from 1922 as an earlier employment of the term (*Empire of Ecstasy*, 397).

In 1966, echoing his mentor Walter Felsenstein's use of the term *Musiktheater* (music theater), Schilling named his company Tanztheater der Komischen Oper Berlin. The label was of course programmatic. The first time a West German choreographer used the term *Tanztheater* was in 1972, when Gerhard Bohner named his company Tanztheater Darmstadt (Schmidt, *Tanztheater in Deutschland*, 7). Pina Bausch began her work with the Tanztheater Wuppertal in 1973.

As this abbreviated chronology of the term *Tanztheater* demonstrates, to dismiss Schilling's work as not being *Tanztheater* holds up neither historically nor programmatically. Schilling used the term to align his work with the progressive approach to opera at the Komische Oper Berlin in East Germany and to signal his rethinking of stage dance in relation to ballet and modern dance. West German choreographers such as Pina Bausch, Gerhard Bohner, Reinhild Hoffmann, and Susanne Linke similarly utilized the term to indicate a break with traditional dance productions, mostly the ballet that dominated theatrical dance in West Germany after World War II. These choreographers are often united under the umbrella term *Tanztheater*, even though their work is far from uniform and inevitably evolved over the course of their individual careers.

13. Schmidt, *Tanztheater in Deutschland*, 220.

14. Goeschen, "From Socialist Realism to Art in Socialism," 46.

15. Ibid., 46.

16. Manning, *Ecstasy and the Demon*, xxii.

17. Goeschen, *Vom sozialistischen Realismus zur Kunst im Sozialismus*, 7.

18. Baakmann and Craven, "An Introduction to Modernism–Fascism–Postmodernism"; Goeschen, "From Socialist Realism to Art in Socialism."

19. Berman, *Preface to Modernism*, 3.

20. Ibid., 3.

21. Habermas, *Die Moderne*, 33.

22. Ibid., 34.

23. Jameson, *A Singular Modernity*, 99; Lefebvre, *Einführung in die Modernität*, 197.

24. Jameson, *A Singular Modernity*, 99.

25. Friedman, "Definitional Excursions," 501.

26. Albright, *Traces of Light*.

27. Funkenstein, "Engendering Abstraction," 390.

28. Ibid., 403.

29. These are features that have been repeatedly mentioned in the literature on modernism. They are, of course, debatable and have been debated over the decades. It becomes clear how much they are informed by Greenbergian and U.S. discourse on modern dance more generally. How much a definition of modernism has been unified retrospectively becomes apparent, however, when even contemporary German dance scholars rely on these features and not, for instance, Adorno's much more politically conscious *ästhetische Moderne* in their discussions of *Ausdruckstanz* or modern dance. See, for instance, Huschka, *Moderner Tanz*; Siegmund, *Abwesenheit*; and Brandstetter, "Still/Motion." As I explain, my utilization of this definition is determined by the East German rhetoric decrying modernism, formalism, and decadence.

30. Morris, *A Game for Dancers*, 12.

31. Even Harold Rosenberg, who in his 1952 "American Action Painters" includes the body and its art making into the definition of modern art, had to accept the dominating power of Greenberg's definition. For a sophisticated critique of Rosenberg's position and its reduction of Pollock's body to a rhetoric, see Jones, *Body Art/Performing the Subject*, 72–73. See also Greenberg's "Avant-Garde and Kitsch." Here, he establishes some of the important characteristics of modern art, which he clarifies in his 1960s "Modernist Painting." Interestingly enough, at the time of the publication of "Avant-Garde and Kitsch," Greenberg regarded socialism as the future savior of genuine art from the takeover by kitsch.

32. Greenberg, "American-Type Painting," 208–29.

33. Jones, *Body Art/Performing the Subject*, 74–76.

34. Ibid., 271n77.

35. Franko, "Some Notes on Yvonne Rainer, Modernism, Politics, Emotion, Performance, and the Aftermath," 290.

36. Auslander, "Motional Abstraction," 159.

37. Ibid., 166.

38. Morris, *A Game for Dancers*, 182.

39. Morris is referring to both Nikolais's and Cunningham's work as modern dance and not—as many scholars do—as postmodern dance. I agree with her, based on U.S. definitions of modernism that were—as I explain in this chapter—defined by art historical

discourse and thus highly political. For a discussion of the relationship between modernism and postmodernism, see the ever-interesting debate between Sally Banes and Susan Manning.

40. Morris, *A Game for Dancers*, 201.

41. Ibid., 203.

42. In 1985, the Dresden Opera moved back into the rebuilt Semperoper building. The company is now the Sächsische Staatsoper Dresden.

43. Even though East Berlin was technically not a part of East Germany but an independent area, the GDR used it as its seat of government and labeled it Berlin, capital of the GDR. To emphasize its special place, the government invested in the city and supplied more funding for the arts there. The most important East German theatrical institutions had their seat in East Berlin and censorship was exercised more cautiously, due to the international visibility of these institutions.

44. German theaters and operas commonly house several of the performing arts under one roof. The *Intendant* (director) of such houses is a very powerful person who oversees the entire production in all disciplines and effectively shapes the artistic direction of the house.

45. In reality, Felsenstein saw more than just this one choreography and more than the two dancers in *La Mer*. See the 1986 video *La Mer*.

46. Fuchs, *The Music Theatre of Walter Felsenstein*, 14.

47. Hasche, Schölling, and Fiebach, *Theater in der DDR*, 14.

48. Ibid., 15.

49. Hintze, Risi, and Sollich, *Realistisches Musiktheater*.

50. Fuchs, *The Music Theatre of Walter Felsenstein*, 15.

51. Köllinger, *Tanztheater*, 8.

52. Schilling's utilization of ballet, folk (German and non-Western), modern, jazz, and pedestrian vocabularies is evident in many of his choreographies. It is also manifested in descriptions of his choreographies by his assistants and dramaturges. See, for instance, Joachim Ahne and Hermann Neef's description of the prologue to *Schwarze Vögel*, in which he refers to a Cébron arabesque and a fourth ballet position (*Dokumentation zur Uraufführung des Balletts "Schwarze Vögel" von Köllinger, Katzer, Schilling*, 54).

53. Ahne and Neef, *Dokumentation zur Uraufführung des Balletts "Schwarze Vögel" von Köllinger, Katzer, Schilling*, 39.

54. Willi Bredel, Lion Feuchtwanger, and Bertolt Brecht served as editors of *Das Wort*, which was established in 1935. Bredel left the journal in 1937 to participate in the Spanish Civil War. Fritz Erpenbeck filled this position from then on.

55. Herd and Obermayer, *A Glossary of German Literary Terms*, 250.

56. Hawthorn, *A Glossary of Contemporary Literary Theory*, 205.

57. Kwiatkowski, *Schüler-Duden*, 384.

58. I am using the term "reality" in line with its employment by socialist propaganda. I am fully aware that there is no such thing as an objective reality.

59. After his return from exile in the Soviet Union in 1954, Kurella became one of the most influential cultural politicians in the GDR and worked tirelessly for the implementation of socialist realism. Balázs, who eventually returned to his native Hungary, is mostly known for his film theoretical work. Lukács also returned to his native Hungary and continued to influence Marxist aesthetics and politics.

60. Stuber, *Spielräume und Grenzen*, 73. Stuber focuses on the two decades after the founding of the GDR and on the impact of social developments during these years on the theater practice of the 1970s and 1980s. Stuber carefully draws connections among a selected wealth of material, demonstrating a complex cause-and-effect relation between art and politics. Her approach demystifies history and reveals how history is constructed through social interaction.

61. The position of all three authors stands in a close relationship to that of the First Congress of Soviet Writers in 1934, as articulated by Andrej A. Zhdanov in his speech, in which he called for relying on tradition rather than new inventions and in which he rejected the idea of experimentation in socialist art. The Communist Party of Germany came to a similar conclusion by focusing on the German classical tradition in the fight against fascism at the party's convention in Brussels in October 1935; see Stuber, *Spielräume und Grenzen*, 72.

62. Realists, such as Thomas Aquinas, maintain that the thing behind the name exists independently of us and that it is possible to understand the essence of all things through their names. As a result, Aquinas's school of thought defines the names as real. Nominalists, on the other hand, among them Ockham, take the terms and the essence to be only names (*nomina*).

63. Stuber, e-mail to author, Dec. 4, 2000.

64. As for instance in the articles that were signed by "Orlow." "Orlow" functioned as pseudonym for a number of Soviet and East German authors who critiqued developments in all realms of art in the Soviet Occupation Zone and during the first years of the GDR's existence; see Stuber, *Spielräume und Grenzen*, 112.

65. Ibid., 120. The plenum took place March 15–17. The function and form of art in the GDR was debated only on the last day. The second day dealt with sports and body culture, suggesting the importance of both of these to the creation of a socialist national identity.

66. Qtd. in Stuber, *Spielräume und Grenzen*, 127, emphasis in original.

67. Ibid., 103. Among the excluded writers and philosophers were several representatives of German Romanticism, who questioned the continuity of history and the idea of objective truth (Heinrich von Kleist, E. T. A. Hoffmann, and both Schlegel brothers), Nietzsche, who critiqued history, truth, and order, and the expressionists, dadaists, surrealists, and functionalists, all of whom challenged the established division between art and reality and fought for an emancipation of art.

68. Stalin, "Marxism and the National Question."

69. Stuber, *Spielräume und Grenzen*, 104. This list appeared in an article by Wilhelm Girnus titled "Wo stehen die Feinde der deutschen Kunst? Bemerkungen zur Frage des Formalismus und des Kosmopolitismus" ("Where Do the Enemies of German Art Stand? Notes on the Question of Formalism and Cosmopolitanism)"; it was published Feb. 13–18, 1951.

70. Staatliche Kommision für Kunstangelegenheiten, *Zur Diskussion: Realismus im Tanz*, 5.

71. Ibid., 8. Martin Sporck was a pseudonym used by Gustav Just, who at the time was the head of the SED's art division; see Stabel, "Die grosse Geste," 217.

72. Staatliche Kommision für Kunstangelegenheiten, *Zur Diskussion: Realismus im Tanz*, 13.

73. Even their terminology varied, as they referred to *Ausdruckstanz, Neuer Künstlerischer Tanz*, and modern dance.

74. Staatliche Kommision für Kunstangelegenheiten, *Zur Diskussion: Realismus im Tanz*, 77.

75. Ibid., 60.

76. Ibid., 62.

77. East German dictionaries have remarkably few entries on terms such as "Moderne," "ästhetische Moderne," "Modernität," and "Modernismus" that relate to modernism. In German, the term "Modernismus" refers to a movement in the Catholic Church during the nineteenth and twentieth centuries that attempted to align Catholic dogma with modern developments in Western societies. Most of the "Modernismus" entries in East German dictionaries refer to this development.

78. Fiedler and Gurst, *Meyers Jugendlexikon Philosophie*, 141–42.

79. Ibid., 142.

80. Greenberg, "Avant-Garde and Kitsch," 21–33.

81. Lukács in the expressionism debate as well as early Soviet socialist realist discourse appealed to both of these concepts.

82. Fiedler and Gurst, *Meyers Jugendlexikon Philosophie*, 74. See also Böhme et al., *Kleines politisches Wörterbuch*, 120, 204, for earlier definitions of decadence and formalism. The similarity of these definitions illustrates that East German rhetoric did not update its definition of modernism over the years.

83. Fiedler and Gurst, *Meyers Jugendlexikon Philosophie*, 39.

84. Rebling, *Ballettfibel*, 65. Schilling always cites the music as his main inspiration for *La Mer*.

85. Liepold, "Der Kampf gegen den Formalismus, Teil 2 1958–1965."

86. I base my analysis on the 1980 restaging of *La Mer* that was filmed and subsequently broadcast on DFF, the East German TV station. Pictures of earlier productions show leotards with abstractly painted waves or simple long leggings for the male dancer.

87. Köllinger, *Tanztheater*, 74. Köllinger was one of the most visible dance scholars in East Germany. He published numerous books on Schilling's *Tanztheater* that often elaborate on the dramaturgy of specific works and situate them inside the socialist discourse on dance.

88. Köllinger, *Der Tanz*, 34–35.

89. Rebling, *Ballettfibel*, 45. The term "Ballett" in German not only connotes classical or Romantic ballet utilizing ballet techniques and ballet conventions but can also be used to refer to other choreographies that depart from ballet technique. See Gommlich, *Showtanz*, 47. Thus, Rebling's ballet history references a variety of dance works.

90. Franko, *Dancing Modernism / Performing Politics*, xi.

91. Köllinger, *Tanztheater*, 40.

92. As an important artist, Schilling was accorded the privilege of traveling outside socialist countries and thus had knowledge of nonsocialist dance. He was able to meet and keep in contact with international choreographers and follow their work. East German officials supported such exchange in the hope that it would result in East German dance becoming an internationally recognized form. Despite *Match*'s similarities to Vaslav Nijinsky's *Jeux* (1913), it is not likely that this early modernist choreography was a major influence on it. Millicent Hodson and Kenneth Archer's reconstruction of

Jeux was performed in 1996 by the Teatro filarmonic of the Arena di Verona, twenty-five years after the 1971 premiere of *Match*; see Acocella, "The Lost Nijinsky."

93. My analysis is based on a broadcast of *Rhythmus* by the DFF.

94. Hasche, Schölling, and Feibach, *Theater in der DDR*, 53.

95. Albright and Gere, *Taken by Surprise*, xv.

96. Ibid., 4.

97. Gommlich, *Showtanz*.

98. Ibid., 12.

99. Interestingly enough, Werner Gommlich was one of the key critics of the dance.

100. Köllinger, *Tanztheater*, 46.

101. Gommlich, *Showtanz*, 38.

102. Ibid., 36–37. Gommlich cites the Russian literary critic Vissarion G. Belinsky, who advocated realistic literature that had a moral stance and that was socially conscious and thus capable of transforming society.

103. Morris, *A Game for Dancers*; Franko, *Dancing Modernism/Performing Politics*.

104. Franko, *Dancing Modernism/Performing Politics*, xi.

105. Just to provide a context for the enormity of these numbers, Mühlhausen, the Thuringian city where Thomas Müntzer lived, preached, and was later executed, was, with ten thousand inhabitants, one of the largest cities in fifteenth-century "Germany." Cologne was the largest with around forty thousand.

106. See Engels, *Der deutsche Bauernkrieg*, or, in English, Engels, *The Peasant War in Germany*.

107. Tübke's painting is in itself a very interesting work of art. The whole project was commissioned and supported by the East German government and was in particular promoted by the then minister of culture, Hans-Joachim Hoffmann. Yet, Tübke, one of the most famous and influential painters (of the now famed Hochschule für Grafik und Buchkunst in Leipzig that trained Neo Rauch, currently one of the most famous German painters), only agreed to the project because he was granted complete artistic control. The painting ended up not being a naturalist depiction of the battle, which was the original intent and in line with socialist realist imperatives, but a fascinating meditation on the Renaissance world and society in general. The painting is created in an allegorical and Renaissance style and allows a variety of interpretations, ranging from a pessimistic depiction of the doom of the world to that of a foretelling of the end of East German society. The 18- × 44-meter-long painting is still on exhibit in Bad Frankenhausen and makes for fascinating viewing.

108. Köllinger, *Tanztheater*, 50.

109. Köllinger's phrasing is hard to translate, because it is one of many of his statements that sound interesting but that on closer reading don't always make sense. The German reads "Nicht Bewegungs-'Realismus', sondern bewegender Realismus bestimmte die Szene" (*Tanztheater*, 50).

110. Ibid., 51.

111. The audience of the Tanztheater der Komischen Oper Berlin was more loyal and younger than that of the neighboring Staatsoper unter den Linden. The Staatsoper presented much more of the classical ballet repertoire. Schilling's audience was also aware of these productions (and given the affordable ticket prices probably also saw them), but they preferred Schilling's experimentation over tradition.

112. The program notes describe the prologue as a ritual dance from ancient times conjuring up the return of spring (Ahne and Neef, *Dokumentation zur Uraufführung des Balletts "Schwarze Vögel" von Köllinger, Katzer, Schilling*, 73).

113. Bausch premiered *Le sacre du printemps* as part of an evening of dance called *Frühlingsopfer* together with *Wind von West* and *Der zweite Frühling* on December 3, 1975, in Wuppertal. For a thorough analysis of Bausch's *Le sacre du printemps* using different methodological approaches, see Brandstetter and Klein, *Methoden der Tanzwissenschaft*.

114. An emphasis on the primitive in this sequence of Schilling's choreography is also an important aspect of his modernist approach. In his description of an earlier choreographic version of the prologue, Schilling's assistant Joachim Ahne refers to the scene as a primitive or pagan ritual that depicted the still-existing unity between human-kind and nature (Ahne and Neef, *Dokumentation zur Uraufführung des Balletts "Schwarze Vögel" von Köllinger, Katzer, Schilling*, 53).

115. Some of the scenes in *Schwarze Vögel* are reminiscent of Graham's *Appalachian Spring*, in which a narrative seems present and yet the characters don't develop and remain as types.

116. *Kammertanz* is a choreographic form for just a few dancers or even soloists. It stands in contrast to larger group and mass choreographies. The term originated in small choreographies performed in bourgeois living rooms in Germany. East German officials used the term to emphasize choreographies that focused on individuality and the personal.

117. See *Tom Schilling: Zum 70. Geburtstag.*

118. For an account of surveillance and defection in relation to East German dance, see Stabel, *IM "Tänzer."*

119. Köllinger, *Tanztheater*, 53.

120. Goeschen, "From Socialist Realism to Art in Socialism," 47. Even as late as 1986, the SED was still insisting on the term "socialist realism" (Sozialistische Einheits-partei Deutschlands, *Protokoll des Verhandlungen des XI. Parteitages der Sozialistischen Einheits-partei Deutschlands*, 84).

121. Goeschen, "From Socialist Realism to Art in Socialism," 47. The time frame for dance needs to be shifted slightly forward; there were new developments at the end of the 1970s.

Chapter 3. Resistive Motions in the East

1. Barba has confirmed my evaluation; see his "Research into Corporeality," 87.

2. Barba uses the term "reenactment" to highlight his striving for accuracy in the reconstruction. He wanted to create an "illusion of authenticity" ("Research into Corporeality," 84). Christel Stalpaert, the European scholar who mentioned Barba to the group of us sitting around the conference table, celebrates his approach as not just reproducing but highlighting the differences between the iconic archival body of Wigman and his own body as a living archive ("Reenacting Modernity").

3. For an analysis of the lecture performance as a stage genre, see Bleeker, "Lecture Performance as Contemporary Dance."

4. She didn't mention Betsy Fisher's reconstruction from 1998–99 either. Fisher, a professor at the University of Hawaii at Manoa, worked with Hoyer's heir Waltraud Luley and Thomas Schallmann on the reconstruction and Laban's notation of the dances. It would be an interesting project to speculate on the reasons why the West

German dance scholar did not mention this reconstruction, but that would go beyond my argument here.

5. Literature on Hoyer's choreography and the reconstructions use the spelling *Affectos humanos* and *Afectos Humanos*. I asked Siegert about her spelling and she replied that Hoyer used the Spanish spelling because she was in La Plata when she started to engage with Spinoza's work (Siegert, e-mail to author, Jan. 20, 2012). The Deutsches Tanzarchiv Köln, which holds Hoyer's archive, affirmed that Hoyer was inconsistent in her spelling of the title. Even her program notes from 1962 used "Affectos Humanos" on March 13 and "Affektos Humanos" on June 1. Hoyer also used "Afectos Humanos" in her notebooks (DHNh.19, Obj. Nr 32658, S 114, Hesse, Deutsches Tanzarchiv Köln, e-mail to author, March 29, 2012). I decided to use Siegert's spelling because her work is central to my investigation.

6. Kaiser and Petzold, *Boheme und Diktatur in der DDR*, 24.

7. The petition, dated November 17, 1976, stated: "Wolf Biermann was and is an inconvenient poet—he shares this with many poets of the past. Considering Marx's words in his 'Eighteeenth Brumaire,' where he states that the proletarian revolution has to critique itself constantly, our socialist society, unlike other anachronistic forms of societies, should be able to take such inconveniences in a relaxed and thoughtful manner. We do not identify with each of Biermann's words and actions, and we distance ourselves from the attempt to use the events around Biermann against the GDR. Despite his critique, Biermann himself has never, not even in Cologne, left any doubt which of the two German states he supports. We protest against his expelling and ask that you please consider this measure" (Krug, *Abgehauen*, 166).

8. Enzensberger, "Baukasten zu einer Theorie der Medien," 163.

9. For a description of the function of the media in the GDR, see Bisky, "Massenmedien und sozialistische Kultur," 64–66.

10. As early as 1962, Renft was prohibited from recording and performing. The band was allowed to perform again between 1967 and 1974, but after the final ban in 1975, members of the band emigrated to West Germany (see the history on the band's website, http://www.renft.de/pages/historie.php, accessed June 3, 2011).

11. See Kaiser and Petzold, *Boheme und Diktatur in der DDR*, for further documentation on this generational divide.

12. Ibid., 15–17.

13. For critiques of Habermas's theory, see Fraser, "Rethinking the Public Sphere"; Hardt and Negri, *Commonwealth*; and Hardt and Negri, *Multitude*.

14. Habermas, *The Structural Transformation of the Public Sphere*, 74.

15. Ibid., 159.

16. Andrew Hewitt effects just such a reductive application of Habermas's understanding of the development of the public sphere to dance; see *Social Choreography*, 32.

17. One aspect would be the construction of a national identity through female dance in the public sphere. See Tomko, *Dancing Class*; and Ross, *Margaret H'Doubler and the Beginning of Dance in American Education*.

18. Habermas, *The Structural Transformation of the Public Sphere*, 128, 139, 129.

19. This is often the Western notion of dance in East Germany or socialism in general.

20. Nickel, "Women in the German Democratic Republic and in the New Federal States," 144, 139.

21. For an elaborate analysis of women's position in the GDR and its depiction in media, see Dölling, "'Unsere Muttis arbeiten wie ein Mann.'"

22. Amt für Information der Regierung der Deutschen Demokratischen Republik, *Die Verfassung der Deutschen Demokratischen Republik*, 15, 23.

23. I am using the terms "materialism" and "materialist" in the Marxist sense, referring to Marx's theorization of human society in his historical materialism. I am not referring to consumerism.

24. See, for instance, Fenemore, *Sex, Thugs and Rock 'n' Roll*, 22, on female teenage embodiment.

25. *Familiengesetzbuch*, 3.1.2.

26. Böhme et al., eds., *Kleines politisches Wörterbuch*, 195.

27. Habermas, *The Structural Transformation of the Public Sphere*, 139.

28. Ibid., 178.

29. Only the Republic of Romania was not a part of this association. Chris Chesher, who demystifies "virtual reality" (VR) in his article "Colonizing Virtual Reality," dates the appearance of VR to 1989, the year of the fall of the Berlin Wall. Besides explaining why he doesn't share the enthusiasm of most academics for VR and cyberspace, Chesher also illuminates the production of computer history by what he calls its "VR fraternity."

30. Poster, "Databases as Discourse," 190.

31. Since the GDR still functioned as a modern society, dreaming of the ideal of the socialist personality, it is not surprising that it made a distinction between the mass body and the individual body. The relation between the secret and the nonsecret, which are connected to issues of public and private, are also important to this issue. For an elaboration on these issues in connection with a deconstruction of the archive, see Derrida, *Archive Fever*.

32. Poster, "Databases as Discourse," 186.

33. Ibid., 190.

34. Bourdieu, "The Objective Limits of Objectivism"; Bourdieu, "Structures and the Habitus."

35. Cresswell, *In Place / Out of Place*, 21–27.

36. Gramsci, *Prison Notebooks*, 233–38.

37. Despite Scott's awareness of performed compliance in public areas and resistance in hidden parts, he still defines the latter as similar in their form. Such lack of distinction is problematic as this chapter with three very different kinds of resistances establishes.

38. Foster, *Choreographing History*, 5.

39. A wealth of material exists on East German oppositional groups and individuals, yet none of it looks at embodiment and choreography as a resistive practice. See, for instance, Kowalczuk, *Endspiel*; Neubert and Eisenfeld, *Macht Ohnmacht Gegenmacht*; Fricke, *Opposition und Widerstand in der DDR*; Gehrke and Rüddenklau, . . . *das war doch nicht unsere Alternative*; Kowalczuk, *Freiheit und Öffentlichkeit*; Kowalczuk, Sello, and Weber, *Für ein freies Land mit freien Menschen*; Neubert, *Geschichte der Opposition in der DDR 1949–1989*; Pollack, *Politischer Protest*; Poppe, Eckert, and Kowalczuk, *Zwischen Selbstbehauptung und Anpassung*; Prokop, *1956*; Rüddenklau, *Störenfried*; Scheer, *Vision und Wirklichkeit*; Subklew-Jeutner, *Der Pankower Friedenskreis*; and Klein, *Frieden und Gerechtigkeit*.

40. Schmidt, "Sensibel aber mit voller Kraft auf der Suche nach dem Eigenen," 18.

41. As Siegert notes, Schilling had just lost several dancers who defected during a tour and so was disillusioned at the time (ibid.).

42. Ibid., 20.

43. Schmidt, *Tanztheater in Deutschland*, 220.

44. See Ladopoulos, "Die Rolle der Improvisation in Geschichte und Gegenwart des modernen Tanzes in Dresden"; and Kaiser and Petzold, *Boheme und Diktatur in der DDR*, 145–90.

45. Landschaften, *Progreß*, program notes.

46. Frede and Siegert, "'Sich Aufmachen, Schöpferisch Sein': Gespräch mit Arila Siegert," 34.

47. Vogelsang wrote *Gedanken zur Situation des Neuen Künstlerischen Tanzes*, *Gedanken über die Technik des Neuen künstlerischen Tanzes und Vorschläge zu ihrer Fixierung*, and *Gedanken über die Pädagogik des Neuen Künstlerischen Tanzes*, all of which were written between 1951 and 1953 (Kant, "*Was bleibt?*," 139). Kant updates Kurt Peters's evaluation from 1997 in which he categorizes Vogelsang's writings only as an extension of Wigman's and Laban's pedagogy from 1936 (Peters, "Ausdruckstanz," 8).

48. See Schnelle, "Reflexionen über Marianne Vogelsang."

49. Schmidt, *Tanztheater in Deutschland*, 220.

50. Famously, Wigman also refused to create a codified technique and have her dances preserved. Recently, Irene Sieben has complicated that refusal by emphasizing a remark made by Wigman in which she envisions the return of a past creation at another time: "A dance piece has its time, just as the dancer is caught in his own time, which allows him to use his body as an expressive instrument. That is the fate of dance. We have all experienced it and must recognize it. But this 'process' is not in vain. All experiences and creations made from that experience receive and fulfill their purpose. They live and continue to effect, under the skin, in a way under the surface, stimulating and fertilizing others. If it is a truly creative idea, it will rise from its burial place, and, freed from the weight of its ballast, emerge again at the right place and at the right time" ("Remembrance with a Future").

51. Helen Thomas states that the story of the reconstruction of Mikhail Fokine's *The Dying Swan* "raises questions about the origin of a work of art and the search for a definitive, authentic version" ("Reconstruction and Dance," 42). She elaborates, noting that ownership, copyright, and intention become complex issues in the transition of the work from one body to another, mediated or not. Rebecca Schneider, who asks about the myth of originality in her discussion of solo works, also brings up issues of authenticity, authorship, copy, and repetition ("Solo Solo Solo," 26). Schneider problematizes, among multiple other terms, the authority of the great singular canonical work and exposes its replication of a patriarchic lineage of artistic creation.

52. Siegmund, "Affekt, Technik, Diskurs," 15, 17. Mark Franko foreshadows Siegmund's assessment on the distinct issues raised by dance from different eras through an investigation of modern dance and baroque dance reconstructions; see "Repeatability, Reconstruction and Beyond."

53. See Siegel, *Watching the Dance Go By*, which set off a whole school of this kind of theorization of dance. Simone Willeit, however, postulates a shift in the 1990s in the aim of reconstruction from a preservation of the past to a historiographic practice. She is interested in the "continuities and breaks" that create a rhizome among old and new works ("Stolpern und Unzulänglichkeiten," 15).

54. Thomas points out that there are hierarchies in dance reconstructions, which value culture either as in high art or in folk traditions. Dance has to be either theatrical or connected to the national culture to ensure an archival and reconstructive effort ("Reconstruction," 34). I would argue that even though modern—and to a certain extent

postmodern—dance programmatically challenges the theatrical institution by often not appearing on stages but instead in alternative performance spaces such as salons, outdoors, churches, and galleries, these dances achieve their institutionalization through other means. Modern choreographers often established companies, schools, and standing companies. Approaches from postmodern dance became the template of choreography classes in Western dance departments. Non-Western dance forms achieve reconstructive value by becoming part of ethnographic projects or as indicators of culture. This uneven application of reconstruction raises ethical questions or at the very least simply highlights existing hierarchies in dance.

55. Müller, Peter, and Schuldt, *Dore Hoyer.*

56. See the 1967 DVD *Afectos Humanos.*

57. Willeit, "Stolpern und Unzulänglichkeiten," 52. The extent to which this was a choice or Linke's general approach to dance can be debated.

58. See Nachbar, "ReKonstruct."

59. Nachbar's title is already so conceptual that it is impossible to translate. He evokes the idea of the original, picking up, keeping, erasing, sublating just with these words. The term "Aufhebung" is also a philosophical term used by Hegel and explored in its complexity by Derrida.

60. Nachbar also used part of the episode in his lecture in 2000.

61. See Willeit, "Stolpern und Unzulänglichkeiten," 19, for a different take on the same scene and Nachbar, "ReKonstruct," 91, for the earlier version of the joke.

62. See Sieben, "Tanz-Rekonstruktionen."

63. Fisher also reconstructed work by Lotte Goslar, Rosalie Chladek, Mary Wigman, Marianne Vogelsang, Hanya Holm, Alwin Nikolais, Murray Louis, Hanna Berger, and Beverly Blossom (Rouhiainen, "Embodying Modern Dance History"). See also Fisher, *Creating and Re-Creating Dance.*

64. Jérôme Bel, Xavier Le Roy, Thomas Plischke, Thomas Lehmen, Meg Stuart, Janez Jansa, and Martin Lofsnes are other artists working with reconstructions.

65. Siegmund, "Affect, Technik, Diskurs," 19.

66. "Original and Revival: Geschichts-Schreibung im Tanz," University of Bern, Switzerland, Nov. 2008.

67. Franko, *The Work of Dance,* 11.

68. Interestingly enough, Susan Manning told me that she felt the same way about Linke's *Afectos Humanos.*

69. For instance, *Viktor* was produced in 1986 in collaboration with Teatro Argentina and the city of Rome.

70. Schmidt, *Tanztheater in Deutschland,* 111.

71. I am drawing on Franko's distinction between emotion and affect. He defines emotion as an individually and historically specific feeling, whereas he sees affect as essential and impersonal and thus universal (*The Work of Dance,* 9). As I elaborate in the previous chapter, the expulsion of emotion and focus on universal expression is modernist (Franko, *Dancing Modernism / Performing Politics,* xi). Thus, Nachbar's refocusing away from emotion, expression, and affect negates the modernist stance of Hoyer's choreography.

72. Siegmund, "Affekt, Technik, Diskurs," 17.

73. Franko asks if reconstruction is comparable to "historical references in post modern art." And following Hal Foster he queries whether reconstruction could "lead to revisionism for an empty culture-effect, which is for the sake of gesture alone" ("Repeatability, Reconstruction and Beyond," 57).

74. Hammergren, "Dance, Democracy and Open Source Movement."

75. Lehmann, "Musik Schafft Eine Welt." Nachbar used the recording of the same performance for his reconstruction. He "found" it in the library of P.A.R.T.S. in Brussels in 1999, where he was studying; see Nachbar, "SPU(E)REN/LESEN: Ein Versuch über das Tanzarchiv," 125.

76. *Afectos Humanos*, program notes, 1989.

77. Ibid.

78. *Protokoll des XI. Parteitages der Sozialistischen Einheitspartei Deutschlands*, 84.

79. The second one would eventually be Paula Guggi, who quit her job with the Gera company to found Guggi and Paul in 1987.

80. Siegert explicitly affirms this in an interview in 1988 (Richter, "Von der Palucca-Elevin zur Ballett-Chefin").

81. Peters, "Ausdruckstanz."

82. See Richter, "Von der Palucca-Elevin zur Ballett-Chefin."

83. Schmidt, *Tanztheater in Deutschland*, 222.

84. See Siegert, "Konzeption Tanzsolo 'Liebe.'"

85. "Ostmodern" is a term coined by Petra Stuber to connote the specific developments in East German art that were not just the same or a duplication of Western postmodern approaches (*Spielräume und Grenzen*, 244).

86. "Sie 'ignorierten die DDR in den Schranken der DDR'" was phrased by the painter Moritz Götze, who was born in 1963 (Kaiser and Petzold, *Boheme und Diktatur in der DDR*, 68).

87. Schütt, *Die Erotik des Verrats*, 19.

88. Artists were aware of the way the term "decadence" was used in socialist rhetoric and purposely reappropriated it to connote a lifestyle different from that demanded by socialist standards.

89. Kaiser and Petzold's 1997 *Boheme und Diktatur in der DDR* was one of the first publications to appear on this topic. See also Michael and Seufert, *Die Einübung der Außenspur*; Fritzsche and Löser, *Gegenbilder*; and *Eigenart und Eigensinn*.

90. The housing program was called "Wohnungsbauprogramm" in East Germany.

91. *Protokoll der Verhandlungen des X. Parteitages der Sozialistischen Einheitspartei Deutschlands*, 42–43.

92. Every larger city in East Germany had an old, nearly abandoned area near its center. In Leipzig it was Connewitz, in Dresden it was parts of the Neustadt, and in Berlin it was the Scheunenviertel and parts of Prenzlauer Berg. These areas of the city were in various stages of decay. Leipzig was probably the most deteriorated city. A friend of mine, who squatted—as all of us did—in one of the unoccupied apartments, was woken up one morning by the sound of his outer bedroom wall, which was the front of the building, literally tumbling down.

93. Both cotton and leather were rarely available on the East German market.

94. Kaiser and Petzold, *Boheme und Diktatur in der DDR*, 17. Köhler stressed that in her opinion this was an apolitical stance.

95. Ibid., 18.

96. Stuber, *Spielräume und Grenzen*, 241.

97. Ladopoulos, "Die Rolle der Improvisation in Geschichte und Gegenwart des modernen Tanzes in Dresden," 3.

98. Ibid., 65.

99. The only scholarship on Kwiatkowski is an unpublished thesis ("Im Osten

nichts Neues?") by Ulrike Melzwig that includes a very good interview with and a short description of her. I relied on some of her information for this chapter.

100. For instance, I received this evaluation with four other dancers (Katrin Filipic, Elke Hunstock, Wolgang Maas, Marko E. Weigert) in the mid-1980s as soloist of the Tanzbühne Leipzig, a student ensemble. This permitted the group to perform for payment outside our own theater, the Beyerhaus. Filipic, Maas, and Weigert are still active as professional dancers and dance pedagogues.

101. Melzwig, "Im Osten nichts Neues?," appendix 5.

102. Kösterke, "Wege zwischen Irrlichtern."

103. As Peggy Phelan has famously observed, "Performance's only life is in the present. Performance cannot be saved, recorded, documented or otherwise participate in the circulation of representations of representations: once it does so, it becomes something other than performance. . . . Performance's being . . . becomes itself through disappearance" (*Unmarked*, 146).

104. See Brandstetter, "Still/Motion," 129, for a thorough summary of postmodern choreographic principles and foci, such as process, play, reorganization of material, chance, individual movement codes, montage, even energy, dancer's body (and not character), simplicity, and physical presence.

105. See Melzwig, "Im Osten nichts Neues?"; Schmidt, *Tanztheater in Deutschland*; Cramer, "Warfare over Realism"; and "Wahrnehmungsstörungen im Schatten des Gummibaums."

106. Kwiatkowski continues to improvise across all borders, as in *criducoeur2010*, which problematizes borders in a global context.

107. For a summary of German gay and lesbian culture, see Giersdorf, "Germany," 398–99.

108. I am referring to Charlotte von Mahlsdorf as a transvestite and using the female personal pronoun to conform to her self-identification. While she can be described in terms of the system of pre-op/post-op and transsexual/transgender common in the United States, as Henry S. Rubin, Judith Halberstam, and C. Jacob Hale suggest, I want to highlight the national specific terminologies by insisting on von Mahlsdorf's self-definition; see Rubin, "Phenomenology as Method in Trans Studies"; Halberstam and Hale, "Butch/FTM Border Wars"; Halberstam, "Transgender Butch"; and Hale, "Consuming the Living, Dis(re)membering the Dead in the Butch/FTM Borderlands."

109. I am recounting the standard version of von Mahlsdorf's biography. There are doubts about the validity of some main facts. Yet the recognition of such incongruities lies at the center of my argument because it conceptualizes von Mahlsdorf's retelling of her biography as another layer of her performance. It also acknowledges history as a construct.

110. Sieg, "Deviance and Dissidence," 94. The Röhm affair and the subsequent prosecution of gays and lesbians by the fascist regime, along with homophobic rhetoric in communist media at the time, show that both the National Socialists and the Communists used accusations of homosexuality as a defamatory tool. For a detailed discussion of the conflation of fascism and homosexuality, see Hewitt, *Political Inversions*.

111. Stümke, *Homosexuelle in Deutschland*, 63, 99.

112. Defining itself as antifascist, the GDR reverted to the prefascist law. In contrast, West Germany kept the fascist version of Paragraph 175.

113. As previously established, the public sphere in East Germany was differently

structured from its capitalist counterparts. Restaurants were few and hard to get into. A café and bar culture existed generally only in larger cities. Groups of people would meet mostly in private homes.

114. This design period roughly corresponds to the North American arts and crafts movement. Gründerzeit heavily influenced architecture in many German cities, leading to the subsequent influence of art nouveau or art deco on furniture and architecture.

115. The East German government prohibited a planned national lesbian meeting at von Mahlsdorf's museum in 1978 and any subsequent gatherings there. For a lesbian perspective on these earlier developments, see Sillge, *Un-Sichtbare Frauen*.

116. Even though the East German state supported atheism, the constitution guaranteed religious freedom. The Protestant Church (Evangelische Kirche) was the largest church in the GDR.

117. The gay rights activist Olaf Brühl was one of those few who pointed at the symptomatic abandoning of Marx's historic and dialectic materialism in the government's approach to homosexuality in the GDR. See Thinius, "Vom grauen Versteck ins bunte Ghetto," 42-44; and Brühl, "Fünf Begegnungen mit 'homosexuellen BürgerInnen,'" 131-36.

118. Compare especially reports by Erich Honecker (head of state and general secretary of the SED) on teaching and communist education. See *Protokoll der Verhandlungen des X*, 104-16; and *Protokoll der Verhandlungen des XI*, 72-86.

119. Still, in 1989, twenty-three church groups and only twelve to fifteen government-sponsored groups existed in East Germany (Brühl, "Fünf Begegnungen mit 'homosexuellen BürgerInnen,'" 131).

120. By this time, Paragraph 151 had not been enforced for years (Leser, "Homosexuelle in der DDR," 40).

121. Thinius provides the following exchange to exemplify the ironic and confident approach. Question: "Are homosexuals not suited for particular professions?" Answer: "Yes, if they have a tree pollen allergy, they should probably not become a woodsman" ("Vom grauen Versteck ins bunte Ghetto," 60).

122. Soukup, *Die DDR, die Schwulen, der Aufbruch*, 19.

123. For instance, when the East Germans closed it in 1963, von Mahlsdorf preserved the furniture of the Mulackritze (a gay and lesbian bar that had opened at the end of the nineteenth century, and was frequented by Bertolt Brecht, Magnus Hirschfeld, and Marlene Dietrich, among others).

124. In chapter 4, I explain the impact of the awareness of possible observation on corporeality and movement vocabulary.

125. Von Mahlsdorf, *Ich bin meine eigene Frau*, 182.

126. Even though von Mahlsdorf reports on a variety of sexual practices with male partners, her refusal to have surgery to become a transvestite means that it is not easy to define her sexuality in terms of either gay or straight.

127. For one theorization of gender crossing, see Elliot and Roen, "Transgenderism and the Question of Embodiment."

128. I purposefully use the term "mimicry" to describe von Mahlsdorf's resistance rather than the term "mimesis." See Diamond, "Mimesis, Mimicry, and the 'True-Real.'"

129. Bhabha, "Of Mimicry and Man," 86.

130. Von Mahlsdorf, *Ich bin meine eigene Frau*, 191.

131. As Henry S. Rubin stresses in his reevaluation of phenomenology to theorize transsexual and transgender experiences, "Transsexual men know all too well that they have female bodies. They are not psychotic" ("Phenomenology as Method in Trans Studies," 263–82). Von Mahlsdorf acknowledges her male body and integrates it into her female gender identity as well as practiced sexuality without erasing it.

132. De Certeau, *The Practice of Everyday Life*, xi–xxiv.

Chapter 4. Border Crossings and Intranational Trespasses

1. See Benjamin, *Das Passagenwerk*. Benjamin's employment of "Flanieren" refers also to the German use of the word that connotes more than simple strolling. It also connotes walking along some scenic path, in a park, or along window displays. The action is as much about enjoying the surroundings as being seen while doing so.

2. Armed border patrols guarded those checkpoints along the border between West and East Berlin. After the building of the wall, the East German government established those checkpoints to allow West Berlin citizens to come to the East. However, the reverse movement of East Berliners toward the West was highly restricted and mostly took place at Bahnhof Friedrichstrasse.

3. This awareness of one's own corporeal identity has been captured by one of the most famous writers in the GDR, Christa Wolf, in her novel *Was bleibt* (*What Remains*). *Was bleibt* was written in the summer of 1979 and reworked in November 1989, the month of the fall of the Berlin Wall. The novella describes a day in the life of the author. It elaborates how she physically and psychologically reacted to her surveillance by the Stasi during a period of intense intimidation of intellectuals, and in particular, artists. The book records her increasing awareness of her own body, her movements, her fear, and her psychic insecurity. By writing about the surveillance and her reaction to it, Wolf attempted to realize the changes of her own body and movement. The obvious and constant observation resulted in an increased self-observation. Every move and each body posture could reveal something to the observer. The smallest detail became important. The only comparison I can make to help the reader to understand effects of surveillance on the body is to consider how the body is affected by an illness. There is always the possibility of getting sick. Everyone knows that. The experience of pain in and of itself produces a different awareness of one's own body. But then this awareness is magnified dramatically after one is diagnosed with an illness. From this time on, the whole body, each movement, body posture, and even motionlessness is understood in terms of the illness.

4. This unofficial uniform consisting of leather jacket and polyester bag became a signifier for members of the Stasi. Thus, East German citizens were often able to spot the undercover agents and observers. Of course, there is the likelihood that the Stasi wanted us to see some of their agents to create a panoptical situation in Foucault's understanding.

5. The bridge is Oberbaumbrücke, which served during the fall of the wall as one of the first hastily opened makeshift checkpoints.

6. See Foster, "Dancing Culture." In this book review, Foster makes the suggestion that a re-creation of embodiment in writing is the only way to theorize the double relationship between society and the body, an idea she would subsequently develop into a full-fledged theory.

7. In the walk, East German citizens crossed the bridge between the two separated German countries from the east to the west. This movement reversed a movement that West German citizens were always able to perform. My view on the walk across the border and the two dance productions is informed by this unexpected reversal as well as my former East German citizenship.

8. Dance scholars theorize a variety of bodies. Very often, we are confronted with scholarship that applies the term "body" in an abstract or metaphorical way. An example would be Hewitt, *Social Choreography*, who writes about the body from literary theory and German studies perspectives. Even though he repeatedly emphasizes physicality and choreography, Hewitt uses the terms to denote discursive strategies. There is nothing wrong with such uses of the term "body" or "choreography." However, we can distinguish among the various levels of abstraction. What is the relationship between bodies as flesh and the metaphorical use of the term "body?" In her essay "Bodies-Cities," Elizabeth Grosz describes how society culturally influences the body's possibilities through disciplining, regulating, administration, and training. Grosz goes on to argue that individual bodies interconnect with other bodies and objects. Considering this definition we could endeavor to interrogate the connection of the body to its abstractions, within ideological, cultural, religious, or technological reconfigurations.

9. I work in a tradition of dance scholarship that draws on this notion of corporeal agency put forward by such authors such as Susan L. Foster, Susan Manning, Mark Franko, Marta Savigliano, Randy Martin, Janet Adshead-Lansdale, Ramsey Burt, and Lena Hammergren.

10. De Certeau, *The Practice of Everyday Life*, 91–110, 98, 102.

11. Ibid., 96, 92–93.

12. Wigman's choreographies react against the narrative form and the position of women in story ballets by emphasizing movement interrogation and blurred gender connotations through her use of costume and mask. Her dances move the individual dancer into an abstract structure. Often, her choreographies revolve around the relationship of a leader and a group, reflecting an elitist view regarding the position of the leader through dance. As I established in chapter 3, Wigman employed improvisation as a working tool, yet she repeatedly spoke out against improvisation as a stage form. See Manning, *Ecstasy and the Demon*.

13. Even though the social and artistic movement of contact improvisation, in which two or more dancers negotiate weight and space based on democratic values, offers principles for a way to move, it does not provide a set vocabulary. Contact dancers are encouraged to pay close attention to their bodies, which are approached and employed as intelligent systems. The parameters of the choreographic choices vary depending on the school and training of the participants. Cynthia Novack provided the first survey of contact improvisation as both an artistic and social movement; see *Sharing the Dance*. The School of New Dance Development in Amsterdam is strongly influenced by a North American–based approach to contact improvisation, which has come under critique as a nearly exclusively white, often middle-class dance form that by emphasizing its pioneering inventiveness and break with any preceding tradition does not always recognize its place in a complex dance genealogy. For a comprehensive analysis of the use of Afro-Caribbean and Asian choreographic principles in contact improvisation and other forms of improvisation, see Foster, *Dances That Describe Themselves*. Building on the research

of dance scholars who interrogate the influence of nonwhite dance forms on modern dance as well as scholarship on jazz and improvisation in music, Foster establishes a genealogy that questions the established narrative of the self-generating origin of contact and improvisation in North America in the 1970s.

14. She founded the company in collaboration with Jochen Sandig.

15. For an overview of her impressive choreographic and managerial activities, see http://www.sashawaltz.de.

16. For a discussion of Fabian's work at three distinct stages of his career and for an abridged and earlier version of the analysis of *Pax Germania*, see Giersdorf, "The Dance Theatre of Jo Fabian."

17. Off-theater in Germany is any theatrical enterprise that exists outside city and national theater institutions. However, the off-theater scene still relies mostly on government, state, and city funding.

18. Fabian, *Whisky & Flags*, program notes.

19. For a more thorough discussion of the politics of this restaging, see Giersdorf, "'Hey, I Won't Let You Destroy My History.'"

20. *Whisky & Flags* premiered at the Theater unterm Dach, where Fabian predominantly performed at that time. He and his company DEPARTMENT restaged the piece at the Hebbel Theater in 2003, partly to thank Nele Hertling, the director of the Hebbel Theater, for her support over the preceding ten years. Fabian and his DEPARTMENT left the Hebbel Theater at the end of the 2003 season. During this time, Germany had the largest financial crisis, with a deficit of over €70 billion, since the post–World War II era (Höll and Hoffmann, "Öffentliches Defizit").

21. This is recounted in a press release dated January 3, 2001, from the Irvine Barclay Theatre and Cheng Hall: "'I started by simply ringing doorbells,' recalls Sasha Waltz. The search for a new ideal led her into a world she never knew: life in a former East Berlin quarter in a street called 'Allee der Kosmonauten,' where apartments all had the same layout. Despite different furnishings, the focal point of each apartment was always the sofa, which stood in exactly the same part of the living room."

22. "The strangers who answered were at first reluctant to talk to me, but soon the ice was broken, and once we established a trust, they began to tell me stories of their lives."

23. This relationship could be compared to the relationship of minority citizens' stance to law enforcement units in the United States.

24. Interestingly enough, Waltz seems to have become aware of her choreography's universal stance. The German description of the piece on her website now states that "the repeatedly awarded portrait of a family from Marzahn or Bombay has been filmed and performed more than 150 times all over the world." Marzahn is the area in which the Allee der Kosmonauten is located. Bombay, obviously, is not.

25. Spivak, "Can the Subaltern Speak"; Said, *Orientalism*. There is of course a difference between the racially marked other and the other that is marked by political systems, nationhood, and class. However, not only does dance studies have to employ appropriate methodologies and tools from other disciplines but it also has to theorize the visually and nationally undifferentiated other, such as the citizens of many Eastern European countries. This analysis would have to focus on the interdependence of class, nationality, and culture in relation to already established notions of a racially marked other, because the already-existing predominantly North American discourse on race

rarely encompasses the racial differences inside Europe, which are often related not only to class but also to nationhood.

26. In an interview with the *Berliner Zeitung*, Waltz explained her current return to more abstracted dance pieces. She expressed that she arrived with her more narrative work at a dead end and subsequently rediscovered the more fragmented and abstracted approach of her earlier work such as *Twenty to Eight*. Schlagenwerth, "Jedes Mal ein Schritt über die Grenze."

27. Waltz described them as three generations (*Allee der Kosmonauten*, program).

28. I have witnessed two very different audiences while watching Waltz's choreography. The first audience consisted of mostly hip East and West Berliners for the premiere run of the piece at the Sophiensale in 1996. The second was a much older and more conservative audience attending the performance at the Barclay Theatre in Irvine, California, in 2001. The audience observing *Allee der Kosmonauten* rarely reacted as a homogeneous group to the choreography. Yet I observed shared moments of enjoyment and discomfort during both performances.

29. See Banes, *Terpsichore in Sneakers*.

30. In 2000, three years after *Pax Germania*, Fabian returned with *Steinberg—Born to Be Wild*, in which he engages in a choreographic interrogation of the post-reunification process and its implications for the citizens of the unified Germany.

31. Cooke, *Representing East Germany since Unification*, 2.

32. I saw *Pax Germania* at the Theater am Halleschen Ufer, which is known for its support of independent dance productions in Berlin. I deliberately unify differing individual spectators into a general audience body in my reading of Fabian's choreography. I am able to do this because Fabian's piece forces the audience into movements and actions comparable to the one that moved across the border. The growing frustration compels a reaction in the spectators that changes the space in which that reaction occurs, just as it did with respect to East German citizens crossing the border. This kind of change is only possible because the critical mass participates as a unified movement of individual bodies.

33. Rouse, "Heiner Müller and the Politics of Memory," 65. Rouse's article appears in *Theatre Journal*'s special issue on German theater about the fall of the wall. The articles display an astonishing variety of views on the development in German theater and approaches to historicizing of the social changes in Germany. Yet, nearly twenty years after the publication of this special issue, one can't help but read a shared nostalgia and uncertainty in several of the articles that react to the dramatic transformations in East German social and cultural landscape at that time, which eventually erased large parts of East German culture and history. Meanwhile, East Germany has since that time mostly been represented in the form of memories and has been relegated to anecdotal material. See, among several publications that structure East German history as anecdotal memory, Hensel, *Zonenkinder*; Aehnlich, *Wenn ich groß bin, flieg ich zu den Sternen*; Osang, *Die Nachrichten*; and Osang, *89*. Nevertheless, it is still interesting to study this erasure and appropriation process not just to understand the different function that such memories now have in Germany but also to gain a better understanding of transformations during such processes as the ongoing merger in the European Union or further globalization.

34. www.ny2dance.com/projects/view/Berlin-Wall/info.

35. Caruth, *Trauma*, 170.

36. Ibid., 171.

37. White, *The Content of the Form*, 24.

Chapter 5. Toward a Transnational History of East German Dance

1. This plot became known as the 2006 transatlantic aircraft plot in which terrorists attempted to detonate liquid explosives on board at least ten planes from different airlines. The plot was foiled by the British police, but it became the reason for the still-in-place security measures that restrict carrying on of liquids.

2. Kühl, *Patricio Bunster*, 53; Winkler, *Der moderne Tanz nach 1945*, 21.

3. Winkler, "Ausdruckstanz in der DDR," 57.

4. *Tanztheater International*, 64.

5. Ibid., 73; Kant, "Dance in Exile," 41.

6. This was true even when I saw it nearly forty years later in 2006.

7. Kühl, *Patricio Bunster*, 18.

8. Joan Turner, who was married to Bunster, later married Víctor Jara and took his name. However, publicity material of Espiral refers to her as Joan Turner and so I refer to her that way.

9. Kühl, *Patricio Bunster*, 33.

10. Ibid., 35.

11. Bloch, *Das Prinzip Hoffnung*.

12. Borchers, "In Bewegung denken," 135.

13. Interestingly enough, *Trotz alledem!* was also the name of Erwin Piscator's revue from 1925.

14. When I watched *Porque tenemos sólo una vida—Denn wir haben nur ein Leben* in 2005 at the Tanzarchiv in Leipzig with Susan Foster, she saw gender conflicts and *Ausdruckstanz* vocabulary and all I saw was class conflict and Chilean folk. I am mentioning this discrepancy in our analysis to point to the subjective nature of analysis, inside of and across reference systems.

15. *Tanztheater International*, 71.

16. *Antología I*, the first retrospective, was staged the year before.

17. Bunster's daughter Manuela Bunster, who also oversees the dance school and the company, told me in an interview that the solo parts of the choreography are based on her mother, Joan Turner, her and her sister, Bunster, and Víctor Jara. Readers might be familiar with Christopher Bruce's *Swansong* (1987) and *Ghost Stories* (1981), in which he also depicts the experience of Víctor Jara specifically and the oppression of the Andean people more generally. Bruce cites his meeting with Joan Turner, among others, as an inspiration.

18. The 1982 documentation of the first dance international workshop for small stages (Petzold, *I. Internationale Tanzwerkstatt ARTAMA Kammertanz*) describes *Venceremos* as an "example of contemporary dance's preservation and application of the best traditions from the proletarian artistic movement and modern dance." Others praised works that came from amateur and folk dance companies.

19. Manuala Bunster, e-mail to author, May 21, 2012.

20. I am rethinking here Althusser's development of Marx's theory of the state in which he describes the necessity of the ideological state apparatus moving into the private sphere and thus normalizing itself and seemingly ridding itself of any ideology (*Lenin and Philosophy and Other Essays*, 143–45).

21. Desai, *Beyond Bollywood*, 7.

Bibliography

Acocella, Joan. "The Lost Nijinsky: Is It Possible to Reconstruct a Forgotten Ballet?" *New Yorker*, May 7, 2001, 211–31.

Adshead-Lansdale, Janet, and June Layson. "Historical Perspectives in the Study of Dance." In *Dance History: An Introduction*, 3–17. London: Routledge, 2006.

Aehnlich, Kathrin. *Wenn ich gross bin, flieg ich zu den Sternen.* Lemfoerde: Gustav Kiepenheuer, 1998.

Afectos Humanos. Produced by Hessischer Rundfunk. Performed by Dore Hoyer. Cologne: Deutsches Tanzarchiv, 1967. DVD.

Ahne, Joachim, and Hermann Neef, eds. *Dokumentation zur Uraufführung des Balletts "Schwarze Vögel" von Köllinger, Katzer, Schilling.* Material zum Theater 83. Berlin: Verband der Theaterschaffenden der Deutschen Demokratischen Republik, 1975.

Albright, Ann Cooper. *Traces of Light: Absence and Presence in the Work of Loïe Fuller.* Middletown, CT: Wesleyan University Press, 2007.

Albright, Ann Cooper, and David Gere, eds. *Taken by Surprise: A Dance Improvisation Reader.* Middletown, CT: Wesleyan University Press, 2003.

Allee der Kosmonauten, program. Sophiensäle, Sept. 9–Oct. 20, 1996.

Althusser, Louis. *Lenin and Philosophy and Other Essays.* London: New Left Books, 1971.

Amt für Information der Regierung der Deutschen Demokratischen Republik. *Die Verfassung der Deutschen Demokratischen Republik.* 2nd ed. Berlin: VEB Deutscher Zentralverlag Berlin, 1958.

Anderson, Benedict R. *Imagined Communities: Reflections on the Origin and Spread of Nationalism.* London: Verso, 1991.

Auslander, Philip. "Motional Abstraction: Alwin Nikolais' Formalism." In *The Returns of Alwin Nikolais: Bodies, Boundaries and the Dance Canon,* edited by Claudia Gitelman and Randy Martin, 154–69. Middletown, CT: Wesleyan University Press, 2007.

Baakmann, Susanne, and David Craven. "An Introduction to Modernism–Fascism Postmodernism." *Modernism/Modernity* 15, no. 1 (2008): 1–8.

Banes, Sally. *Terpsichore in Sneakers: Post-Modern Dance.* Middletown, CT: Wesleyan University Press, 1987.

Barba, Fabián. "Research into Corporeality." *Dance Research Journal* 43, no. 1 (2011): 83–89.

Baxmann, Inge. "Der Körper als Gedächtnisort." In *Deutungsräume,* edited by Inge Baxmann and Franz Anton Cramer, 15–35. Munich: Kieser, 2005.

————. *Mythos, Gemeinschaft: Körper- und Tanzkulturen in der Moderne*. Munich: Fink, 2000.

Benjamin, Walter. *Das Passagenwerk*. Frankfurt am Main: Suhrkamp, 1982.

Berlant, Lauren. "National Brands/National Body: Imitation of Life." In *The Phantom Public Sphere*, edited by Bruce Robbins, 173–208. Minneapolis: University of Minnesota Press, 1993.

Berman, Art. *Preface to Modernism*. Urbana: University of Illinois Press, 1994.

Bhabha, Homi K. *The Location of Culture*. London: Routledge, 1994.

————. "Of Mimicry and Man: The Ambivalence of Colonial Discourse." In *The Location of Culture*, 85–92. London: Routledge, 1994.

Bisky, Lothar. "Massenmedien und sozialistische Kultur." In *Kulturtheorie Ästhetik: Studientexte für die Ausbildung an Ingeneur- und Fachschulen*, edited by Kurt Kießling and Gerhard Volk, 64–66. Leipzig: VEB Verlag Enzyklopädie Leipzig, 1985.

Bleeker, Maaike. "Lecture Performance as Contemporary Dance." In *New German Dance Studies*, edited by Susan Manning and Lucia Ruprecht, 232–46. Urbana: University of Illinois Press, 2012.

Bloch, Ernst. *Das Prinzip Hoffnung*. Frankfurt am Main: Suhrkamp, 1985.

Boehn, Max von. *Der Tanz*. Berlin: Wegweiser, 1925.

Böhme, Waltraud, et al., eds. *Kleines politisches Wörterbuch*. Berlin: Dietz, 1967.

Borchers, Susanne. "In Bewegung denken: Zur Arbeit mit Patricio Bunster." *Tanzforschung* 5 (1994): 133–36.

Bourdieu, Pierre. "The Objective Limits of Objectivism." In *Outline of a Theory of Practice*, 1–31. Cambridge: Cambridge University Press, 1977.

————. "Structures and the Habitus." In *Outline of a Theory of Practice*, 72–95. Cambridge: Cambridge University Press, 1977.

Bradley, Karen. *Rudolf Laban*. New York: Routledge, 2009.

Brandenburg, Hans. *Der moderne Tanz*. Munich: Müller, 1913.

Brandstetter, Gabriele. "Still/Motion: Zur Postmoderne im Tanztheater." In *Bewegung im Blick*, edited by Claudia Jeschke and Hans-Peter Bayerdörfer, 122–36. Berlin: Vorwerk 8, 2000.

Brühl, Olaf. "Fünf Begegnungen mit 'homosexuellen BürgerInnen': Ein Nachtrag." In *Die DDR, die Schwulen, der Aufbruch: Versuch einer Bestandsaufnahme*, edited by Jean Jacques Soukup, 131–36. Göttingen: Schriftenreihe Waldschlösschen, 1990.

Bürger, Peter. *Theory of the Avant-garde*. Minneapolis: University of Minnesota Press, 1984.

Butt, Gavin. *Between You and Me: Queer Disclosures in the New York Art World, 1948–1963*. Durham, NC: Duke University Press, 2005.

Carter, Alexandra, ed. *Rethinking Dance History: A Reader*. London: Routledge, 2004.

Caruth, Cathy. *Trauma: Explorations in Memory*. Baltimore, MD: Johns Hopkins University Press, 1995.

Certeau, Michel de. *The Practice of Everyday Life*. Berkeley: University of California Press, 1984.

Chesher, Chris. "Colonizing Virtual Reality. Construction of the Discourse of Virtual Reality, 1984–1992." *Cultronix* 1, no. 1 (1994): n.p.

Climenhaga, Royd. *Pina Bausch*. London: Routledge, 2009.

Cooke, Paul. *Representing East Germany since Unification: From Colonization to Nostalgia*. Oxford: Berg, 2005.

Cramer, Franz Anton. "Warfare over Realism: *Tanztheater* in East Germany, 1966–1989."

In *New German Dance Studies*, edited by Susan Manning and Lucia Ruprecht, 147–66. Urbana: University of Illinois Press, 2012.

Cresswell, Tim. *In Place/Out of Place: Geography, Ideology, and Transgression*. Minneapolis: University of Minnesota Press, 1996.

Daly, Ann. *Done into Dance: Isadora Duncan in America*. Bloomington: Indiana University Press, 1995.

Derrida, Jacques. *Archive Fever: A Freudian Impression*. Chicago: University of Chicago Press, 1996.

Desai, Jigna. *Beyond Bollywood: The Cultural Politics of South Asian Diasporic Film*. New York: Routledge, 2004.

Diamond, Ellen. "Mimesis, Mimicry, and the 'True-Real.'" *Modern Drama* 32, no. 1 (1989): 58–72.

Die andere Liebe. Directed by Helmut Kißling and Axel Otten. DEFA, 1988.

Doerwaldt, Edith, ed. *Der Volkstanz: Katalog der methodischen Ausstellung*. Leipzig: Zentralhaus für Laienkunst, 1957.

Dolling, Irene. "'Unsere Muttis arbeiten wie ein Mann': Ein Blick zurück auf Frauenbilder in DDR-Zeitschriften der vergangenen Jahre." In *So nah beieinander und doch so fern: Frauenleben in Ost und West*, edited by Agnes Joester and Insa Schöningh, 125–38. Pfaffenweiler: Centaurus, 1992.

Draeger, Volkmar. "Auf der Suche nach Profil: Tanzforum Berlin (Umorientierung Eines Armee-Ensembles)." *Tanz International* 7/8 (1990): 74–75.

Eigenart und Eigensinn. Bremen: Forschungsstelle Osteuropa, 1996.

Elliot, Patricia, and Katrin Roen. "Transgenderism and the Question of Embodiment: Promising Queer Politics." *GLQ* 4, no. 2 (1998): 231–62.

Engels, Friedrich. *Der deutsche Bauernkrieg*. Berlin: Neuer Weg, 1946.

———. *The Peasant War in Germany*. New York: International Publishers, 2000.

Enzensberger, Hans Magnus. "Baukasten zu einer Theorie der Medien." *Kursbuch* 20 (1970): 159–86.

Fabian, Jo. *Whisky & Flags*, program notes. Hebbel-Theater, May 8–11, 2003.

Familiengesetzbuch. Berlin: Staatsverlag der DDR, 1965.

Fenemore, Mark. *Sex, Thugs and Rock 'n' Roll*. New York: Berghahn Books, 2007.

Fernandes, Ciane. *Pina Bausch and the Wuppertal Dance Theater: The Aesthetics of Repetition and Transformation*. New York: Peter Lang, 2001.

Fiedler, Frank, and Günter Gurst, eds. *Meyers Jugendlexikon Philosophie*. Leipzig: VEB Bibliographisches Institut, 1979.

Fisher, Betsy. *Creating and Re-creating Dance: Performing Dances Related to Ausdruckstanz*. Helsinki: Theatre Academy of Finland, 2002.

Foster, Susan Leigh. *Choreographing Empathy: Kinesthesia in Performance*. London: Routledge, 2010.

———, ed. *Choreographing History*. Bloomington: Indiana University Press, 1995.

———. *Choreography and Narrative: Ballet's Staging of Story and Desire*. Bloomington: Indiana University Press, 1998.

———, ed. *Corporealities: Dancing, Knowledge, Culture, and Power*. London: Routledge, 1996.

———. *Dances That Describe Themselves: The Improvised Choreography of Richard Bull*. Middletown, CT: Wesleyan University Press, 2002.

———. "Dancing Culture." *American Ethnologist* 19, no. 2 (1992): 362–66.

———. Introduction. In *Worlding Dance*, edited by Susan Leigh Foster, 1–13. New York: Palgrave Macmillan, 2009.

———. "An Introduction to Moving Bodies: Choreographing History." In *Choreographing History*, edited by Susan L. Foster, 3–21. Bloomington: Indiana University Press, 1995.

———. *Reading Dancing: Bodies and Subjects in Contemporary American Dance*. Berkeley: University of California Press, 1986.

Foucault, Michel. "Nietzsche, Genealogy, History." In *The Foucault Reader*, edited by Paul Rabinow, 76–100. New York: Pantheon, 1984.

Franko, Mark. *Dancing Modernism/Performing Politics*. Bloomington: Indiana University Press, 1995.

———. "Mimique." In *Bodies of the Text: Dance as Theory, Literature as Dance*, edited by Ellen W. Goellner and Jacqueline Shea Murphy, 205–16. New Brunswick, NJ: Rutgers University Press, 1995.

———. "Repeatability, Reconstruction and Beyond." *Theatre Journal* 41, no. 1 (1989): 56–74.

———. "Some Notes on Yvonne Rainer, Modernism, Politics, Emotion, Performance, and the Aftermath." In *Meaning in Motion: New Cultural Studies of Dance*, edited by Jane Desmond, 289–303. Durham, NC: Duke University Press, 1997.

———. *The Work of Dance: Labor, Movement, and Identity in the 1930s*. Middletown, CT: Wesleyan University Press, 2002.

Fraser, Nancy. "Rethinking the Public Sphere: A Contribution to the Critique of Actually Existing Democracy." *Social Text* 25/26 (1990): 56–80.

Frede, Matthias, and Arila Siegert. "'Sich Aufmachen, Schöpferisch Sein': Gespräch mit Arila Siegert." *Theater der Zeit* 5 (1988): 34.

Fricke, Karl Wilhelm. *Opposition Und Widerstand in der DDR: Ein Politischer Report*. Cologne: Wissenschaft und Politik, 1984.

Friedman, Susan Stanford. "Definitional Excursions: The Meanings of Modern/Modernity/Modernism." *Modernism/Modernity* 8, no. 3 (2001): 493–513.

Fritzsche, Karin, and Claus Löser. *Gegenbilder: Filmische Subversion in der DDR, 1976–1989; Texte, Bilder, Daten*. Berlin: Janus Press, 1996.

Fuchs, Peter Paul. *The Music Theatre of Walter Felsenstein: Collected Articles, Speeches, and Interviews*. London: Quartet Books, 1991.

Funkenstein, Susan Laikin. "Engendering Abstraction: Wassily Kandinsky, Gret Palucca, and 'Dance Curves.'" *Modernism/Modernity* 14, no. 3 (2007): 389–406.

Gehrke, Bernd, and Wolfgang Rüddenklau, eds. *. . .das war doch nicht unsere Alternative: DDR Oppositionelle zehn Jahre nach der Wende*. Münster: Westfälisches Dampfboot, 1999.

Giersdorf, Jens Richard. "Dance Studies in the International Academy: Genealogy of a Disciplinary Formation." *Dance Research Journal* 41, no. 1 (2009): 23–44.

———. "The Dance Theatre of Jo Fabian: Blown Away, Pax Germania, and Prometheus." *Theatre Forum* no. 15 (1999): 90–96.

———. "Germany." In *Gay Histories and Cultures: An Encyclopedia*, edited by George E. Haggerty, 388–89. New York: Garland, 2000.

———. "'Hey, I Won't Let You Destroy My History': East German Dance Theater and the Politics of Restaging." *Maska* nos. 82–83 (2003): 17–22.

Goeschen, Ulrike. "From Socialist Realism to Art in Socialism: The Reception of

Modernism as an Instigating Force in the Development of Art in the GDR." *Third Text* 23, no. 1 (2009): 45–53.

———. *Vom sozialistischen Realismus zur Kunst im Sozialismus.* Berlin: Duncker und Humblot, 2001.

Goewe, Jürgen "Folklore Heute." In *II. Kolloquium,* 3–11. Neustrelitz: Staatliches Folklore-Ensembles der DDR, 1976.

Goldschmidt, Aenne. *Handbuch des deutschen Volkstanzes: Systematische Darstellung der gebräuchlichsten deutschen Volkstänze.* Stuttgart: Kögler, 2001.

Goldschmidt, Aenne, Rosemarie Lettow, and Albin Fritsch. *Der Tanz in der Laienkunst.* Leipzig: Zentralhaus für Laienkunst, 1952.

Gommlich, Werner. *Showtanz.* Leipzig: Zentralhaus-Publikation, 1989.

Gottschild, Brenda Dixon. *Digging the Africanist Presence in American Performance: Dance and Other Contexts.* Westport, CT: Greenwood, 1996.

Gramsci, Antonio. *Prison Notebooks.* Edited by Joseph A. Buttigieg. New York: Columbia University Press, 1992.

Green, Richard C. "(Up)Staging the Primitive: Pearl Primus and 'the Negro Problem' in American Dance." In *Dancing Many Drums: Excavations in African American Dance,* edited by Thomas F. DeFrantz, 105–42. Madison: University of Wisconsin Press, 2002.

Greenberg, Clement. "American-Type Painting." In *Art and Culture: Critical Essays,* 208–29. Boston: Beacon, 1961.

———. "Avant-Garde and Kitsch." In *Pollock and After: The Critical Debate,* edited by Francis Frascina, 21–33. New York: Harper and Row, 1985.

———. "Modernist Painting." In *Modern Art and Modernism: A Critical Anthology,* edited by Francis Frascina and Charles Harrison, 5–10. New York: Harper and Row, 1982.

Grosz, Elizabeth. "Bodies-Cities." In *Sexuality and Space,* edited by Beatriz Colomina and Jennifer Bloomer, 241–53. New York, Princeton Architectural Press, 1992.

Grundmann, Uta, Klaus Michael, and Susanna Seufert, eds. *Die Einübung der Aussenspur: Die andere Kultur in Leipzig, 1971–1990.* Leipzig: Thom, 1996.

Habermas, Jürgen. *Die Moderne—ein unvollendetes Projekt.* Leipzig: Reclam, 1994.

———. *The Structural Transformation of the Public Sphere: an Inquiry into a Category of Bourgeois Society.* Cambridge, MA: MIT Press, 1989.

Halberstam, Judith. "Transgender Butch: Butch/FTM Border Wars and the Masculine Continuum." *GLQ* 4, no. 2 (1998): 287–310.

Halberstam, Judith, and C. Jacob Hale. "Butch/FTM Border Wars: A Note on Collaboration." *GLQ* 4, no. 2 (1998): 283–85.

Hale, C. Jacob. "Consuming the Living, Dis(re)membering the Dead in the Butch/FTM Borderlands." *GLQ* 4, no. 2 (1998): 311–48.

Hammergren, Lena. "Dance, Democracy and Open Source Movement." "Dance and Spectacle," Society of Dance History Scholars Conference, Jul. 9–11, 2010, University of Surrey, UK.

Hardt, Michael, and Antonio Negri. *Commonwealth.* Cambridge, MA: Belknap Press of Harvard University Press, 2011.

———. *Multitude: War and Democracy in the Age of Empire.* New York: Penguin, 2004.

Hardt, Yvonne, and Kirsten Maar. *Tanz, Metropole, Provinz.* Hamburg: Lit, 2007.

Hasche, Christa, Traute Schölling, and Joachim Fiebach. *Theater in der DDR: Chronik und Positionen.* Berlin: Henschel, 1994.

Hawthorn, Jeremy. *A Glossary of Contemporary Literary Theory*. London: E. Arnold, 1992.

Heising, Elvira, and Sigrid Römer. *Der Tanz im "künstlerischen Volksschaffen" der DDR: Amateurbühnentanz, Volkstanz zum Mitmachen*. Remscheid: Deutscher Bundesverband Tanz, 1994.

Hensel, Jana. *Zonenkinder*. Reinbek bei Hamburg: Rowohlt, 2002.

Herd, E. W., and August Obermayer. *A Glossary of German Literary Terms*. Dunedin: Dept. of German, University of Otago, 1992.

Hewitt, Andrew. *Social Choreography: Ideology as Performance in Dance and Everyday Movement*. Durham, NC: Duke University Press, 2005.

———. *Political Inversions: Homosexuality, Fascism, and the Modernist Imaginary*. Stanford, CA: Stanford University Press, 1996.

Hintze, Werner, Clemens Risi, and Robert Sollich. *Realistisches Musiktheater: Walter Felsenstein: Geschichte, Erben, Gegenpositionen*. Berlin: Theater der Zeit, 2008.

Höll, Susanne, and Andreas Hoffmann. "Öffentliches Defizit—Schwerste Finanzkrise der Nachkriegszeit." http://www.sueddeutsche.de/politik/oeffentliches-defizit-schwerste-finanzkrise-der- nachkriegszeit-1.800542. Accessed Mar. 31, 2011.

Huschka, Sabine. *Moderner Tanz: Konzepte, Stile, Utopien*. Reinbek: Rowohlt, 2002.

Husemann, Pirkko. "Choreographie als Kritische Praxis: Arbeitsweisen Bei Xavier Le Roy Und Thomas Lehmen." Transcript, 2009.

Jameson, Fredric. *The Political Unconscious*. Ithaca, NY: Cornell University Press, 1981.

———. "Reflections in Conclusion." In *Aesthetics and Politics*, by Ernst Bloch et al., 196–213. London: Verso, 2007.

———. *A Singular Modernity*. London: Verso, 2009.

Jones, Amelia. *Body Art/Performing the Subject*. Minneapolis: University of Minnesota Press, 1998.

Jooss, Kurt. "Die Sprache des Tanztheaters" (1935). *Ballett: Chronik und Bilanz des Ballett-jahres* 34, no. 6 (1935): 17.

Jürgens, Birgit. *Zur Geschichte des BDM (Bund Deutscher Mädel) von 1923 bis 1939*. Frankfurt am Main: Peter Lang, 1994.

Kaiser, Paul, and Claudia Petzold. *Boheme und Diktatur in der DDR: Gruppen, Konflikte, Quartiere 1970–1989*. Berlin: Fannei und Walz, 1997.

Kant, Marion. "Dance in Exile: The Latin American Connection" *Performance Research* 3, no. 1 (1998): 32–42.

———. "The Moving Body and the Will to Culture." *European Review* 19, no. 4 (2011): 579–94.

———. "*Was bleibt?* The Politics of East German Dance." In *New German Dance Studies*, edited by Susan Manning and Lucia Ruprecht, 130–46. Urbana: University of Illinois Press, 2012.

Karina, Lilian, and Marion Kant. *Hitler's Dancers: German Modern Dance and the Third Reich*. New York: Berghahn Books, 2003.

Klaus, Georg, and Manfred Buhr. *Philosophisches Wörterbuch*. Leipzig: VEB Bibliographisches Institut, 1974.

Klein, Gabriele. "Inventur der Tanzmoderne." In *Tanzforschung und Tanzausbildung*, edited by Claudia Fleischle-Braun, Ralf Stabel, and Sabine Kaross, 71–83. Berlin: Henschel, 2008.

Klein, Thomas. *Frieden und Gerechtigkeit! Die Politisierung der unabhängigen Friedensbewegung in Ost-Berlin während der 8oer Jahre*. Cologne: Böhlau, 2007.

Kleist, Heinrich. "Über Das Marionettentheater." In *Der Zweikampf, Die heilige Cäcilie, Sämtliche Anekdoten, Über das Marionettentheater und andere Prosa*, 84–92. Stuttgart: Reclam, 1984.

Klotzsche, Volker, and Sigrid Römer. *Tanz in Sachsen: Betrachtungen zum Amateur- und Volkstanz im 20. Jahrhundert*. Norderstedt: Book Demand GmbHs, 2006.

Köllinger, Bernd. *Der Tanz: 10 Versuche*. Berlin: Henschel, 1975.

———. *Tanztheater: Tom Schilling und die zeitgenössische Choreographie*. Berlin: Henschel, 1983.

Kösterke, Doris. "Wege zwischen Irrlichtern." *Frankfurter Rundschau*, Dec. 28, 1996.

Kowalczuk, Ilko-Sascha. *Endspiel: Die Revolution von 1989 in der DDR*. Munich: Beck, 2009.

———, ed. *Freiheit und Öffentlichkeit: Politischer Samisdat in der DDR 1985 1989*. Berlin: Robert-Havemann-Gesellschaft, 2002.

Kowalczuk, Ilko-Sascha, Tom Sello, and Gudrun Weber, eds. *Für ein freies Land mit freien Menschen: Opposition und Widerstand in Biographien und Fotos*. Berlin: Robert Havemann-Gesellschaft, 2006.

Kraut, Anthea. *Choreographing the Folk: The Dance Stagings of Zora Neale Hurston*. Minneapolis: University of Minnesota Press, 2008.

———. "Dance Copyright and Migrations of Choreography." CORD conference, Nov. 8–11, 2007, Barnard College, New York City.

Krug, Manfred. *Abgehauen*. Düsseldorf: ECON, 1996.

Kühl, Edith, ed. *Patricio Bunster: Wege—Begegnungen*. Berlin: Akademie der Künste, Sektion Darstellende Kunst, 1990.

Kwiatkowski, Gerhard. *Schüler-Duden Die Literatur*. Mannheim: Duden, 1980.

Ladopoulos, Susanne. "Die künstlerische und pädogogische Arbeit Hanne Wandtkes in der Tradition des Ausdruckstanzes." *Tanzforschung* 5 (1994): 115–26.

———. "Die Rolle der Improvisation in Geschichte und Gegenwart des modernen Tanzes in Dresden." Diplom thesis, University of Leipzig, 1993.

La Mer. Performed by Frank Bey, Hannelore Bey, Roland Gawlik, Edith Löffler, and Jack Theis. Abenteuer Tanztheater, 1986. Video MDR.

Lammel, Rudolf. *Der moderne Tanz*. Berlin: Oestergaard, 1928.

Landschaften, Medea. *Progreß*, program notes. Leipziger Oper, 1992.

Langfeld, Rita. "Das Profil einer sozialistischen Tänzerpersönlichkeit im Erich-Weinert-Ensemble der NVA." Staatsexamensarbeit, Humboldt University, 1972.

Lefebvre, Henri. *Einführung in die Modernität: Zwölf Präludien*. Frankfurt am Main: Suhrkamp, 1978.

Lehmann, Ulrike. "Musik schafft eine Welt." *Die Deutsche Bühne*. http://www.die-deutsche-buehne.de. Accessed Jan. 1, 2010.

Lepp, Nicola, Martin Roth, and Klaus Vogel. *Der Neue Mensch: Obsessionen des 20.* Ostfildern-Ruit: Cantz, 1999.

Leser, Olaf. "Homosexuelle in der DDR: Versuch eines historischen Überblicks." In *Die DDR, die Schwulen, der Aufbruch: Versuch einer Bestandsaufnahme*, edited by Jean Jacques Soukup, 39–46. Göttingen: Schriftenreihe Waldschlösschen, 1990.

"Letters from Sally Banes and Susan Manning." *Drama Review* 33, no. 1 (1989): 13–16.

Liepold, Alexander. "Der Kampf gegen den Formalismus, Teil 2 1958–1965." Kopie nach Originalen. http://www.carl-bechstein-gymnasium.de/schueler/stuff/projekte/ddr-kunst/period1/period1_5.htm. Accessed June 8, 2010.

Lukács, Georg. "Critical Realism and Socialist Realism." In *Realism in Our Time: Literature and the Class Struggle*, 93–135. Translated by John and Necke Mander. New York: Harper, 1971.

Mahlsdorf, Charlotte von. *Ich bin meine eigene Frau: Ein Leben*. Munich: Deutscher Taschenbuch, 1995.

Manning, Susan. *Ecstasy and the Demon: Feminism and Nationalism in the Dances of Mary Wigman*. Berkeley: University of California Press, 1993.

———. "Modernist Dogma and Post-Modern Rhetoric: A Response to Sally Bane's *Terpsichore in Sneakers*." *Drama Review* 32, no. 4 (1988): 32–39.

Markard, Anna. *The Green Table: A Dance of Death in Eight Scenes*. Book and choreography by Kurt Jooss. Edited by Ann Hutchinson Guest. New York: Routledge, 2003.

Material für die Bildungs- und Erziehungsarbeit der Volkskunstgruppen: Tanz. Leipzig: Zentralhaus für Laienkunst, 1953.

Melzwig, Ulrike. "Im Osten nichts Neues?" Diplom thesis, Fachhoschschule Potsdam, 2003.

Morris, Gay. *A Game for Dancers: Performing Modernism in the Postwar Years, 1945–1960*. Middletown, CT: Wesleyan University Press, 2006.

Müller, Hedwig, Ralf Stabel, and Patricia Stöckemann. *Krokodil im Schwanensee: Tanz in Deutschland Seit 1945*. Frankfurt am Main: Anabas, 2003.

Müller, Hedwig, Frank-Manuel Peter, and Garnet Schuldt. *Dore Hoyer: Tänzerin*. Berlin: Hentrich, 1992.

Münz, Rudolf. "Theatralität und Theater: Konzeptionelle Erwägungen zum Forschungsprojekt 'Theatergeschichte.'" *Wissenschaftliche Beiträge der Theaterhochschule Hans Otto*, no. 1 (1989): 5–20.

Nachbar, Martin. "ReKonstruct." In *Moving Thoughts*, edited by Janine Schulze and Susanne Traub, 89–97. Leipzig: Vorwerk 8, 2001.

———. "SPU(E)REN/LESEN: Ein Versuch über das Tanzarchiv." In *Are 100 Objects Enough to Represent the Dance*, edited by Janine Schulze, 122–37. Munich: Epodium, 2010.

Ness, Sally. *Body, Movement, and Culture: Kinesthetic and Visual Symbolism in a Philippine Community*. Philadelphia: University of Pennsylvania Press, 1992.

Neubert, Ehrhart. *Geschichte der Opposition in der DDR 1949–1989*. Berlin: Links, 1998.

Neubert, Ehrhart, and Bernd Eisenfeld, eds. *Macht, Ohnmacht, Gegenmacht: Grundfragen Zur Politischen Gegnerschaft in der DDR*. Bremen: Temmen, 2001.

Nickel, Hildegard Maria. "Women in the German Democratic Republic and in the New Federal States: Looking Backward and Forward (Five Theses)." In *Gender Politics and Post-communism: Reflections from Eastern Europe and the Former Soviet Union*, edited by Nanette Funk and Magda Mueller, 138–58. New York: Routledge, 1993.

Novack, Cynthia Jean. *Sharing the Dance: Contact Improvisation and American Culture*. Madison: University of Wisconsin Press, 1990.

Osang, Alexander. *89: Helden-Geschichten*. Berlin: Links, 2002.

———. *Die Nachrichten*. Frankfurt am Main: Fischer, 2000.

O'Shea, Janet. "Roots/Routes of Dance Studies." In *The Routledge Dance Studies Reader*, edited by Alexandra Carter and Janet O'Shea, 1–15. 2nd ed. London: Routledge, 2010.

Partsch-Bergsohn, Isa. *Modern Dance in Germany and the United States: Cross Currents and Influences*. Chur: Harwood Academic Publishers, 1994.

Partsch-Bergsohn, Isa, and Harold Bergsohn. *The Makers of Modern Dance in Germany: Rudolph Laban, Mary Wigman, Kurt Jooss.* Hightstown, NJ: Princeton Book, 2003.

Pence, Katherine, and Paul Betts. Introduction. In *Socialist Modern: East German Everyday Culture and Politics*, edited by Katherine Pence and Paul Betts, 1–36. Ann Arbor: University of Michigan Press, 2008.

Petermann, Kurt. "Aufgaben und Möglichkeiten der Tanzwissenschaft in der DDR." *Material zum Theater* no. 125 (1980): 49–65.

Peters, Kurt. "Ausdruckstanz—Wurzeln und gegenwärtige Bedeutung." *Ausdruckstanz: Möglichkeiten und Grenzen* no. 225 (1989): 5–14.

Petzold, Fred, ed. *I. Internationale Tanzwerkstatt ARTAMA Kammertanz.* Leipzig: Zentralhaus-Publikation, 1982.

Phelan, Peggy. *Unmarked: The Politics of Performance.* London: Routledge, 1993.

Poggioli, Renato. *The Theory of the Avant-Garde.* Cambridge, MA: Belknap Press of Harvard University Press, 1981.

Pollack, Detlef. *Politischer Protest: Politisch Alternative Gruppen in der DDR.* Opladen: Leske und Budrich, 2000.

Poppe, Ulrike, Rainer Eckert, and Ilko-Sascha Kowalczuk, eds. *Zwischen Selbstbehauptung und Anpassung: Formen des Widerstandes und der Opposition in der DDR.* Berlin: Links, 1995.

Poster, Mark. "Databases as Discourse; or, Electronic Interpellations." In *Computers, Surveillance, and Privacy*, edited by David Lyon and Elia Zureik, 175–92. Minneapolis: University of Minnesota Press, 1996.

———. *The Mode of Information: Poststructuralism and Social Context.* Chicago: University of Chicago Press, 1990.

———. *The Second Media Age.* Cambridge, UK: Polity, 1995.

Praunheim, Rosa von. *Ich bin meine eigene Frau.* Berlin: Rosa von Praunheim Filmproduktion, 1992.

Prokop, Siegfried. *1956—DDR am Scheideweg: Opposition und neue Konzepte der Intelligenz.* Berlin: Homilius, 1992.

Protokoll der Verhandlungen des X. Parteitages der Sozialistischen Einheitspartei Deutschlands im Palast der Republik in Berlin, 11. Bis 16. April 1981. Berlin: Dietz, 1981.

Protokoll der Verhandlungen des XI Parteitages der Sozialistischen Einheitspartei Deutschlands. Berlin: Dietz, 1986.

Rebling, Eberhard. *Ballet.* Leipzig: VEB Breitkopf und Haertel, 1963.

———. *Ballettfibel.* Berlin: Henschel, 1974.

Richter, Ricarda. "Von der Palucca-Elevin zur Ballett-Chefin." *Tribüne Berlin*, Dec. 27, 1988.

Roach, Joseph R. *Cities of the Dead: Circum-Atlantic Performance.* New York: Columbia University Press, 1996.

Rodekamp, Volker. *Sportschau: Ausstellung Deutsche Turnfeste 1860 bis 2002.* Leipzig: Stadtgeschichtl Museum, 2002.

Ross, Janice. *Margaret H'Doubler and the Beginning of Dance in American Education.* Madison: University of Wisconsin Press, 2000.

Rouhiainen, Leena. "Embodying Modern Dance History: Betsy Fisher's Approach." Teatterikorkeakoulu. http://www2.teak.fi/teak/Teak202/7.html. Accessed Aug. 27, 2010.

Rouse, John. "Heiner Müller and the Politics of Memory." *Theatre Journal* 45, no. 1 (1993): 65–74.

Rubin, Henry S. "Phenomenology as Method in Trans Studies." *GLQ* 4, no. 2 (1998): 263–81.

Rüddenklau, Wolfgang. *Störenfried: DDR-Opposition 1986–1989: Mit Texten aus den "Umweltblättern."* Berlin: BasisDruck, 1992.

Sach, Curt. *World History of the Dance.* New York: Norton, 1965.

Said, Edward W. *Orientalism.* New York: Pantheon, 1978.

Savigliano, Marta. "Worlding Dance and Dancing Out There in the World." In *Worlding Dance,* edited by Susan L. Foster, 163–90. New York: Palgrave Macmillan, 2009.

Scheer, Udo. *Vision und Wirklichkeit: Die Opposition in Jena in den Siebziger und Achtziger Jahren.* Berlin: Links, 1999.

Schlagenwerth, Michaela. "Jedes mal ein Schritt über die Grenze." *Berliner Zeitung,* June 9, 2001.

Schmidt, Jochen. "Sensibel aber mit voller Kraft auf der Suche nach dem Eigenen." *Frankfurter Allgemeine Zeitung,* Sept. 18, 1992.

———. *Tanztheater in Deutschland.* Frankfurt am Main: Propyläen, 1992.

Schmidt-Feister, Karin. *Canto General—Poem für Tänzer.* Berlin, 1989.

Schneider, Rebecca. "Solo Solo Solo." In *After Criticism: New Responses to Art and Performance,* edited by Gavin Butt, 23–47. Malden, MA: Blackwell, 2005.

Schnelle, Manfred. "Reflexionen über Marianne Vogelsang." http://www.arila-siegert.de/knz/vogls.htm. Accessed Aug. 22, 2010.

Schulze, Janine, and Susanne Traub. *Moving Thoughts: Tanzen ist Denken.* Berlin: Vorwerk 8, 2003.

Schütt, Hans-Dieter. *Die Erotik des Verrats: Gespräche mit Frank Castorf.* Berlin: Dietz, 1996.

Scott, James C. *Domination and the Arts of Resistance: Hidden Transcripts.* New Haven, CT: Yale University Press, 1990.

Shay, Anthony. *Choreographic Politics.* Middletown, CT: Wesleyan University Press, 2002.

Sieben, Irene. "Remembrance with a Future—Reenacting Mary Wigman." Translated by Leanore Ickstadt. Proceedings of Conference Presentation Tanzkongress, Nov. 7, 2009, Hamburg.

———. "Tanz-Rekonstruktionen: Neugier auf das tänzerische Erbe." Goethe-Institut, June 2009. http://www.goethe.de/kue/tut/tre/de4695509.htm. Accessed Aug. 25, 2010.

Sieg, Katrin. "Deviance and Dissidence: Sexual Subjects of the Cold War." In *Cruising the Performative: Interventions into the Representation of Ethnicity, Nationality, and Sexuality,* edited by Sue-Ellen Case, Philip Brett, and Susan L. Foster, 93–111. Bloomington: Indiana University Press, 1995.

Siegel, Marcia B. *Watching the Dance Go By.* Boston: Houghton Mifflin, 1977.

Siegert, Arila. "Konzeption Tanzsolo 'Liebe.'" http://www.arila-siegert.de/knz/liebe.htm. Accessed Aug. 28, 2010.

Siegmund, Gerald. *Abwesenheit: Eine performative Ästhetik des Tanzes.* Bielefeld: Transscript, 2006.

———. "Affekt, Technik, Diskurs." In *Original und Revival: Geschichts-Shreibung im Tanz,* edited by Christina Thurner and Julia Wehren, 15–26. Zürich: Chronos, 2010.

———. *William Forsythe: Denken in Bewegung.* Berlin: Henschel, 2004.

Sillge, Ursula. *Un-Sichtbare Frauen: Lesben und Ihre Emanzipation in der DDR.* Berlin: Links, 1991.

Soukup, Jean Jacques, ed. *Die DDR, die Schwulen, der Aufbruch: Versuch einer Bestandsauf-nahme.* Göttingen: Schriftenreihe Waldschlösschen, 1990.

Spivak, Gayatri Chakravorty. "Can the Subaltern Speak?" In *Marxism and the Interpretation of Culture*, edited by Cary Nelson and Lawrence Grossberg, 271–313. Urbana: University of Illinois Press, 1988.

Staatliche Kommision für Kunstangelegenheiten. Hauptabteilung Kommission Künstlerischer Nachwuchs und Lehranstalten. *Zur Diskussion: Realismus im Tanz.* Dresden: VEB Verlag der Kunst, 1953.

Stabel, Ralf. "Die grosse Geste—Der sozialistische Realismus im Ballett." In *Bewegung im Blick*, edited by Claudia Jeschke and Hans-Peter Bayerdörfer, 213–24. Berlin: Vorwerk 8, 2000.

———. *IM "Tänzer": Der Tanz und die Staatssicherheit.* Mainz: Schott, 2008.

———. "Und so wird daraus nichts." In *Neuer Künstlerischer Tanz*, edited by Eve Winkler and Peter Jarchow, 99–117. Dresden: Tanzwissenschaft e.V., 1996.

———. "Keine Tabus mehr: Der Tanz in die 'Entwickelte Sozialistische Gesellschaft'—die 70er und 80er Jahre in der DDR." In *Krokodil im Schwanensee: Tanz in Deutschland seit 1945*, edited by Hedwig Müller, Ralf Stabel, and Patricia Stöckemann, 218–59. Frankfurt am Main: Anabas-Verlag, 2003.

———. *Tanz, Palucca! Die Verkörperung einer Leidenschaft.* Berlin: Henschel, 2001.

Stalin, Joseph V. "Marxism and the National Question." Marxist Internet Archive. http://www.marxists.org/reference/archive/stalin/works/1913/03a.htm#s1. Accessed May 22, 2011.

Stalpaert, Christel. "Reenacting Modernity: Fabian Barba's 'A Mary Wigman Dance Evening.'" *Dance Research Journal* 43, no. 1 (2011): 90–95.

Stuber, Petra. *Spielräume und Grenzen: Studien zum DDR-Theater.* Berlin: Links, 1998.

Stümke, Hans-Georg. *Homosexuelle in Deutschland: Eine politische Geschichte.* Munich: Beck, 1989.

Subklew-Jeutner, Marianne. *Der Pankower Friedenskreis: Geschichte einer Ost-Berliner Gruppe innerhalb der Evangelischen Kirchen in der DDR 1981–1989.* Osnabrück: Der Andere, 2004.

SUPERillu Spezial. Berlin: SUPERillu, 1999.

Tanztheater International. Material zum Theater 213. Berlin: Verband der Theater-schaffenden der Deutschen Demokratischen Republik, 1988.

Taylor, Diana. *The Archive and the Repertoire: Performing Cultural Memory in the Americas.* Durham, NC: Duke University Press, 2003.

Thiess, Frank. *Der Tanz als Kunstwerk: Studien zu einer Ästhetik der Tanzkunst.* Munich: Delphin, 1920.

Thinius, Bert. "Vom grauen Versteck ins bunte Ghetto: Ansichten zur Geschichte ostdeutscher Schwuler." In *Schwuler Osten: Homosexuelle Männer in der DDR*, edited by Kurt Starke, 11–90. Berlin: Links, 1994.

Thomas, Helen. "Reconstruction and Dance." In *Rethinking Dance History*, edited by Alexandra Carter, 32–45. London: Routledge, 2004.

Toepfer, Karl Eric. *Empire of Ecstasy: Nudity and Movement in German Body Culture, 1910–1935.* Berkeley: University of California Press, 1997.

Tomko, Linda J. *Dancing Class: Gender, Ethnicity, and Social Divides in American Dance, 1890–1920.* Bloomington: Indiana University Press, 1999.

Tom Schilling: Zum 70. Geburtstag. Berlin: Sender Freies Berlin, 1998. DVD.

Volkstanz-Sammlung. Leipzig: Junge Welt, 1952.

"Wahrnehmungsstörungen im Schatten des Gummibaums." *Frankfurter Rundschau*, Aug. 6, 2002.

Weidt, Jean, and Marion Kant. *Auf der großen Straße: Jean Weidts Erinnerungen.* Berlin: Henschel, 1984.

Weiss, Peter. *Die Ästhetik des Widerstands.* Frankfurt am Main: Suhrkamp, 2005.

White, Hayden V. *The Content of the Form: Narrative Discourse and Historical Representation.* Baltimore: Johns Hopkins University Press, 1987.

Willeit, Simone. "Stolpern und Unzulänglichkeiten." In *Original und Revival: Geschichts-Shreibung im Tanz*, edited by Christina Thurner and Julia Wehren, 47–58. Zurich: Chronos, 2010.

Winkler, Eva. "Ausdruckstanz in der DDR." *Tanzforschung* 5 (1994): 53–58.

———. *Der moderne Tanz nach 1945—Sein Einfluss auf die Entwicklung des Tänzernachwuchses in der DDR.* Material zum Theater 225. Berlin: Verband der Theaterschaffenden der Deutschen Demokratischen Republik, 1989.

Winkler, Eva, and Peter Jarchow. *Neuer Künstlerischer Tanz.* Dresden: Tanzwissenschaft e.V. and Palucca Schule Dresden, 1996.

Wolf, Christa. *What Remains and Other Stories.* Translated by Rick Takvorian and Heike Schwarzbauer. Chicago: University of Chicago Press, 1993.

Wong, Yutian. *Choreographing Asian America.* Middletown, CT: Wesleyan University Press, 2010.

Index

Note: Page numbers in italics refer to illustrations.

STUDIES IN DANCE HISTORY
A Publication of the Society of Dance History Scholars

The Origins of the Bolero School, edited by Javier Suárez-Pajares and Xoán M. Carreira

Carlo Blasis in Russia by Elizabeth Souritz, with preface by Selma Jeanne Cohen

Of, By, and For the People: Dancing on the Left in the 1930s, edited by Lynn Garafola

Dancing in Montreal: Seeds of a Choreographic History by Iro Tembeck

The Making of a Choreographer: Ninette de Valois and "Bar aux Folies-Bergère" by Beth Genné

Ned Wayburn and the Dance Routine: From Vaudeville to the "Ziegfeld Follies" by Barbara Stratyner

Rethinking the Sylph: New Perspectives on the Romantic Ballet, edited by Lynn Garafola (available from the University Press of New England)

Dance for Export: Cultural Diplomacy and the Cold War by Naima Prevots, with introduction by Eric Foner (available from the University Press of New England)

José Limón: An Unfinished Memoir, edited by Lynn Garafola, with introduction by Deborah Jowitt, foreword by Carla Maxwell, and afterword by Norton Owen (available from the University Press of New England)

Dancing Desires: Choreographing Sexualities on and off the Stage, edited by Jane C. Desmond